Wind

Despite making every effort to be accurate and researching carefully,
the authors respectively editor and the publisher take no responsibility
and accept no liability for the content provided.

1st Printing © 2021 Pantauro
by Benevento Publishing Salzburg – München,
a brand of Red Bull Media House GmbH,
Wals near Salzburg

All rights reserved, in whole or in part, especially the right of public lecture/recitation, the right to transmit by radio and television, and the translation right. No part of this publication may be reproduced in any form or by any means – graphic, electronic or mechanical (which includes but is not limited to: photocopying, recording, taping or storing information) – without the written permission of Red Bull Media House GmbH.
Typeset in Tisa Pro und LL Akkurat

Owner, publisher and editor:
Red Bull Media House GmbH
Oberst-Lepperdinger-Straße 11–15
5071 Wals near Salzburg, Austria

Translation: Ezra Fitz
Design: wir sind artisten
Cover: Gustavo Cherro, Francisco Vignale
Photography: Santiago Lange Family archive, Gustavo Fazio, Gustavo Cherro,
Matías Capizzano, Roman Hagara Archive, Carlo Borlenghi, Sailingshots by María Muiña

Printed by GGP Media GmbH, Germany
ISBN 978-3-89955-006-1

Santiago **Lange**

with Nicolás Cassese

Wind

The journey
of my life

Translated
from Spanish
by Ezra E. Fitz

To Yago, Theo, Borja, and Klaus, my children

Table of Contents

Introduction
9 **Under the Christ with the Open Arms**

Chapter One
27 **Discipline at Home, Freedom on the River**

Chapter Two
41 **The Friend I Could Never Beat**

Chapter Three
57 **From Río de la Plata to Southampton**

Chapter Four
79 **This One's for You, Dad**

Chapter Five
97 **Industry Dreams**

Chapter Six
115 **The Olympic Flame Has Been Lit**

Chapter Seven
125 **A New Method**

Chapter Eight
141 **The Happy Image Machine**

Chapter Nine
151 **Catching the Wind**

Chapter Ten
161 **Why Didn't We Win in Athens?**

Chapter Eleven
179 **A Boat Is a Living Being**

Chapter Twelve
193 **He Didn't Leave, He Now Rests in the Sea**

Chapter Thirteen
213 **What If We Try Sailing Together?**

Chapter Fourteen
227 **An Unexpected Wind**

Chapter Fifteen
241 **Wounded Lion**

Chapter Sixteen
257 **Recovered Lion**

Chapter Seventeen
271 **Work Your Magic, Old Man**

281 **Epilogue**

286 **Acknowledgements**

Introduction

Under the Christ with Open Arms

It will be hot today, but it's still early, and I barely break a sweat as I bike at a steady pace through Flamengo Park on the coast of Rio de Janeiro. It's a regular circuit for me, but the wide range of characters I come across every morning continues to amaze me. There's a runner proud of his gym-honed physique. Fleet of foot, he dodges a couple of gringos walking around with their heads on a swivel, perhaps nervous about the rumors alleging a lack of safety. A drunk, beer in hand, sitting on one of the nearby exercise machines could indeed confirm those fears. Nearby, a wrinkled man listening to music while sunbathing in his Speedo shows them the other side—free and uninhibited—of this wonderful city. Without even thinking, I start to hum a tune by Mercedes Sosa: *I'm grateful for this life that has given me so much / It has brought me laughter and it has brought me tears / It's how I know the difference between bliss and brokenness / The two themes that make up my song.*

I'm well aware of the privilege of experiencing this moment. The stakes are high, but that pressure doubles as a source of joy. It makes me feel alive, and it will drive me to perform at my best. I'm fifty-five years old, I'm appearing in my sixth Olympic Games, and this bike ride on the morning of August 16, 2016, brings me to the race that will determine whether or not I will achieve what I've been pursuing for nearly three decades: the gold medal in sailing.

In a short while, Cecilia Carranza will also be biking to the marina where we keep our boat, a Nacra 17 catamaran debuting in the mixed events at these Olympic Games. She has downloaded the Argentine national anthem onto her phone, though it's a version performed by Los Piojos, a rock band from her generation. She listens to that song on repeat, again and again. It's from a live performance, and the howling of the crowd with which the song starts lends it a sense of power, connecting it with the task we came here to do. Ceci has grown a lot during the time we've been sailing together. A short while ago, at breakfast, I noticed the confidence in her eyes. We didn't talk much, not even a few words of encouragement. There was no need to.

Yesterday, the day off before the final competition, her nephew Berna dropped in for a visit.

"Tía, they told me not to say anything to you, but I'm so nervous!" he said.

Ceci laughed and explained that we had trained for this moment as best we could. Win or lose, we would lay everything on the line. That much was certain. The road that brought us here was a long and winding one, to be sure. Among many other things, I had never sailed with a woman before, which is a requirement in this category. Also, we came from different sets of experiences, something which created an uneven relationship and a lot of tension. "Take a better tone with Ceci. Never raise your voice or pressure her again," I jotted down in my little red notebook after one particularly difficult day. I don't know if I'll end up with a medal around my neck this afternoon, but one thing I'll definitely take with me from Rio is an advanced degree in how to relate with a woman twenty-six years younger than me. Ceci and I joke that, after these Games, I'll be ready to get married again.

I've been competing for nearly half a century, and I know that the important work has already been done. Now, all that's left to do is unfurl everything we've spent so much time practicing. I feel calm, and the scenery helps. Before me lies the imposing Guanabara Bay. Watched over by the statue of Christ the Redeemer surrounded by hills lush with vegetation, this mirror-like water has been the center of our lives for the past nine months. Rife with uncertainty and behind in terms of preparation, we decided that the only way to get to the Games with a chance—even a hope—of a medal was to move here immediately. And so we did. We became locals. We sailed in order to discover the secrets and capriciousness of this devilish geography. We're experts in each and every current crossing the bay, and we know the infinite winds that sweep across it.

The effort has paid off. After the initial twelve races, we have arrived here, on the final day of the Games, with a five-point advantage over second place. But our sport is a cruel one. Your finishing position in each regatta is added to your total score, but this final competition, the medal race, is worth twice as much as the previous ones. The team that accumulates the fewest points wins the title. We're in a good position, but if we have a bad day today, we could be left off the podium completely.

I take a minute to gaze out at the sea. I'm looking for signs that might confirm the forecast we received earlier from our meteorologist, Elena Cristofori. One of the things I love about sailing is that the playing field is constantly changing due to the wind and currents. That makes sailing an unpredictable game. Chess played on a dynamic board. Sailors combine the meteorological reports we receive with our own ability to read the wind in the middle of a race. It's a fascinating art, but the wind can be a rebellious thing. It's always hiding something. So it's not just about knowing what's happening in the moment; you also have to be prepared for what will happen in the following minutes. We collect data on the cloud formations, the colors of the water, the way the flags on the coast are flying, and the ways in which the rival ships are moving. But despite all of this, intuition plays a fundamental role.

To this we add the expertise to execute maneuvers and the tactics to respond to the movements of our competitors. In the final race, which will begin in just a few hours, the top ten teams will compete to see who can best combine these variables while maintaining their balance as they hang from the trapeze: the only thing connecting us to a fast and unstable vessel.

Lying on the bed in the dark, having surrendered myself to the healing hands of Eva Álvarez, our kinesiologist, I let go and share part of my story with her. It was during one of our first treatment sessions that she had discovered my scar. It's small and it has healed well. In the middle of my chest at the level of my ribs. It's hard to see at first glance, but she found it and worked it gently, looking to restore some elasticity to the skin. I told her where it came from: the cancer for which they had to remove the entire upper lobe of my left lung. After the operation I was unable to speak, let alone make even the slightest physical effort. "Single cylinder," my friends used to call me.

They had resected roughly thirty percent of my pulmonary system. Over time, what was left of the organ would expand to fill the vacant space, but at first it was very difficult to breathe. The surgery was less than a year ago, and today I'm about to compete in the final sailing event of the Games. And what an irony it is: the International Olympic Committee had incorporated the Nacra catamaran because they wanted a fast and agile vessel that would entice young viewers, and yet here I am, the oldest sailor competing in Rio, and just recovered from cancer.

I ride my bike through a short tunnel that passes under an avenue. When I reemerge in the park, I recall the epic cycling workouts with which I began my rehabilitation in Cabrera de Mar, a rugged Spanish mountain town just over sixteen miles from Barcelona. It's my second home. Immediately, the images of Theo and Borja, my twins, come to mind. They were my support group after the surgery and throughout the entire period of recovery.

They're not sailors. They just didn't inherit my passion for the sport. Although they enjoy physical activity, it's a strong artistic inclination that prevails in them, one which comes from their mother, Silvina. Still, in one month we logged nearly 300 together on our bikes. Spending time with them during the recovery period was an opportunity to get to know them better. Instead of a competitive impulse, they both prefer a more relaxed approach to life. I worried about it at times, but in the moment, I was able to understand and appreciate it. As I ride on, the memories of those days fill me with energy.

I have two other sons, Yago and Klaus. They compete together in the 49er skiff, one of the most dynamic and explosive Olympic classes. And they're very different athletes. Yago shares my obsession with planning and tactics. He's the oldest, and may have suffered the most when Silvina and I separated and I decided to make a living as a competitive sailor, forcing me to spend long periods of time outside the country. Klaus, the youngest, is pure sensitivity. We spend a lot of time together, and he greets me with an effusive hug every time we pass one another in the marina. The two of them are also in Rio, competing in their first Olympics. Just over a week ago, the three of us, plus Ceci, paraded together during the opening ceremony. The moment we entered the Olympic Stadium, celebrating with the other athletes, was worth more to me than the two bronze medals I had won during previous Games. In a world rife with conflicts, inaugurating the Olympics is a sign that different peoples and cultures can come together in peace: a message that's even more important to me than the sport itself.

Sharing this experience with them in Rio justifies the effort that I'm demanding of my body. I always trained hard throughout my career and suffered a few injuries. I play squash with Yago and Klaus, and the matches are even. My weak point are my knees. I had surgery on both meniscuses before I started competing in Nacra and they can be quite painful. Crouching down, which is a common position to find yourself in on a catamaran, was torture. I was clearly suffering, and Ceci looked at me with concern. Before the Games, I had traveled to Brasilia to participate in a road race, the Red Bull World Run, and had to stop after only a hundred meters. I warmed up and was able to continue, but I prefer using the bike for training purposes. This Scott road bike I'm riding towards the Olympic marina is the same one I have used all these months to climb up to the statue of Christ the Redeemer at the top of Corcovado.

It wasn't just my knees that ended up paying a heavy price for my lifestyle. I know the decisions I've made have affected my relationships. There were times when I'd spend nine months out of the year competing around the globe. I understand how difficult it is to maintain a healthy relationship with your partner with that sort of schedule. I've been alone for quite some time. It's not something I've sought out for myself.

At some point I began questioning my vocation. What's the point of putting so much effort into something that apparently isn't very relevant? I would compare myself with my uncle Wolfgang, a doctor who saved lives and cared for the health of his patients. And what have I done instead? I spent decades trying to be the best at steering a boat between a couple of buoys. What does that mean? What am I contributing to society through my daily efforts?

Having arrived at the marina, we prepare our catamaran before venturing forth into battle. There are a few hours left before the final race, and the routine won't be altered. The final day of an Olympic competition is no time for innovation. Everyone knows what to do. The ship has three sails. I'll handle the mainsail while Ceci takes care of the other two, the jib and the spinnaker. Our team is there to assist us, but they know that Ceci and I like to check the rigging, cotter pins, bolts, and other systems, as well as set all the battens with precision in order to give just the right amount of tension to the sails. It's a way of making sure that nothing is worn out and at risk of breaking. Preparations also include decisions about which materials to use based upon the wind conditions we expect to find.

Yesterday, Mariano Parada and Mateo Majdalani, our coaches, did the hardest of all maintenance jobs: putting a final polish on the hull so it offers the least possible resistance to the water. They're one of the reasons we're here with a serious chance of winning gold. Cole, as Mariano is known, is a great friend and highly experienced sailor himself. We competed together in other classes, including the 2000 Sydney Olympics and two Snipe Class World Championship Regattas, which we won. We brought him on board a year ago to balance Mateo's youth with his own extensive experience.

At twenty-two years of age, Mateo is a prodigy, and a close friend of my youngest son Klaus. They were competing together in the junior classes and I could already see their enormous talent. After having asked his father for permission to make him an offer, we called him up as soon as we started our campaign. He'd never been a coach, much less faced Olympic-level competition. We had already worked with young, promising sailors during previous Games, and they were a guarantee of enthusiasm and commitment. They were also a way for us to pass along our approach to the work to newer generations. And with Mateo, the results were exceptional. He is serious, focused, hard-working, and above all, very intelligent, which is key in a sport like this where so many variables are at play. His professional growth will be one of the best things to have come out of this adventure.

In the marina, you're in close contact with your fellow competitors. You can smell the tension. We're lined up in the order of our classification. We are the first. Next to us are the Italians, followed by the Austrians and the Australians: the three greatest threats in the battle for medals. Based on the current standings, it is possible to calculate the final results based on potential finishes. In fact, we have done the maths last night. All that matters to me is the knowledge that, if we finish in the top three, we were guaranteed the gold. And if we are among the first six to finish, we would be assured of a spot on the winner's podium. Ceci had all the other possibilities memorized.

"You have to sail well and that's it," I say. It's not that I don't care. Gold is what I want. I understand the importance of numbers, but what I know is that, when you're on board a Nacra, you can't sail and do mental arithmetic at the same time. If I have to choose, I'll stick with the first one. But just in case, Cole and Mateo had printed out a sheet listing all the possible finishing positions. They had laminated it and stuck it on the boat.

The catamaran is ready and we like being the first to hit the water. But now the winds are changing and the race has been postponed. When this happens, it's important to maintain a sense of balance. If I've learned anything after all these years, it's that being nervous is useless. But dismissing it isn't as easy as it sounds. You've prepared for a specific schedule, and all of a sudden everything is put on hold until further notice. You have no idea when you'll have to get yourself back into the optimal state of mind for competition. I head for an area under a tree where we store our things: a toolbox, a couple of chairs, some bags, and our spare equipment. We have chosen this place specifically because it's remote. When I'm trying to focus, I look for solitude. I'm calm, I lay down in the grass. I block out the sun with my cap, assume the fetal position, and let the time go by.

Ceci, however, is more restless. Cole takes her aside to distract her. They prop themselves up against the hull of our boat, protected by the shade cast by the sail, and talk about what plans they have for after the Games and for their families. Cole is wearing a T-shirt that reads "Ceci and Santi" in that order. It was made by Ceci's parents, who are there in Rio, and she smiles when she sees it. Cole also has an Argentine flag stashed in his backpack in case Ceci needs to celebrate. He's done well to hide it; none of us even allow ourselves to talk about it. Ceci uses the break to have a short visualization session with Daniel Espina, our yoga instructor and sports psychologist.

Sessions with Dani are always individual. You don't need much. Just a mat and a ball for stretching. I had a short one this morning and a more intense session yesterday afternoon. Ceci has a similar routine. At the beginning of the routine, in order to get her out of her thoughts and into a calm state of mind, Dani tells her to visualize herself sitting on the banks of the Paraná River. Vast and mighty, the Paraná is where Ceci first learned to sail. It serves as a beautiful waterfront to Rosario, her home. She adores her city and her river. It's her refuge, it's where her family is. The image makes her feel protected and safe from any insecurity.

Dani played a fundamental role when we had to deal with critical situations between Ceci and I. He listened to both of us and tried to make us understand that it wasn't just about sailing faster, it was about learning to work together. That was the great challenge for this mixed team. It brought out the best and the worst in us. The age difference was never a problem, but we have very different personalities and have had very different experiences. There was a time when we weren't performing particularly well and I would often take my anger out on her. That certainly didn't help the team. Ceci is a tireless worker. When we started out, her attitude was perfect for absorbing information, but the dynamics of our relationship often undermined that learning process. At some point, she got frustrated and began to question whether she was ready for this level of demand.

My demeanor contributed to her mental slump. I'm always looking to see how far we can push the limits, to see just how well we can perform. I need the challenge. When I don't see that desire to give everything and then some, I get anxious. When I'm in my training mode, I can come off as too intense for someone who has a different philosophy when it comes to approaching both sport and life.

There's another factor at play as well: I'm Ceci's teammate, but—based on my experience—I also serve as coach and team leader. This overlapping of roles brought complications. I had to involve not only her, but the rest of the crew in the decision-making process. And in doing so, I made—and continue to make—efforts to reduce the abruptness with which I express myself. "Don't you agree?" Dani says, laughing as he parrots the catchphrase I use whenever I'm seeking approval for one of my ideas.

Before the start of the competition in Rio, we took stock of what these years of preparation had been like. Ceci hit on one of the key factors: the problems we'd faced were enormous, but no more so than our desire to overcome them. Many times she found herself at the edge of her physical and mental capacities. She'd wake up in the morning feeling like she didn't have the energy to get out of bed, wondering whether the fatigue was in her body or just in her head. She questioned whether she could summon the strength to face everything that had to be done not just on that day but every day leading up to the Rio Games. Workouts in the gym, hours upon hours on the water, tuning up the vessel, planning, and traveling to compete in preparatory races. How does one carry all of this forward?

Dani helped Ceci climb the physical and emotional mountain that this Olympic campaign represented. That's what he told her, yesterday, during their session. When they finished, Ceci looked him in the eye and thanked him excitedly.

"I have no doubt that tomorrow, no matter the result, we'll do well, and I'll be able to accept it with nothing but peace and tranquility," she said.

They embraced in silence.

Ceci was the last member to join the racing team that we formally began in 1993. The method we've developed over the years includes Dani's yoga work and visualization techniques mixed with other ingredients, including rigorous planning, relentless physical preparation, long hours out on the water, and pre-competition gatherings where we all share a house together. One of the founding members of the KGB—that's what we jokingly call our team—is Daniel Bambicha, our long-standing trainer. Bambi is a former track athlete. When he was still competing, he traveled to Yugoslavia, which was part of the socialist axis, to train with his national team. It was there that he adopted the steely system of discipline which he later used to punish us in the gym. He liked to push the limits of our endurance, and we all shared a love of a job well done. Although we had had a disagreement that resulted in Bambi not traveling with us to the Games, his contributions were nonetheless crucial.

Bambi's friendly counterpart is Mariano Galarza, another veteran member of the team. If Bambi's role was to push us to the breaking point, Galarza's was to spoil us. A good-natured giant, he was a tremendous injection of positive mentality when he arrived in Rio. He gave us that boost of energy we needed to face the competition. During our earlier Olympic campaigns, he was in charge of our marketing strategy, managing sponsors, setting up travel logistics, and he even looked after my children and ex-wife while I was traveling. But he also had one more function, which he performs now: he cooks and makes sure that we're all comfortable in the house. With the former, he's a real genius. Last night we had pork brochette with potatoes, zucchini, and eggplant. The food was delicious, but even better were the stories that brightened up the dinner table.

Galarza is from Santa Lucía, a small and warm town in the Argentine province of Corrientes, which seemed almost mythical in the ways he worked it into his stories. After so many years, we'd heard almost all of them, but they're still always hilarious when he tells them. Last night he returned to one of his classics: the time when he was a child and the circus came to Santa Lucía, and he and his friends went and caught some stray cats to feed to the tiger during siesta time. We went to bed with sore bellies from laughing so hard. Demanding yet enjoyable: that's the true spirit of Team KGB.

An essential role in this working environment was played by Carlos Mauricio Espínola, another founding member of the team. Camau was the great companion of my Olympic career. It was with him that I learned how to plan a campaign and win medals. He's Galarza's brother-in-law and also from Corrientes, but his personality is just the opposite. Reserved and sullen, he keeps to himself during social gatherings and can come across as unfriendly to those who don't know him. But I do. I know and admire him. I'll never forget the first time I saw him training at the Tarek gym. He was an athlete with a knack for physical preparation that was unprecedented in our sport at the time.

The peak of our performance came during the 2004 Athens Olympics, when we competed in the Tornado, a catamaran that preceded the Nacra. We were so coordinated on board the vessel that we barely even spoke. We each knew what the other had to do, and we trusted that they would do it well. There was an absolute sense of respect between us. Together we garnered two bronze medals, but our level of competitiveness had us going for gold. Not having won left a thorn in my side.

Twenty minutes to go before we launch the boats into the water, and I get my body going with some light exercise, which I do with Dani. I take off my sportswear and put on the neoprene. I don't have a problem changing in front of people, but there are cameras everywhere, so I cover myself with a poncho. I choose the lighter wetsuit, 1.5 millimeters, the short boots, the light blue and white lycra shirt, the calm wind trapeze harness, the life jacket, the cap, and finally the yellow bib which identifies us as the leaders going into this final competition. It's the first day we start out in this position, and I feel a sense of pressure that inspires me, a mix of both strength and pride. The feeling dissipates fast. It's time to get moving.

As soon as the ramp is in place, Ceci holds the vessel steady and removes the trailer. I remove the bow stops on which the hull rests. This is neither the time nor the place for pep talks. Nothing should change the way we do things. The emotion is floating in the air all around us. No need to mention it.

Cole told me later that he'd prepared a short speech. He reminded Ceci about what she'd gone through to be here. He was going to tell me that this was our chance, that I'd fought through a thousand regattas and cancer itself. That day, before the Christ with the open arms and my family who would be cheering us on from the beach, I just had to go out and enjoy it. Luckily, though, he'd spoken with Dani and decided not to. Instead, it was the usual. A slap on the shoulder, a quick hug, a knowing look. Anything else would have been too much.

We start sailing and feel the roar from the grandstands, something unprecedented in our sport. More accustomed to setting sail with no one other than the other competitors and race officials, the cheering overwhelms us. Flags are waving and the famous *Argentina! Argentina!* chant more commonly heard at soccer games resounds through the air. My mother, a few of my siblings, my children, Ceci's family, and hundreds of people we don't know are cheering us on as if we were Messi. There are even a number of Brazilians among them. After all, we're local.

There is little time and much to do before the race begins. The first thing is to test the setting we have chosen for the boat. We have to make sure that the set-up is correct. We base our decisions on the wind conditions in the weather forecasts and what we could see from the land, but we make the final adjustments once we start sailing and can feel how the boat behaves. On the way to the staging area where the course begins, we try a few alternatives and exchange information with Mateo and Cole, who are on the motorboat. When we arrive, we meet with the Swiss team for speed checks and to decide, according to the wind and currents, which is the preferred side to be on. It's a vital choice: there's no point in going fast if you're on the wrong path.

The wind sweeps down from Sugarloaf Mountain, and that creates gusting, which is difficult to predict. Tough conditions, but we'll take them. Not one of the nine other teams have spent as much time sailing in this bay as we have, and that gives us a measure of assurance. I'm confident that when the time comes, we'll sense before anyone else where the winning gust will come from. Everything is going well in the test runs with the Swiss, and we relay our conclusions to our coaches.

"I like the right," I say as I hydrate while Ceci chews on a granola bar.

"Me too," Mateo agrees. "But don't overdo it and get caught up in the pockets of calm."

He's right. If we stick too closely to the coast, we run the risk of losing the wind. We talk about paying close attention so we can choose from which angle to enter the first set of buoys, one of the more complicated segments of the course. In the end, we confirm the strategy for the start of the race we had planned out last night.

The start is a critical moment in a short event like this, the medal race. We begin by positioning ourselves behind an imaginary line set up between two boats as a reference point. We can't cross it until a horn sounds announcing the start of the race. If we do, we have to go back. We could even be disqualified. The whole process begins with a five-minute countdown. The goal is to be in the most favorable position and at maximum speed, with no opponents to worry about and at the exact limits set by the line, when the clock reaches zero. The ten vessels are all looking for the same thing and space is tight.

We decide we want to be towards the left side of the line and aiming towards the right side of the course. This strategy has several advantages, but it also involves a serious risk. Based on the course we've chosen, the rules state that we're required to let all boats coming from the other side pass. There tends to be a lot of crisscrossing at the start of a race, and we'll have to avoid any compromising situations with another boat that has the right-of-way. The judges watch from their motorboats and when they see a foul, they blow their horn: the most feared sign of all. It means you're penalized with a full turn, a slow maneuver that takes you off your planned course.

If everything goes according to plan, taking this risk will allow us to get to the side of the course which we think has the most favorable wind, which would simplify the rest of the competition. It's an aggressive strategy. We could opt for a more conservative approach, playing it safe in hopes of securing a spot on the winner's podium, but I'm driven by my desire for gold.

When it comes to the division of tasks on board the vessel, my responsibility is to execute the tactics. Ceci, on the other hand, besides keeping an eye on the movements of our competitors (among many other duties) keeps track of the time on her stopwatch and checks the flags with which the regatta commission boat announces the type of route and how much time is left until the start. My ignorance when it comes to the flag codes is absolute. I've never learned them, nor do I have any desire to do so. I trust in Ceci.

"Two minutes to go," she says.

At this point it's clear that the majority of the fleet has made a decision similar to ours: start at a slight angle to the right with no right-of-way. We're second from the left end of the starting line. On one side of us are the Austrians, with the English on the other. We try to keep the vessel from moving forward, maintaining our position relative to those next to us. It's not easy. The waves, the wind, and the current are making us anxious. If we want to maintain control, we'll have to tighten the sails and let the catamaran edge forward, but that would bring us dangerously close to the starting line, which must not be crossed. Like racehorses on tight reins, our Nacras are restless when restrained. They vie for every inch.

"One minute," Ceci announces.

A bit of a development appears on the right: the French and Australians are set up to start facing the opposite direction. They'll have the right of way, and we must make sure they can cross in the clear. Otherwise, we could be in violation of the rules.

"Thirty seconds."

The critical element of the start is deciding when to accelerate. Catamarans pick up speed very quickly. If I swing the rudder and change course, one of the hulls will rise up out of the water and we'll take off. I have to do it at precisely the right moment and in a very finely tuned coordination with Ceci, who handles the sails. Not a second before, and not a second after.

The goal is to let the French pass and just miss the Australians. The English, who are downwind, will do the same. This is our most immediate concern. In the next ten seconds, we'll find out who executed the best start. They'll be the first to break to the right, which is where we all want to be.

"Twenty seconds."

I ready myself to pull the trigger and accelerate, while at the same time keeping my eye on the English crew as well as the two vessels crossing in front of us which we'll have to avoid.

"Ten seconds."

Danger! The English set sail first in hopes of getting out in front of the Australians. It's a bad decision and they'll be penalized for it, but that's their problem. Our immediate concern is something else: the Australians will have to avoid the English, putting them on a collision course with us.

"Nine... eight..."

The worst case scenario comes true: the Australians have changed their course drastically and we are now hurtling towards what could be a disastrous head-on collision. The Australian helmsman looks panicked. So do we. If we collide while sailing in opposite directions, our vessels will get hooked together and break apart. It'll be the end of the race and goodbye to the medals.

The Australians miss us by inches. Having dodged this bullet, we tear off. This wasn't the start we'd anticipated, but we're in the race.

Then the horn blows.

I turn my head and I can't believe it. The judge is pointing his flag at us. It's a penalty, but not a fair one. The fault lies with the English crew, while we did everything we could to solve the problem they created. But there's no time to be wasted on speculation. We have to make a complete turn before getting back into the race. It's a complicated maneuver, one we never really train for. Of all the things we had to prepare for, this was not one of the priorities. It comes out slow and rough. The catamaran almost capsizes.

When we finally finish and get back to sailing, I look up and see that we're in last place, far behind the rest of the fleet. Once again, the gold medal seems to be slipping away into the distance. But I don't let myself get upset. It's a short race, but there will be opportunities to recover. The important thing is not to worry. Keep calm and confident. That's the new plan, and in fact, it's the only one we've got. We're going to have to fight our way up from the bottom if we're to have our resurgence.

Chapter One

Discipline at Home, Freedom on the River

It all started as a game. A game that allowed us to be free and happy during a time when we didn't even know the meaning of those words.

The playground where our adventure took place began where the wooded grounds of the Yacht Club Argentino looked out over the river in San Fernando, a suburb on the outskirts of Buenos Aires, and expanded infinitely once we boarded our little boats. We were barely seven years old, and we had the Luján River to ourselves, and beyond that, an estuary of the Río de la Plata, vast and expansive, which opens up just over a mile from the club. Growing up at the exact point where a great confluence of fresh water, a dark and earthy color, forms a delta of islands, islets, rivers, and streams gave me exceptional access to what has always been my great passion: sailing.

Before the rivers and the ocean beyond it, the club's bay spread out before us. It was marked off by two buoys, which was the limit our parents had imposed upon us. We spent hours running races—calling them regattas would be more than a bit overblown—between the ramp where we launched our boats and one of those buoys. Sailboats anchored in the bay became obstacles to navigate around. We lived for those competitions, and soon enough, through those trial runs, we began unlocking the secrets of nature. In order to win, we had to figure out where the wind was blowing the strongest, or react quickly when there was a change in its direction. We did these things intuitively, without even realizing it.

During the excitement of the race, we would occasionally collide with the hulls of anchored boats or get tangled up in their moorings. Most of the time, there was nobody on board, and we could flee quickly to avoid responsibility. But every once in a while we would run into a boat where someone was taking a nap, rocking gently in the swaying waters, who would stand up and shout at us angrily. When we got tired of racing, we played hide and seek in the water. One of us would count to fifty with our eyes closed while the rest would set out and hide behind the larger sailboats anchored in the bay, where they'd lower the mast and hide the sail to avoid being discovered.

The club also featured soccer, Argentina's national sport. I played, just like everyone else, but I didn't like it nearly as much as sailing. And my tall, lanky physique didn't help. Plus, I wore glasses. I still have a scar from the injury I gave myself when I was ten and trying to play without them.

"Watch out! You're blind! You're gonna hurt yourself," Martín Billoch said mockingly.

Quick in the way short kids tend to be, and with a headband to rein in his abundant blonde locks, Martín was two years older than I and much more skilled than I was with the ball. He was also faster in a boat. While the soccer thing didn't much matter to me, his superiority on the water kept me up at night. I'd lie there in bed, wide awake, searching for the answer to the same question I ask myself to this day: how can I become a better sailor?

There were other boys with whom we shared games on land and adventures on the water. Girls were into sailing as well. In that sport, integration almost always came about naturally without gender distinctions. Not many of them had our fanaticism, though. We were rivals, but Martín and I were close. He was the first friend I had out there on the water, which is where I had the best times of my youth.

Weekends always started early in my home in San Isidro, a residential area with a small town feeling located a little under twenty miles from hectic and bustling Buenos Aires. On Fridays, Martín would come for a sleepover. Saturday, after breakfast, we'd pack our bags and step outside to wait for the bus that would take us to the Yacht Club. After a twenty-minute ride, we'd get off on an unpopulated road and begin a seemingly endless hike until we reached the entrance where a sailor in a security post guarded the entrance. Ecstatic and set to go, we finally crossed over into the aquatic side of life where the rules that applied on dry land lost their validity. This was our secret garden, filled with stories known to no-one but ourselves. At school I could come across as shy and a bit reserved. At home I was the youngest of five children under a strict, stern father. But all of that faded away once we walked through the doors of the club and could sense the presence of the nearby river.

The Yacht Club is situated on a peninsula that starts out narrow before widening at the end. As we walked to the sheds where our boats were stored, to the right we could admire some of the finest vessels that sailed the Río de la Plata. We dreamed of one day taking the helm of one of them. We knew all their names and imagined epic regattas, distant seas, and unknown ports which, very soon—it was only a matter of time—we would be visiting.

Martín and I were kids in a club for adults, which was one of the oldest, most traditional in all of Argentina, and proud of that status. Back then, despite the hot summer weather, there was no swimming pool. That would have gone against its principles: sailing was club's one true purpose. Members treated one another with a sense of respect for mores that contrasted sharply with our childish impetuousness. Every once in a while, an older member of the club would tell us to stop yelling or running around, or remind us we couldn't enter the bar area in swimming trunks. But that tended to happen during the day when more people were there. We spent nearly every Saturday night aboard our parents' ships, and the nights were ours. We were the lords and masters of a deserted club. We got the boats ready, and after everyone else had fallen asleep, we slipped out to explore the dark bay. We listened in silence to the thumping sound of the hull against the still water as we slid down to the river's bank. The moon lent an aura of mystery to our adventures.

We quickly became the darlings of the club's sailors and other employees, who appreciated the joy we introduced to a place with such a formal atmosphere. What we liked best about them was that they lacked the censuring tendencies of our parents. I remember Giménez, who worked in the storeroom and gave us access to sails and life jackets, as well as Ávalos and Urrel, who came with the club's motorboats to tow us when we started competing in regattas. Ana María, the sailing instructor, was a woman with a tremendously strong character. We used to have our differences. She was an old school sailor who wanted to teach us how to read buoy markings and nautical charts, but these were theoretical questions that didn't interest us much. All Martín and I wanted to do was sail, to explore the river, and we'd learned how to do that on our own. Other than some basic advice handed down to us from older sailors, nobody gave us much in the way of instruction when we were starting out. One day we simply hopped on a boat and started to learn out there on the water, which is where we really wanted to be. Thus, without even thinking about it, we had begun what would become hundreds of hours of training.

We made up for our lack of a formal education with the freshness that stems from being adventurous children. We would have many frightening moments, and we were certainly in danger at times, as the river can be a treacherous place, but the memories I have of those days is the pure joy of sailing. Back then, we had no coaches and followed no written rules, which allowed us to grow without the fear of making mistakes. That stately and distant club would give us, without even realizing it, the opportunity to learn and discover things at our own pace.

The freedom I felt on the river contrasted sharply with the disciplined routine that my father, Enrique Jorge Lange, exercised at home. Order was his personal obsession. Before going to bed, our tasks included leaving our closets impeccably clean and laying out the following day's clothing on a chair next to the bed. Every so often, my father would conduct an inspection. Once, I remember him grabbing everything in the closet and throwing it on the floor before ordering us to pick it back up and organize it properly. Dinner was always a ceremony. The entire family would wait for my father to come home from work so we could eat together at a large, immaculately set table. Before we could sit down, he would inspect our hair and our hands, and anybody who had missed a spot had to go to the bathroom and tidy up. His nap was sacred. When he lay down to sleep, we were forbidden from playing out in the yard. During the summer we couldn't use the pool—which my older siblings had scrubbed and painted early in the season—until he was up. My friends were afraid of him. Martín, especially, still remembers when he had to take the bus home in the middle of the night, even though we had planned on a sleepover. That was my father's punishment for misbehaving.

He never yelled at us or resorted to corporal punishment. Instead, he imposed himself with a (stern) look and his military ways. He was of German descent and graduated from Argentina's Naval Academy. His parents, Max and Clara, were born in Weimar, in the German state of Thuringia. They emigrated to Argentina with Wolfgang, their eldest son, and my father was born here. I have no memories of my paternal grandfather. My maternal grandmother, whom we called Omama (from "Oma," meaning "grandma" in German) was extremely tough, even tougher than my father. She spoke Spanish with a heavy accent. She would come over on Sundays and knit wool socks for us. We didn't see much of Uncle Wolfgang, but I loved and admired him. He was a renowned physician, a cultured and refined man. Like Omama, he spoke with an accent, and there was a cold and distant manner about him that annoyed my siblings. I liked his seriousness. And while my father would regularly invite him over for Sunday roasts, he rarely came, preferring instead to study.

My father's career as a sailor was short-lived. During the second half of the 20th century, Argentina experienced a period of great political upheaval. Peronism—a movement that sought the support of workers and and unions whlie confronting the nation's traditional sectors—was emerging. My father like most of his colleagues in the Navy, was a liberal who found himself at odds with Juan Domingo Perón, the movement's populist leader. He preferred to avoid politics after the 1955 coup overthrew Perón and put the military in charge of the country. Instead, he turned to the private sector, which garnered him some economic prosperity. Still, though, he was never fully able to stay away from the troubled and violent times that loomed over Argentina.

What my father truly enjoyed was sailing. He owned at least three sailboats in his life and competed in open ocean races. He participated as a substitute in the 1952 Helsinki Games in one of the sailing categories. On the wall of my childhood bedroom I had a poster from those Games with the Argentine flag and the Olympic rings in gold. The funny thing is that I never talked about this with him, like so many other things that went unsaid. When I started sailing at the YCA, as we called the club, he had his boat moored there. At mid-morning on the weekends he'd drive up there in his car. He did his thing; he didn't follow me around or worry about what I might be up to. Maybe he thought that, as long as I was sailing, everything would be fine. The space he gave me there was important. It allowed me to follow my true interests and learn to solve problems on my own. When he was with his friends, he was free-spoken, jovial, and well liked. At least, that's what the other club members who were around his age told me.

There's one day I'll always remember because it would come to define what later became my career in sports. I came home from the club in frustration: I had been on the verge of winning a tournament when a piece of my rudder broke and I was forced to withdraw. It was a cold and windy afternoon, the river was raging, and for once I had been ahead of Martín. On top of my anger over surrendering was the fatigue of having spent an entire day on the water and the long bus ride home, brooding over my bad luck. When I got home and opened the door, I felt what was left of my strength leaving me, and I collapsed on the floor in tears. My dad asked me what had happened, and I told him. It was then that he said something which would stay with me as a tenet:

"Races are won on land."

My obsession with planning strategies and prepping the boats stems from that very day, as does my belief that every outcome is defined by preparation and training.

My father had a hard time expressing affection, but he taught me to be responsible, committed, and respectful. And, above all, he gave me the freedom to seek out my own path and grow. I was a quiet, introverted kid who kept to himself and was fascinated by boats. Everything else was relegated to the background. There's a line that my siblings jokingly repeated every time I failed to appear at some family event: "Santi couldn't be here 'cause he's out sailing." On my mother's birthday, they put my face on a cardboard cutout and placed it in the photos as a way of poking fun at the fact that, once again, I wasn't there. This passion for sport and my tendency to put it above all other things would define not only my childhood but my adult life as well. Ever since I was a kid, I knew that all I ever wanted to do was become the best sailor I could, and I put an enormous amount of effort into achieving that dream. The rest of the family had no choice but to learn to deal with my absences.

My siblings say my father had a special place in his heart for me. According to them, the love we shared for the river had softened his stern exterior to the point where he became almost kind towards me. One Christmas, my dad gave me an Optimist, a small, single-handed dinghy. I was stunned. My father tried to hide what was obvious—that he'd gotten it for me—by claiming it was to share with my brother Sebastián who was a year and a half older than me. We called him Pololo; he loved rugby and he hated sailing. Nevertheless, when we got to the club and assembled the boat, my brother, who had always been confrontational with my father, stood up and announced that he would be the one to launch it. It was his right, he argued, as the older brother.

"Let Santiago do it," my dad said curtly.

The Optimist, the world's most popular boat for children and young teenagers, was inspired by a soap box derby car that kids from Clearwater, Florida, used for holding street races in the late 1940s. Clifford A. McKay, an American military officer who was looking for a simple, cheap design, used it as a model for a small sailboat for his son. The idea was picked up by the Scandinavians, who adapted and standardized it. It was an immediate hit, and in 1962, the first world championship for the class was run.

News of the boat that was revolutionizing ways of learning how to sail soon reached Argentina. The first Optimist arrived from England aboard the Fortuna, the Navy's training vessel. One version of the story—which I could never confirm—alleged that my dad was on board that same vessel. They took it to the YCA, which was the country's sailing capital, and immediately it became a toy favored by Martín, who would have been nine, and me, around seven.

It was a wooden craft and came disassembled. Patricio Billoch, Martín's father, who would later go on to be the first president of the IDOA, the Optimist Dinghy Association in Argentina, followed some plans he'd gotten in Denmark and put it all together. The sail was white with blue stripes and printed with the letter K, nomenclature for English ships, and the number 701. Martín and I had been on other boats, but the Optimist gave us our first opportunity to be out on the water alone. We were finally on our own. Before us stretched the river and a world of possibilities. Soon, other kids from the club wanted to come and join in the fun.

I remember going with my dad to a shipyard run by Jorge Cavado, who had been commissioned to manufacture the first six Optimists on Argentine soil. Like everything else at the time, they were made from varnished wood, and they had a copper bottom with a white waterline. Martín had the number "1" on his sail and dubbed his boat the Tiki. Mine was number "3." When my father gave it to me for Christmas, I named it What Do I Know. To this day, if I close my eyes, I can still see it floating there in the bay.

Martín and I were an inseparable pair. Best friends and rivals. We needed each other in order to gauge our progress. Later on we were joined by the boys from the Club Náutico San Isidro, located a few miles downriver, where the Luján River merges with an estuary of the Río de la Plata. With a wide range of sports other than sailing, the Náutico had more of a family atmosphere. The close proximity fostered connections and rivalries between the two clubs. As ambassadors of this new vessel, we put on an exhibition, and thus the Optimist became the Náutico's official training vessel. They placed another order with the Cavado shipyard and added a number to their own fleet.

In order to get to the race course we had to learn how to navigate the Luján River. Sometimes a larger boat would tow us there. If not, we'd make our own way using the nautical knowledge we were starting to acquire. The center of the canal was off limits because the current was stronger there and it had much more traffic. Choosing the best side was essential to shorten the trip. Martín still has nightmares about slogging through the reeds, his feet sinking into the muddy bank of the river as we dragged the Optimist behind us when the wind gave out and the current was against us. When that sort of thing happened, the return trip was long and tiring, especially in winter. We didn't have high-tech athletic clothing at the time, and instead sailed in jeans and wool sweaters that got heavy and cold as soon as they got the slightest bit wet. We'd get home, chilled to the bone, and immediately dive into a shower hot enough to burn our skin.

The alternative was to spend the night at the Club Náutico, a solution that was both practical and fun. We'd set sail from our yacht club early Saturday morning, compete in the regattas, and then head for the Náutico, which was closer. We'd spend the night curled up in an armchair in front of the fireplace, fighting back the cold and hiding from Ponce and El Tucu, two employees who would have sent us packing. If we were absolutely starving, we'd raid the bar for a sandwich or an alfajor, a shortbread sandwich cookie with a dulce de leche center. On Sunday we'd be up with the sun, sail in our regattas, and return, exhausted, to the YCA. Monday morning meant the beginning of a tedious week of school and life away from the water which I endured by daydreaming about becoming a sailor.

Just as my father set the rules that defined our childhood, my mother, Ana María Robertie de Lange, or Chuqui to her friends, was in charge of the day to day household activities. Affectionate, sociable, and chatty, but also temperamental on occasion. Heiress to a family of French origins that had earned a small fortune distributing coffee, she lost her mother as a young woman. She had no relationship with her father to speak of. As she put it, he was a womanizer who abandoned them. Instead, she was raised by her absent father's sisters: two adorable, single aunts, Francina and Paulette, who were our de facto grandmothers. They lived in a spacious apartment in an elegant part of the city. Generous, intelligent, and endowed with a great deal of common sense, they were the emotional pillars of our childhood.

Polú (as we called her) was determined and organized. She'd suffered from polio as a child which left her with a limp. She ran the house while Fanchi busied herself with more recreational or artistic tasks such as bookbinding. We were all concerned about how Fanchi would do when Polú died. That happened in 1982, and Fanchi lived on to the ripe old age of ninety-nine. She continued her hobby of embroidering even after she could barely see anymore. Her longevity may have been due to her curious diet of black cigarettes, a whiskey before every meal, and fernet—a dark, bitter Italian liqueur—after dessert. Both were quite wise. Traditional in their way of living, but generous in their manner of thinking. They had the ability to offer true love without expecting anything in return. That was their greatest quality. I never heard a single complaint about the fact that I, always immersed in my own world, somewhat neglected them. Sebastián recently gave all the siblings a framed photo of the two of them. We all keep it in a prominent place in our homes.

We would see our great-aunts often throughout the year, and even more so during the summer, when we would invade their home in the Uruguayan seaside resort of Punta del Este. With a marina and a peninsular geography that results in two very different coastlines—La Mansa, which is protected and barely has any waves, and La Brava, which is exposed to the strong Atlantic winds—Punta del Este was our refuge during the hot season. We would settle there in December, when school was out, and return in March shortly before school began again. With its homes with large yards, the forests, and the promenade overlooking the ocean, the city was a child's paradise. Our general routine included the beach in the morning, a siesta around noon, and bike rides, tea with the aunts, fishing in the port, and more beach in the afternoons. I liked to dive directly into the onrushing waves, to roll around in the surf. I remember the joy of trundling home with a bucket filled with silversides to cook and eat later that same night. Bike races around the block were another classic summer activity. A tight turn around a corner could result in a bad crash thanks to the sand that collected in the streets. The scrapes burned even worse the next day when we went back in the ocean.

Fanchi and Polú's house had two stories and was known as Luna Nueva. The upper level was for the grownups, and each couple had their own room. The ground floor amounted to one giant bedroom where all the Lange children slept. There were so many of us, not to mention the girlfriends, boyfriends, other friends, and friends of friends. Meals were organized in an ironclad fashion: it was the only way to feed so many people. There was a massive dining room table large enough to seat fifteen, but there were at least twice that many of us, so we introduced a two-shift system: you ate your first course while feeling your replacement breathing down your neck behind you. In charge of (all) the social arrangements was my mother, the great organizer of family life, who enjoyed the help of two housekeepers. After having managed to accommodate every last one of us, she would engage in her favorite pastime there in Punta del Este: go out for a long walk on the beach with my father.

According to my mother, her relationship with my father first had to overcome her French family's resistance to a relationship with a German man. The trauma of the Second World War had reached as far as Argentina. But a photograph of her had absolutely captivated my father, and he wouldn't rest until he had convinced the Roberties to accept him. They got married and two years later, Máximo, the first of my siblings, was born, followed in short order by Martín, Inés, Sebastián, myself, and finally Enrique. Theirs was an old-fashioned marriage. They shared an active social life, but there were also nights when my mother stayed at home while my father hung out with friends. This was an unspoken pact marked by a clear signal: the blue jacket. If my father left in the morning wearing his blue jacket, my mother knew he wouldn't be home for dinner. It could have been a meeting of the Yacht Club board of directors, which my father was on, or something completely different. In those days, explanations weren't given.

When their family began to grow, my parents looked for a suburban neighborhood to settle and a school for their children. This is how we moved from downtown Buenos Aires to San Isidro. The Colegio San Juan el Precursor, founded by a group of Catholic families, didn't seem like the most logical of choices for my dad, who wasn't especially spiritual and who a more worldly character about him. But that's where they registered us. I imagine he approved of the strict dress code required of all students: brown shoes, gray socks and pants, a light blue shirt with a blue tie, and a corduroy blazer during the winter, which could be replaced by a light blue sweater during the hotter months of the year.

The most important thing about school, which is what my classmates and I would take with us for the rest of our lives, was an emphasis on friendship. Those same boys with whom I shared a classroom are, to this day, five decades later, still my dear friends. We grew together, we developed together, and that bond has had a lot to do with the kind of people we've come to be.

In San Isidro, my siblings and I played in the cobblestone streets, we walked back and forth between our friends' houses, and every morning we hopped on our bikes and rode to school. We enjoyed a level of independence we would never have had in a big city like Buenos Aires. Plus, just a few blocks from home was El Sesenta, the number 60 bus route, which I could ride to San Fernando. There I could reunite with the river and with the untamed sense of freedom that I felt welling up every Saturday morning as I watched my boat slip into the water.

Chapter Two

The Friend I Could Never Beat

Martín Billoch always beat me. My only consolation in the face of each and every loss was that he didn't just beat me, he beat everyone. Martín trained extensively and was so obsessed with sailing that, at night, in bed, he would go through the motions of the different maneuvers required during a regatta. In 1974, he traveled to Lake Silvaplana, in Switzerland, to compete in the first Optimist World Championship in which Argentina was a participant. He didn't know anybody, nobody knew him, and he competed against a hundred other young sailors, many of whom already had international experience. On top of that, he had to rent a plastic boat because the ones we were using back home were still made of wood. And even so, he won. In the final race, he outpaced the second-place finisher, a Swede who had been favored to win it all and who had been insulting him throughout the competition. When Martín prevailed, his defeated opponent confronted him, looking to fight. Luckily, officials were able to separate them. Weighing in at eighty pounds and standing at just four foot nine, Martín had obvious competitive advantages out on the water, but not as a boxer.

He was welcomed back to Buenos Aires with a festival in his honor. A large group of friends from both school and the Yacht

Club were waiting to greet him at Ezeiza Airport, along with photographers and journalists. They ran a story on him and invited him to appear on a popular TV show where the country's most famous host, Mirtha Legrand, would have lunch with prominent figures from all sorts of backgrounds. At just fourteen years of age, Martín coolly answered all the questions and showed off one of the prizes he won: a Swiss watch that dangled from his skinny wrist.

Along with Martín, there were four other Argentines who had sailed well enough in qualifying to earn the right to go to the first World Championships: Hugo Castro, Gonzalo Campero, Norma Lasalle, and Gonzalo Pérez Mendoza. I was left on the outside looking in. At the time I had a rather slow boat. After the original wooden Optimists came the second generation, the Bordolani, which were made from plastic and vastly superior. Thanks to my dad's frugality, I was one of the last to change ships. Plus, when my father finally did agree to buy me the new plastic Optimist, I got a bad one, over thirteen pounds heavier than the others. And while that may not have been the primary reason, the name I gave it was nonetheless appropriate: Obelix, after the ever-famished character from *Asterix the Gaul*, a French comic I was a fan of. It was black and bore the number 303 on the sail.

But what separated Martin from me was never the ship. Nor was it the support of his father, who accompanied him to every regatta. The difference was talent, something which he had in abundance. Martín was born with skill and when it came to the Optimist that made a significant difference. This feeling of asymmetry defined our relationship and had a key effect on my career: it was the incentive I needed to improve, to always go for more. Deep down, I knew I could achieve it through dedication and work. My friend forced me to get better, to improve myself as a sailor, and to become mentally tougher so defeats wouldn't get me down or cause me to lose my focus. Not even Martín won every race he entered.

The only talent I would say was innate in my skillset as a sailor is being able to fly with the wind pushing the boat from behind. Running downwind, as this point of sail is called, requires a special sensitivity in order to adjust your body and accommodate the boat. You have to get it to ride the waves and bear down, like you're on a surfboard. A headwind requires a more laborious and predictable response, but when the wind comes from the stern it offers a free and intense communion with the waves. That's where I can make a difference: with speed. The sensation of sliding across the face of a wave while leaving your opponents behind is one of the most pleasant things I've ever felt on board a vessel. I have always had a knack for that. Everything else—the athletic and emotional resources which allowed me to improve myself and win championships—came to me through effort.

I made my debut as a sailor at the age of six, alongside my older brother Máximo. We competed in the Cadet class, a youth category where you sail in pairs. The helmsman can be up to seventeen years old, and the crew member is usually a child. The only thing I remember from that baptism on the water was my brother screaming about my complete lack of ability. It was a bad experience altogether and I went home in tears. El Chino, as we called him, was a good sailor who went on to achieve some local success. He was the way I was back then: quiet, calm, and reserved. He failed a few classes not because he was rebellious but because he simply wasn't interested in studying. When summer school came around, he would focus harder on the books and passed all of his exams. And he applied that ability to concentrate throughout his college career. After finishing high school, he set up shop in a small utility space next to the kitchen and locked himself in there until he graduated as an architect. He'd been interested in designing things since he was a kid, building balsa wood model ships. Martín Billoch and I looked up to him with admiration.

On the sibling scale, Máximo is followed by Martín, with whom he shared a bedroom. They are polar opposites when it comes to appearance and personality. Martín is over six feet tall and effusive. He also enjoyed sailing, as we all did. When I started in the Cadet class with Máximo, he had another Martín—Martín Billoch—as a crew member. They may have been a competitive duo, but in fact the only real memory I have is of the song my brother hummed during those regattas: "Jugo de tomate frío," or "Cold Tomato Juice," a song by Manal, a pioneering Argentine rock band from the late 60s. But Martín preferred rugby to sailing, and played for the San Isidro Club, one of the local teams. He also did a lot of volunteer work and social activism. With the prevailing trends in the country being what they were at the time, that vocation provoked strong discussions with my father.

Martín grew up during troubled times. Many young Catholics who did relief and advocacy work in poor neighborhoods were drawn to Peronism. They challenged the political order and confronted their parents. Some groups became radicalized and, in the 1970s, they resorted to violence as a means of promoting revolutionary change. Those were the times of attacks and kidnappings against the police, the military, and businesspeople. The Armed Forces, which staged a coup against Isabel Perón's administration in March of 1976, responded with a wave of brutal repression that included kidnappings, disappearances, murders, and secret detention camps.

While Martín didn't condone violence, he had friends who had taken a step down that path, a fact that left him extremely anxious. When he was stopped at a checkpoint in the street, he had no way of knowing whether the uniformed men were members of the military or a guerrilla group… nor was he sure which to be more afraid of. Martín graduated from San Juan El Precursor, his high school, in 1972. During his time there, at least five students had disappeared: young people killed by the dictatorship and whose remains were never found.

The ideological debates between my dad and Martín were tense yet respectful. My brother questioned his status as a sailor and as an executive with a multinational company: two institutions he believed were perpetuating an unjust system that oppressed the poor. My father countered that Martín and his friends were delusional, that they were being manipulated by a small group of violent men, and that all this political turmoil was going to end badly. These discussions turned dramatic when one of my brother's best friends, Alejandro Sackman, disappeared. Martín was scared and distraught, and my father sought to protect him with recommendations which he had no choice but to follow.

Besides these heated discussions, Martín now prefers a more typical memory of our father. It's from his first regatta, which went across the Río de la Plata to Punta del Este. My brother would have been around fourteen at the time, and our dad sat him in one of his friend's sailboats as a crew member. It was autumn, and they arrived at the finish line around six in the evening, when it was getting dark and starting to get cold.

"Put on your swimming trunks," ordered my father.

"Why?" Martín asked.

"So you can jump in the water and clean all the scum off the hull."

"But Dad, it's cold as shit!"

"Doesn't matter. You have to be a man to be on board a ship."

Martín says it took him years to lose the rigidity we inherited from the way our dad raised us. Still, though, the relationship between my father and my brother never erupted. Instead, it happened once... with my mother. I don't remember exactly why, but one night she kicked him out of the house. For the better part of a year, Martín lived with Aunt Fanchi and Aunt Polú. But despite these conflicts, both Máximo and Martín had a closer relationship with our parents than the rest of us younger children. They had them when they were still young and full of energy. At night they would engage in hotly contested truco competitions, a traditional Argentine card game. Máximo played with my father and Martín with my mother.

Inés, the third child and only girl, was my father's spoiled darling. She made friends easily, which was helpful because she had to change schools a number of times, either because she was being held back or kicked out, but when it came to her there were no punishments. She was the only one of us with her own room. As a child, she used her younger siblings as dolls. She'd comb our hair, dress us up, and play mommy with us. Her sailing partner was Claudia Billoch, Martín's sister. She had plenty of boyfriends until she ended up getting pregnant out of wedlock. My mother was outraged. A rushed marriage had to be arranged to prevent her from becoming a single mother, which was a serious social stigma at the time. After that rocky start, Inés is to this day still married to Alejandro Miglio, her boyfriend at the time, and living in Bariloche in southern Argentina. Our family was always about harmony, and she had an effortless way of bringing the most amiable smile to my father's face. She has never been intimidated by her loudmouthed brothers, and when we all get together, she's quick to raise her own voice so she can be heard above the din. Every once in a while she succeeds.

Inés was followed by Sebastián. He and Martín are the siblings with truly outgoing personalities. He's also a big, emotional guy, whether it's expressing anger or affection. He's the one who clashed most with my dad. They had tremendous confrontations. I can still hear him cursing under his breath when we were told to wash our hands before dinner. One of their most epic battles took place one day when Pololo showed up at home in a pair of overalls. He would have been around seventeen at the time, and was working nights as a DJ. My dad grabbed a pair of scissors, and sliced off the bib while Sebastián was still wearing it and suspenders to make them look like a regular pair of jeans. Outraged, my brother confronted him. The two of them locked eyes.

"Not in my house," my father said.

The dress code imposed upon us by our father—short hair, shirt tucked in, loafers when going into the city—disgusted Sebastián. Restless and fidgety, to him sailing seemed like a tedious endeavor. He hated the cold, the long hours out on the water, and the bus ride to the Yacht Club. He preferred rugby and played as a winger at the San Isidro Club. Unfortunately, he was injured during the only match our father came to watch. "This is the last time I'll come watch you play," he told him as they loaded him into an ambulance with a concussion. Sebastián was, and still is, the most critical among us when it comes to our father. But despite all that, he's willing to admit that he did in fact inherit some of his manic tendencies. "I still roll up the garden hose in a perfect spiral, just like he did, and I lose it if any of my kids do it any other way," he said, laughing, at a recent family cookout.

While I understand that sentiment when it comes to our father, I don't necessarily share it. I reacted to all of his directives differently. Instead of expending energy fighting them, I adapted. I did what he told me to do and I minded my own business, which was a more efficient way of dealing with his demands. Sebastián and I talked about all these sorts of things in the bedroom we shared in the family home. When we were little, when he had a nightmare, he'd climb into my bed. But we also fought. I didn't like the fact that he stole my allowance—I was organized and economical, and managed it better than he did—or that he would get out of the car to yell at another driver who cut him off at a light when he was driving me to the club. Despite our personality differences, we've always been close companions. There's a curious symmetry to our lives: we both got married and separated in the same years. Plus, he was in the same three Olympic Games where I medaled. He says he brings me luck. Which could well be true. What I know for certain is that we were allies in the adventure of growing up in a large family. Today, our family gatherings are always held at his home. I've always admired his heart of gold.

There was a sixth Lange sibling, Enrique, a year younger than me. We were children when he died. Quique, as we called him, slept in our room. I have vague memories of what happened. According to my older siblings, after one Christmas which he spent doing laps around the dining room on his new tricycle, Quique started feeling bad. My parents took him to the hospital and he passed away suddenly, just a couple of days later, on December 28th. I was four years old. He was a happy little boy and his death, which was determined to have been caused by measles, had a devastating effect on my mother. She fell into a state of depression until my father was able to convince her that she'd mourned Quique's death long enough and that she had five other children to raise. After that, there wasn't much talk in the home about the brother we lost as a child.

Those who know me will say I've always been focused. Maybe it's because, when I was still a child, I had discovered a world that captivated me and which I made my own. The ability to concentrate has helped me throughout my career. Even back during my Optimist days I was adopting some of the habits that have stuck with me to this day, such as exhaustive training and analyzing each and every variable in a regatta with a clinical eye. I took advantage of the winter holidays to sail. Every morning I'd head down to the river, alone and freezing, determined to get better. When I was eleven, I became obsessed with making the rudder and centerboard—the two parts that sit beneath the surface of the water and set the ship's course—more efficient. I bought paints and brushes at Don Ramón, the neighborhood hardware store, and set up shop in the garage where I got down to work.

When he turned fifteen, the statutory age limit, Martín retired from the Optimist with the double satisfaction of being a both a world champion and undefeated in our personal duel. I told myself I'd get my revenge later, in a different class. For now, I had two seasons left without my dear rival, and I needed to take advantage of them. But there was another outstanding competitor, Hugo Castro, who had even beaten Martín the previous year.

While I was focusing all my energy on sailing, the country's political turmoil hit our family. As a manager with Renault, my father was a possible target of the guerrilla movement which, in the mid-1970s, was kidnapping businessmen. There was a scary moment when his offices in downtown Buenos Aires were shot at, and he occasionally carried a gun in his car. When he traveled, he did so with a bodyguard. A police detail parked outside our house. My father never wanted this sort of security; to him, it seemed dangerous for the two officers to be so exposed, sitting there in the car.

I remember the commotion at night when we'd hear his car horn. It was the signal to open the gate. He couldn't get out of the car, as per his security protocol, but we didn't want to go outside ourselves, resulting in a tense situation on both sides. It was all very scary to me. I remember the feeling of being exposed and vulnerable whenever I ended up having to do it. "This is where they shoot me," I'd think to myself as I stared into the headlights of some random car driving down the street.

That tense political climate also reached my social group. I was good friends with Jaime Smart, whose father was a judge who'd convicted a group of guerillas back in 1971. Later he was named Minister of Government for Buenos Aires Province during the military dictatorship. Decades later, during the Kirchners' presidential administration and the government-promoted trials, he was sentenced in court for actions he took during the dictatorship. Santiago Van Gelderen and Ignacio Jasminoy were also among that same group of friends. Santiago's older brother, Roberto, earned a law degree and defended workers in their union disputes. He was one of the military's victims and to this day he is still missing, as is José Jasminoy, Ignacio's brother. The Van Gelderens were friends of my parents, but they suffered political violence from the other side of the aisle. That's how complicated and tragic those years were. We didn't talk about these things, neither at home nor in school. Much of what really happened didn't even appear in the newspapers.

At three o'clock in the afternoon of May 13th, 1976, however, violence broke out on our very own doorstep. There was no looking the other way anymore. Sebastián and I were riding home on our bikes. As we turned the corner, we were faced with a swarm of police officers.

"Stop right there!" one of them yelled.

In the midst of all the confusion, we identified ourselves and were immediately rushed inside the house. As we passed the security car, we saw the cause of all the commotion: it was riddled with bullets, and inside lay the two motionless bodies of the officers assigned to keep watch over us. They had been gunned down in a hail of automatic gunfire. To this day Sebastián remembers seeing a bouquet of roses in the back seat.

Family life had just been shattered. The first sign was the heartbroken sobbing with which my mother met us. She hugged us for a good long while before sending us off to our room. We stayed there for the next few hours, wondering fearfully where our dad and older siblings might be and whether they were alright. From our confines we could perceive frantic movements and conversations taking place in other parts of the house. Later that same night, our mother came in and told us to pack a bag of clothes. We were leaving. She offered no further explanation, nor did we ask for any. The next thing I remember is getting into a police car driven by an officer with Sebastián and my mother, while my siblings got into another. We still hadn't heard anything from my father. We took Avenida del Libertador towards downtown Buenos Aires. Sebastián slid over to my side of the back seat. Later he would confess to me that he was terrified. I was too, thinking that every red light we stopped at was the perfect opportunity for someone to pull up and kill the rest of us.

We turned onto Avenida 9 de Julio before finally arriving at the Hotel Presidente, one block from the Teatro Colón, the city's main opera house. My father was waiting for us in a suite on the fifth floor. Finally, all seven of us were together. He asked us if we were all okay, and told us that he never meant to expose us to anything remotely like that. And he was sorry, he added, but we wouldn't be leaving the country. We were going to stay in Argentina and we would be well cared for. It would be a while before we could return home, and in the meantime, we'd be staying in the hotel. The rest of our belongings would be brought over the next day. Sebastián and I settled into one of the suite's rooms, Inés in another, and my parents in yet another. Máximo and Martín slept in another room down the hall on the same floor.

And so began our extraordinary exile. For the first two weeks we were locked up and unable to leave the room. We read, we flipped through the four channels offered by the television, and we tried to study. But most of all, we were bored. I remember room service meals from the hotel restaurant, as well as the surprise when our washed and starched clothes appeared at our door. We were small town kids stuck in a sophisticated world we didn't know or understand. But at the same time, there were also moments of levity. Sebastián was allowed to go down to the kiosk to buy a copy of El Grafico, the leading sports magazine of the time, which had a cover feature on the prize fight between Carlos Monzón, the world champion, and Rodrigo Valdez, his Colombian challenger. The bout took place on June 26th, 1976, in Monte Carlo, and we watched it on TV in our room. Nearly six weeks after the murder on our doorstep, my older brother Máximo left the hotel and went to live with his girlfriend.

Shortly thereafter we went back to school. At first it was a bodyguard who took us, though later it would be Martín, who had graduated and was then working as a teacher's aide at Colegio San Juan. Some afternoons we'd have lunch with mom at our house in San Isidro, which was then being occupied by three guards. We would go back to the hotel to sleep. After three months of this, we moved into an apartment, also in downtown Buenos Aires. We were allowed to travel back and forth by train, and I was even able to sail again. Since the commute from the club to the apartment was a long one, I would often on the weekends sleep over at my friend Jaime's house. We spent nearly two full years in these living arrangements, including the final—and most successful—of my Optimist class career.

The 1975 season—my first without Martín as a rival—had started well. I qualified for the World Championships that year in Aarhus, on the eastern coast of Denmark, and I traveled for the competition. And while I didn't stand out quite like my old friend, I finished 21st out of over 180 participants, which was the best among the five Argentine sailors. Plus, I had a great time. Denmark was an oasis of freedom for me.

While in Aarhus we visited nude beaches and—even better—went to Legoland, which I loved. We slept in tents. The men had open relationships with the girls who were also participating in the competition, which was different from the norms and customs of San Isidro. During that first international event, I discovered that traveling not only helped me to grow as a sailor but also as a person.

During those teenage years I found proof that my shyness went away when I got a bit outside my comfort zone. During my third year of high school, with two more to go before graduation, I was kicked out of Colegio San Juan. This came in the wake of an unfortunate event. I was an average student who generally went unnoticed. I wasn't known for being brilliant, nor did I call attention to myself for being rowdy or lazy either. To pass my Drawing class, I needed a score of seven when it came to my practical work, and I had asked Máximo for help. The work that I turned in was impeccably done, but for some reason the teacher gave me a six. After handing me my work along with a note, I turned away and mumbled an insult under my breath. As luck would have it, this teacher—who was half deaf—somehow managed to hear me loud and clear. He slapped me with the harshest punishment possible. My mother appealed, arguing that this was the first time I was ever cited for a lack of discipline, but the school administrators ruled in favor of the teacher. I was done at Colegio San Juan, and would enroll instead at Martín y Omar, a more demanding school, secular and mixed gender.

 I showed up wearing my blue blazer, but all my classmates were wearing green ones. Standing out like that on my first day was embarrassing, but soon enough I started making friends. And some of them were girls. Up until that point, interacting with members of the opposite sex produced in me a mix of panic and indifference. The established protocol required one to call up a girl on Wednesday in order to set up a date for Saturday, along with a commitment to exclusive attention throughout the night. At Martín y Omar, though, the boys were a minority—there were only five of us—and the exchange with the girls was more relaxed. I'd had a girlfriend at my previous school, but now I was becoming friends with girls for the first time. After a year, I was allowed to return to Colegio San Juan, where I graduated with the rest of my childhood friends.

 My priorities, however, remained unchanged. Upon returning from Denmark, I set out to achieve my first major goal, winning the Argentine Championship, in which sailors from all across the country would be competing. Hugo Castro was the one to beat, having won the title in 1973, 1974 and 1975. His brother, Mariano Castro, had also been sailing very well. They both had the support of their father, who coached them, and they competed out of Náutico San Isidro. As we were being towed to the route, we were humming little tunes to distract the Castros.

 The first thing I would need in order to beat Hugo was a good boat. I finally got my dad to upgrade me from my old Obelix to a new Optimist, which was white with a black stripe and definitely fast. I christened it Swallow. Plus, I was able to get a new sail thanks to a licensing agreement I'd entered with Luis Buglioni, a manufacturer who chose to sponsor me. I had no more excuses. Which brings us to the Argentine Championship, where one of us would emerge as the best. I was fifteen years old and it was my last chance to win a title in an Optimist: the class to which I had dedicated half my life.

After an intense duel with Hugo, I was crowned Argentina's Optimist Class Champion for 1976. There were no fans, no grandstands, just a father (not even mine) who smiled at me from a nearby motorboat. The celebration was a small one. That joyous feeling of completing my task—that sense of satisfaction at having achieved my goal—is something I carry with me to this day. I would go on to win much more significant titles later in life, but that first triumph is still one of my most cherished.

Chapter Three

From Río de la Plata to Southampton

Booommm!!! The deafening sound of something collapsing interrupts my study. I run down the stairs and out into the yard to find the rubble of what had been our bathroom. The toilet is covered with sheetrock from the ceiling, which has collapsed. Everything looks dusty and bleak. With a sigh, I return to my room, resigned to continue studying. We'll fix this somehow. The bathroom is located outside the house, meaning what was once an inconvenience is now an advantage. We can ignore it. Pretend it doesn't exist.

The neighborhood in which we're living is home to prostitutes, skinheads, and immigrants. Nobody here will be bothered by our unsightly property. In fact, it's filled with run-down buildings occupied by run down on their luck. Neighbors are used to such mishaps and worse. It was 1982 and the economic crisis had taken its toll on Southampton, a gray, industrial port city on England's southern coast. This world in which I find myself was far from my childhood home in San Isidro, which might be one of the reasons I'm so comfortable here.

From 1980 to 1983, I studied naval architecture at Southampton College of Higher Education. I learned to design ships, to miss my friends and family, to make ends meet on the tightest of budgets, to persevere through my projects, to plan trips and regattas with limited resources, and to have fun while at the same time working hard to sail at the highest levels of the sport.

Those three years in England shaped and molded me. I arrived as a nineteen-year old boy who was accustomed to the insulated world of the club, the school, and the river. When I finished my degree, I was someone completely different. The decision to go study in England was a pivotal event in my life, but in fact I made it without giving it much thought. Just as I had before, I followed Martín's lead. When I finished high school, I wasn't very interested in college. One option for me—which my father never would have allowed—was to get a job related in some way to sailing and continue dedicating myself to the sport. Regattas were the only thing that mattered to me. I wanted to win a world title in one category or another. For a while I thought about a career in physical education, but quickly gave up on that idea.

Martín, on the other hand, always knew he wanted to design boats. His vocation had already started to appear when he was a boy and we'd admire the balsa wood sailboats that brother Máximo would test in the pool at home. The first naval design class he took was by correspondence. Later he found out about Southampton's program and encouraged me to take a look at it. Without any better alternative, I got on board. It was a way of staying close to the world of sailing and avoiding any further family conflicts. After my father agreed, I filled out the application and was accepted by the school. I graduated from high school in December of 1979, but the Southampton program didn't start until the following September. I took advantage of those free months to save some up some money and sail.

That summer I got my first real job working for a sailing school in Villa La Angostura, a region of southern Argentina known for its lakes, mountains, and forests. I'd be teaching a class on how to operate the Optimist for children from Cumelén, a private neighborhood that lies on the shores of Lake Nahuel Huapi. Since their own athletic experiences were limited to either golf or rugby, the parents of these kids knew nothing about sailing and trusted me with them. I loaded five Optimists onto a truck and, over 1,000 miles later, I settled into a cabin overlooking the lake and surrounding mountains. I discovered that I enjoyed teaching people how to sail. And I was well paid for it. Back in Buenos Aires, I invested my earnings in a new boat, thus inaugurating a tradition which I'd continue throughout my life: working for the money I'd turn around and spend on sailing.

After my career sailing an Optimist came to an end, I had a brief yet productive stint as the helmsman of a Cadet. In 1978 I was Argentine champion with Sergio Ripoll as my crewmember, qualifying for the World Championships which would be held the following year in Torquay, a coastal town in southern England where Agatha Christie was born. Sergio couldn't make the trip so I ran with Miguel Saubidet instead. We didn't win the title, but we sailed well and got along even better. I wasn't sold on the Cadet, though. It was slow and old-fashioned. It was around that time that the first 470 arrived at the YCA: a much faster and more modern sailboat for the time.

The name is a reference to the length of the hull, which measures 4.7 meters, and it's been an Olympic class sailboat since the Montreal Games in 1976. As it did before with the Optimists, the YCA bought and imported the first few vessels, and a competitive fleet was soon established. The best young sailors in Argentina really took to the 470, which has a crew of two and requires greater coordination and a more demanding set-up than youth class sailboats. I made some great friends back then, some of whom—the

Baqueriza and Borgström brothers, especially—I continue to share a passion for sailing with today.

This was the first boat I sailed that included a trapeze: the wire that a crew member uses to hang in a harness when they're hiked out over the water. This technique allows for a much larger sail than other boats. It enables you to scud across the waves in order to gain speed, which can make things a bit unsteady. Under proper conditions, the 470 is a fast, electric, unbridled animal which must be guided with a great deal of skill. I competed with Santiago Martínez Autin, or Sacho as he was known, in a class championship held in Porto Alegre in southern Brazil. It didn't go well. We were still getting the feel of the boat and hadn't quite mastered it yet. Blood was drawn during one of the races, thanks to a self-inflicted blow during a failed maneuver. But that was a small accident compared to the adventure Martín and I experienced during one of our first outings in a 470.

It was a spring afternoon during my last year of high school. After my last class, I ran to the club, changed, and hopped on board the boat which Martín had already prepped to sail. The wind was coming from the southeast, a condition which usually creates a lot of chop on the Río de la Plata. There were a few hours of daylight left, and the idea was to start taming the beast. We hadn't thought of telling anyone about or plans to be out on the river, but we were at least smart enough to bring life jackets.

Martín was at the helm and I was hanging on the trapeze. No sooner had we looked across the bow at the open river than we noticed that the wind, which was already strong, was beginning to pick up. But we were already out there and neither of us was going to tell the other that the sensible thing would be to turn back. After a few minutes, we were gaining confidence and taking greater risks... until a wave hit us with such force that I was knocked overboard.

I tried to swim towards the boat but both the current and the wind were working against me. Martín tried to right the ship, but that only made things worse, as he was drifting further away. Since I couldn't catch my friend, who himself was barely clinging to the capsized boat, I looked for the shore. It was too far away to swim. If I wanted a rescue boat to find me, I'd have to stay as close to the capsized vessel as possible. The problem with that strategy, though, was that since we hadn't told anyone we were going sailing, it could be hours before anyone noticed we were missing and might be adrift in the river. The sun was beginning to set behind the buildings. Martín and the 470 had already drifted far enough away that they would appear and disappear behind the sway of the waves, and I was already dreading the prospect of spending the night afloat, trying to endure the cold that was already beginning to creep into my body.

I tried to banish such thoughts from my mind. I took off my clothes, which were waterlogged and dragging me down. I cursed. I prayed. Some lights on the horizon, which could have been lifeboats, gave me hope. But they could have easily been a mirage created by my exhausted brain. It was getting dark, it had been a stormy day, and the river was deserted. Nobody would be out sailing, other than a couple of crazy young men like Martín and me.

Over an hour passed—at some point I stopped checking my watch—when I thought I heard the sound of a motor in the distance. At first I resisted the urge to look up. I didn't have the strength to bear another disappointment. But then, suddenly, a call cut through the darkness:

"Santi!"

And there was Hugo Castro waving at me from the deck of the Tenax, a launch being steered by one of the club's sailors.

"You okay?" Hugo asked after they had managed to rescue me from the waters.

I eagerly accepted his jacket.

"Where's Martín?"

I pointed in the direction where I thought my friend was, and we sped off in search of him. We found him using the 470 as a life raft, so he was in a better state when we rescued him. Between the four of us, we righted the boat and towed it back to shore, though it was a wreck: the mast had snapped and there were several holes in the hull.

"Well, it could have been a lot worse," Hugo said.

When time came to depart for England, I made quick stop in Texas to compete in a junior World Cup with Sacho. As a result, I missed the first week of classes. But eventually I made it, and I remember my first day quite well. Martín was already there, and on that Monday in September of 1980, he had saved a seat for me next to him. It was the Boat Building class, and the professor, Mr. Child, had an impossible accent. I couldn't understand a word he said.

When it came to maths, the problem wasn't so much the language but the extent of my knowledge. The first thing the professor announced was that he'd be giving us a little quiz to find out where our baseline was. He then proceeded to fill the board with derivatives and integrals. Martín and I looked at each other in fear. We had no idea what he was talking about. The only class in which we could hold our own was Drawing. Martín had previously worked for Germán Frers, the renowned yacht designer, in Buenos Aires, and he helped me along.

That morning, while classes were being taught, I decided to check out my classmates. I was particularly struck by one lad with green hair. Later I found out that he lived in a black bus and his name was Andrew Preece. He was quite an eclectic, cosmopolitan class, to be sure. Back then, Southampton's naval architecture program was the only one of its kind, and it attracted aspiring designers from all corners of the globe. The previous week, before I had arrived, Martín had already identified those who would become our friends.

"He's Santi, he's from Argentina too," he said, introducing me during a break.

"What's up, Che?" joked Eduardo Galofre, a Spaniard whom I immediately understood.

He was from Barcelona and was really into windsurfing. He was there with another Spaniard, Javier Elizalde, whom we called Square Javier. The group of Latinos was completed with the addition of a third Argentine, Javier Etchart, el Bebe. What brought us together was need: Martín and I were struggling with maths, and Javier and Edu helped us catch up.

We soon became inseparable. We were buddies on the same adventure of living far away from home. We played a little soccer and a lot of squash. We went to see *Evita*, the musical based on the life of Eva Perón, which was all the rage at the time. We saw all the major bands like Yes, Genesis, The Who, Talking Heads, Duran Duran and UB40 when they came to town on tour. Once I even traveled to London to see The Rolling Stones at Wembley Stadium. We liked going out at night. Once, we were excited about a club called Manhattan, but we soon came to find that Southampton was a fairly hostile to foreigners.

When we really wanted to have fun, we'd go to Bournemouth, a summer town about an hour away. The environment was kinder there, and every so often someone would get lucky with a girl. This created logistical problems. The Spaniards had a Renault 5 which we all crowded into in order to drive back and forth. If anyone ended up wanting to spend the night in Bournemouth, he had to find company and a place to crash for the rest of the group. The alternative was to sacrifice convenience for love and take the train back the next morning. Martín and I opted for a more efficient solution and bought another car. I announced this to my mother in a letter dated October 13th, 1980, after I had been in England for about a month.

"Let me tell you specifically about the cash I've got," I stated in nervous handwriting. If I remember correctly, I'd arrived in Southampton with four hundred pounds and four gold coins, and it was already almost gone. "I had to buy a lot of textbooks, notebooks, and T-squares… life here is pretty expensive, especially in the beginning, when we don't know all the cheap places." From there I went on to mention the forty pounds I spent on some glasses before bringing up the great deal I thought we got when we bought the car, which was a yellow 1971 Ford Taunus with a 1978 engine in it. "We haggled it down from 350 to 300," I stated, though of course I didn't mention that it was rusty. "A car like that is worth £700 or more, and the guy who sold it to us is a mechanic, so he can fix any problems we might have. We'll take good care of it and won't drive it during the week so we can save on gas." I admitted that the Taunus also cost me two of my gold coins, "but it was money well spent." The point, as I explained, was that I now owe £40 in rent. "Send money as soon as you can," I begged. Unfortunately, I don't have a record of how my parents responded to these financial decisions. We had to cut our expenses quickly, and we started with our accommodations.

Martín's father had set us up with a rented room in an elderly couple's home. The woman, Mrs. Fry, went through her same routine every day.

"Nasty weather," she offered as a greeting while serving up a breakfast of fried eggs, black beans, and tomato sauce.

The house itself was fine. Located at 202 Bitterne Road, a sloping street in a quiet neighborhood less than two miles from campus. We were paying £20 a week, which was a fortune to us and our struggling finances. Expenses were covered by our families, who deposited money in our accounts at the beginning of every month. It was a significant effort on their part. At the start of my second year, my father checked with the financial aid office to see if I qualified for the European citizen tuition discount, since my mother had arranged for me to have a French passport. The answer was no, as I didn't meet the condition of having lived in France for a minimum of three years prior to enrolling. Meanwhile, Andrew, our green-haired partner, had a solution for us: for just two pounds a month, we could move into one of the houses run by a left-wing youth organization. These were semi-abandoned buildings that the city of Southampton made available while the demolition paperwork was being processed. The conditions for occupying one of those buildings were you had to make it habitable and you had to know a trade. We convinced them that Martín and Edu were electricians and I was a painter. The interview went so well, in fact, that we were given a house exclusively for the three of us. One Saturday in April of 1981, we got together with about ten members of the association, who helped us get things up and running. We cleaned up the dirt, ran some wiring, and did a bit of painting, all the while putting on a bit of a revolutionary façade so we didn't fall out of favor with our new friends. But we dropped all pretense the next day when we abandoned the repair work and went cruising in Edu's car.

"You'll never guess how great things are going!" I wrote to my father in a letter dated May 17th. I told him about the house, though I spared him the details, including the lack of heating. Nor did I tell him that we had to put coins in the meter in order to have electricity. Instead, I described how I decorated my room—family pictures and a few photos of me sailing in the 470, the Cadet, and the Optimist—and the drafting table I cobbled together from wood I had found. "I'm doing better than ever now that I can study in peace and have plenty of space to draw," I told him.

After that first winter, when we had finally caught up with our studies, we were starting to feel happier and better adapted. We grew our hair and discovered a trick for making free calls from phone booths where we used a soldering iron and a spoon to simulate dropping in the coins. The rather inconvenient part of occupying these condemned buildings was that they had to be vacated by the time the demolition process was scheduled to begin. The association would assign you another one, but you had to put the work in again to make it habitable. As the cycle wore on, we gradually lost our enthusiasm. "Instead of becoming a draftsman, I'm more of a plumber and electrician," I wrote in a January 1983 letter.

The second house we got was in very bad condition indeed, with broken glass and bricked-up windows. It the winter it felt like a cold, dark hole. The third was even worse, and on top of that, it was located in an impoverished and dangerous neighborhood. As I was designing ships in my room, I could look out the window at a brothel. The constant parade of customers was quite a distraction. This was the house where the bathroom collapsed. For the next several months we had to appeal to the generosity of the bartenders at the corner pub who pretended to be distracted when we popped in to use theirs.

Before making the trip to England, Martín and I had competed in the Olympic Trials to represent Argentina in the 470 class at the 1980 Moscow Games. Martín won with Juan José Grande as his crewmember, and that summer they embarked on a successful European tour. They weren't able to compete in the Olympics because Argentina, like so many other nations, chose not to participate for political reasons. Martín brought the 470 with him to Southampton and we sailed it together, with him as the helmsman and me as the crewmember.

In the earliest letter I still have, dated October 11th, 1980, I ask my siblings to write to me, I announce that my studies are improving—I'm finally beginning to understand physics and maths—before moving on to what's important: "On Saturday we went sailing. The wind was blowing at fifteen knots, and it made me think of dad because there were regattas everywhere."

Martín and I joined Weston Sailing, a small club with a good level of talent that was just twenty minutes by bicycle from where we lived. Members took turns cooking or tending bar or officiating over competitions. Instead of taking a boat and laying out a course according to the wind, the races were held between fixed buoys. Before starting, the officials indicated where the turns should be made. "On Sunday we ran two races and won them both," I wrote in one of the letters, "but we were disqualified because there are a thousand buoys and we lost track of the course." The racing area was a cold, windy channel between Southampton and the Isle of Wight. Sometimes the current was so strong you would barely make any headway. Tides were also a problem, especially during a spring tide, when we occasionally had to drag the boats through the muddy channel back to the club. While it was often tough to sail in such conditions, we enjoyed the challenge. It was our training ground for when we started entering events across Europe where the level of competition was significantly higher.

The European summer of 1981 was a glorious one. I started out as coach of the Argentine Optimist team that competed at the World Championships in Howth, a town south of Dublin, Ireland. They hired me because they could take advantage of both my experience and the fact that I was already in Europe. The President of the

Optimist Class, Guido Tavelli, was highly competitive. He asked me what we would need to win, and I told him to buy Henriksen boats and sails made by a Danish company called Green, and to plan to arrive early enough to get in a few test runs and some training.

The first tournament didn't go well for us, which was to be expected. The boys, all of whom were less than fifteen years old, had made the long trip from Buenos Aires without much in the way of training. My goal was to raise the bar. As coach, I wanted them to have complete control of the boat at all times, and I designed exercises to achieve that. We didn't waste any time and spent long hours out there on the water.

We were in fine form by the time the World Championships came around. The boys won their first race, though we had to fight for it because of the protests filed by some of our competitors. In large competitions, judges are now on motorboats in the water with you and they can resolve conflicts on the spot. But before, if someone thought a competitor had violated the rules, they had to go through a tedious process on land. Despite the fact that a number of protests were lodged against us throughout the tournament, we still won both the individual and team Optimist World Championships. It was the first time Argentina had brought home both titles.

After that victory, I traveled to Quiberon, in western France, to compete in the 470 World Championships with Martín. We didn't have much in the way of cash, so we stuffed ourselves with bread and cheese and slept in the car. Or, as I should say, Martín slept in the car. I was taller, which made it all but impossible for me, especially with the gear shift jabbing into my ribs. I tried sleeping on the beach, and even on the boat. It was torture, and it didn't go well for us. We ended up finishing seventeenth, six spots behind Alejandro Irigoyen, a YCA teammate and our rival in the 470 class.

"Martín doesn't seem interested in the World Championships," I wrote in a letter to my family before the tournament began. "I am." It was a sign of tension between the two of us. Living together was taking a toll on the relationship. Over the past few years, the age difference that had always lent Martín status as an authority figure had faded. We never had a big, one-off argument, but there were a number of little disagreements that were likely signs of exhaustion. We stopped living together and dissolved our partnership in the 470. Martín went on to sail on board larger vessels while I competed in the Europa Moth, a one-person dinghy which was popular in competitions at the time.

Edu, my Spanish friend, became one of my best allies in Europe. During that World Championship summer, we traveled to France with a couple of friends. It took two cars, because everyone brought their own windsurfing board. They loaned me one, and we spent a few days surfing, sailing and camping out on the beach.

It was during those years in Europe that I learned how to sail successfully with limited resources. Seamanship is an expensive thing. You have to invest in boats, sails, and masts, and on top of that you have to consider the costs of travel to the various championships, which can really add up, especially when your home base is Argentina. I've had significant budget constraints throughout my career, though they were never as strict as they were back then. This forced me to be both bold and resourceful when it came to logistics, one example of which came during a trip to Palma de Mallorca, Spain, during the Easter weekend of 1982.

The idea is to compete in the Moth class at the Princesa Sofía regatta, which is one of the most prestigious in the world. An Italian friend of mine was willing to loan me a boat, but—for reasons of better performance—I opted to race with my own equipment.

The hardest part was transporting the mast, a rigid aluminum pole roughly six feet in length, from Southampton to Barcelona. From there it would be loaded onto one of the organization's boats and shipped to the island of Mallorca. Lacking any better options, I decided to take it myself by train and ferry.

I recorded the trip on a cassette tape which I sent back to Argentina. "Dear family, I'm not sending you a letter this time because I want to tell you about this trip to Spain, and I could go on for so long that I don't feel like writing it down," I began, looking forward to the adventure I was about to relate.

I first went from Southampton to London's Waterloo Station, where I had to change to another train to Victoria Station. At each transfer, I had to slide the mast through a window, set it down lengthwise, on the floor, which was where I'd have to travel as well, after looking for my luggage. All of this on a busy train while trying not to attract the attention of security. Civilized English passengers would look at me in amazement before offering to help.

I spent the night in Victoria Station, and the next morning I caught another train to the coast where a ferry to mainland Europe was waiting. Once I arrived in France, I had to order a special taxi to take me from the port to the train station, and still I had to tie the mast to the roof. The train was one of the newer models with no windows. I appealed to the engineer, who was kind enough to allow it. Another, who came on later and was not so nice, wouldn't let me board the train with the mast and threatened to kick me off the train, once he realized I was going to do so whether he liked it or not.

Once I reached Palma, a new problem arose. While dealing with all the last-minute preparations, I had neglected to register for the championships, and the officials wouldn't budge. The deadline had passed and the story of my struggles to get there didn't move them in the least. They just weren't willing to let me compete.

Desperate, I went up and down the marina where the rest of the competitors were prepping their boats. I obtained signatures supporting my entry from a number of rivals, and two hours before the championship began, the officials gave in to my insistence.

"I had such a great time. I went swimming in the Mediterranean every day. Nobody else did, but I was, like, crazy in the sun after so many cloudy days in England," I recorded on the tape. I also mentioned that I shook hands with the King and Queen of Spain when I received the award for finishing the Championship in third place. I was one of the few people there who wasn't wearing a suit, and yet there I was, chatting with a couple of highnesses. "I don't know exactly what they are referred to as," I admitted.

I competed in many events during those years without any resources other than a little bit of money and ingenuity. I slept wherever I could and financed myself by selling some of the sails I'd been given to promote. There were a lot of women in the Moth category—it would become a women's class event at the Barcelona Games in 1992—and that made the competitions even more interesting. I was a half-crazy South American making it on his own and performing well, which made me popular with the girls.

I had no coach. I went out at night and didn't sleep much, even before big events. I started to think it was part of the key to my success, and justified the late nights with the idea that they helped me relax before competing. My friend Edu always likes to tell stories about how he'd drop by at nine in the morning to go sailing, as we'd agreed, but when he rang the bell I was always still asleep. "Just give me five minutes," I'd say while packing a bag and slurping down the last of my coffee.

On the trip back from Palma I ran into an unexpected problem. Argentina and the United Kingdom had started a war in the South Pacific over the Falkland Islands which were claimed by both nations. I was twenty at the time: the age at which you could be conscripted into my country's Armed Forces and sent off to fight against the professional British troops. It was insane. And to make matters worse, the information I was receiving from British television and newspapers contradicted the patriotic optimism that my family was sending me from Buenos Aires, where society was being victimized by the censorship which the Argentine junta had exercised over the media.

"I can't stand the English anymore. You turn on the TV and something about the Falklands comes up, and they're convinced they've got it in the bag," I said on tape. "When we talk on the phone, or when we get a letter from Argentina, we wonder if what they're saying here is true, because as soon as you turn on the TV for a minute, none of it makes any sense."

In the end, the English news reports were true. The war was brief and bloody. Argentina was defeated.

Nights in Southampton got even more difficult. If someone noticed our accent at a pub, we said we were Brazilian or Spanish. And if they pressed, which happed once, we had no qualms about running away. My French passport saved me from any complications when crossing the border, but Martín had some problems returning to the UK after a vacation.

Summers of sailing across Europe were followed by long winters of studying, with little sun and even less money. Some of my letters home reflected my state of mind. "I've been thinking about Dad all day," I once wrote to my sister Inés. "Since I'm so far away, I want to send him a little gratification. I know he deserves it, so I try to work as hard as I can. I want to find some way to thank him for everything he does for us. You know I'm not very expressive, and that's part of the problem, because I don't know how to show them how much I love them. Ine, please take care of them and write to me and tell me exactly what's going on, because Mom won't. She doesn't want me to stress or worry about anything. But when you miss someone this much, it's even harder because of how your mind works."

This letter was dated February of 1983, the last year I spent in England. It's one of the few times I allowed myself to express the anguish I felt after learning that my father had been diagnosed with cancer.

It was a long and painful convalescence. I know my dad was experiencing unbearable, shooting pains, but I was so far away and very much out of the loop. My father didn't talk about it with me. In the cassette tapes she sent me, my mother asked for my help with the guided imagery therapy he was starting. It was supposed to help alleviate my father's suffering, and while it wasn't a miracle cure, she believed it could help slow the progression of the disease.

"Dad knows I do guided imagery, but he thinks it's for my own sake," my mother admitted to me, after having received the approval of the priest who takes her confession. My father started to improve, and that excited her. "We're really helping dad with guided imagery," she told me in the recording. "We're sending him our energy. We're visualizing the tumors shrinking. It sounds crazy when you say it like that, but then you see the results." She asked me to join in the efforts, even from as far away as England. "The more people we have doing the exercises, the more energy we bring."

Sebastián also brought up the subject in a recording he made for me early one morning. Between filling me in on the latest headlines from El Gráfico, my brother explained the technique and its benefits in his sleepy voice. "You try to make things better through these exercises. If you draw up a program, you can complete it. It's helpful for studying, too, or anything else, for that matter," he says. So I started doing the exercises myself, which served as a precursor to the visualization techniques which I would later incorporate into my athletic training.

In addition to my father's illness, the other big issue to come up during that European spring of 1983 was my own future. I'd be graduating in just a few months, and I had to decide what I was going to do. My options boiled down to returning to Argentina or staying and working abroad.

The best bet for staying was a contact with a naval architect from La Rochelle, France. From what I can gather from the tapes, my mother was more excited about the possibility than I was. "I made a name for myself in Argentina," I said from England. "I can compete in regattas there. If I need to step up and compete in bigger boats, I can do that. But in La Rochelle, I'd be starting from scratch."

What I really wanted to do was compete at the highest levels of the sailing world, and there was a real possibility of doing so. The Los Angeles Olympics were coming up in 1984, and my dream was to represent my nation in the 470 class. But there was a lot of competition in Argentina. Martín and Irigoyen were still my two great rivals. The trials to determine who would travel to the Games would take place in early 1984. I called up Sacho, and we decided to take our shot at it.

I needed my father's approval. I wanted to show him I wasn't wasting all the tremendous sacrifices he'd made for me to get my degree. At the same time, though, I was harboring doubts of my own. I needed to start generating my own income, and at that time, the sport of sailing represented nothing but expenses. A college degree had set me up for a profitable livelihood as a naval architect, but that would also come at the expense of my athletic career. I found myself faced with the dilemma which would accompany me throughout much of my life: the tension between my work responsibilities and my desire to compete.

"Dad, I'd like your opinion on this," I said to him in a recording. "This is a pretty big moment. I'm about to get my degree, and it might not make much sense to devote myself to sailing anymore." I followed that up with my plans: "In Europe, representing your country in the Olympics is an incredible honor. If I were to do that, it wouldn't just be because I like it and enjoy it. It would also be to open up possibilities for me as an architect, to get interesting jobs and to sail on quality boats. If I'm going to become an architect one day, I have to know how to sail."

Clearly I was looking for parental support. It was around that time that I received a five-minute long recording from my father. I could tell from the tone of his voice just how much affection he had for me. And while he didn't say this openly, as I listen to this tape again after many, many years, I understand he was trying to dispel the uncertainty he had detected in my own voice from my own recording.

"I'd like to reflect," he said. "I listened very carefully. I just need to take some time to digest everything, to chew it over, to touch base with folks in Buenos Aires and see what possibilities there might be for supporting your projects, all of which I find very interesting. You're taking a smart approach to things. It would be wonderful if you could represent Argentina in the Olympics, but don't forget that the competition here is pretty good as well." At this point, he offers me his support, and encourages me to step out from underneath his watchful gaze: "I'll support you, but you have to remember that this is your life. You're the one who has to make the decision."

At the end of the tape, he offers more encouragement in a display of affection that was unusual for our exchanges. "Sending you a big hug, an even bigger kiss, and the best of luck with your final exams. I know you're on the verge of becoming a great naval architect. And I agree completely with you… in order to design great ships, you will have to know your niche, you'll have to operate in your niche, which is competing. And that's why you can count on I promise you my full support," he says. He signs off by offering to send money, in case I need any during the final stretch of my stay, before an elated farewell: "More hugs. Keep it up and don't ever be intimidated. Sempre avanti!"

Around that same time, my mother sent me a recording of her own regarding the matter. In it, she's loving, supportive, and empathetic, and it offers a glimpse of the position my parents had taken. I could tell that they had discussed the matter and come to an agreement. "We're going to support you as much as we can, but you're the one who has to choose your destiny," she said. "Your father and I are fifty-eight and fifty-three, and we're finishing up our lives. But yours is about to begin." The drama in her words, which would have been understood by my dad, who at the time had less than two years left to live, seemed excessive in this particular instance. "Think about it. Do the guided imagery. Talk to God. Talk to yourself and come to a conclusion. Your father and I will be behind you no matter what you decide." To this day, I'm still moved by these tape recordings, and by the unconditional support of my parents when I was still just twenty-one years old.

That final year of college, like the ones before it, I took a few months off from sailing to focus on studying. I passed my final exams and graduated as a naval architect. And then I returned to Argentina, where I trained with Sacho in the 470 and competed in the 1984 Olympic Trials. We failed to qualify, but from that sense of frustration, the long-awaited opportunity to measure myself against the finest sailors in the world was born.

Chapter Four

This One's for You, Dad

The autumn breeze carries my father's ashes to the waters of the Río de la Plata, his final resting place. Along with my mother and my siblings, we said goodbye to him aboard the Fortuna, the Naval ship he sailed through the world's oceans. We're accompanied by many other boats manned by dozens of friends.

As I look out across the river, I think about the fact that my dad never got dejected, even when the bladder cancer he suffered from limited both his mobility and possibility of living a full life. He continued to work and to sail—his two passions—and he was my single greatest source of both emotional and financial support during my collegiate years in England. As we sat with him during one of his final nights, we all laughed as we reminisced over the respect he commanded during his nightly bedroom inspections. He could be severe, of course, but that's not the image he leaves me with as he bids his farewell. Instead, what I hold onto are the encouraging letters he sent me while I was trying to decide what to do with my life as I came to the end of my stay in Southampton, the warm memories of his friends, and his teachings on the virtues of work and commitment. I owe him for instilling in me the most important values in life… including, of course, my love for this great, puma-colored river.

I look up to see the lighthouse that marks the access channel to the Club Náutico San Isidro. The first time I sailed through it was with him, on board his boat. I was still just a boy. I tell myself that this, the place where the river widens to become the estuary that turns into the sea beyond, is my place in the world. My dad will now rest in these waters. He is already a part of them. From this day forward, the Club Náutico lighthouse will be my own private monument. Every time I pass it by, it is like a little intimate ceremony in rememberanc of my father.

I think about what's coming up in just two days: the trip to Punta del Este, where we'll compete for the South American Championship. I was going to withdraw, but now I realize that would have been a mistake. My dad chose to endure the pain and stay active until the end. With that example of toughness, quitting was not an option. I'll make the trip, and I'll do my best to win. That will be my tribute.

On the calendar for that year, 1985, Monday, the 25th of November, had been circled in red: it was the day the Snipe World Championships were slated to begin at the Náutico San Isidro. The opportunity to compete in a regatta of that magnitude at home drew the finest sailors from all across Argentina. Still frustrated at having failed to qualify for the Olympics, I sold the 470 and focused instead on the Snipe, a ship designed in 1931 and sailed by a crew of two. I wanted to win my first World Championship.

The first thing I needed to do was find a good crew member. I immediately thought of Miguel Saubidet, my partner from the Cadet World Championships whom I later trained when he was competing in an Optimist. Miguel was pure talent. It was a pleasure just to watch him sail. He had an innate gift for getting as much speed out of a ship as possible. He was never wrong in his maneuvers, and he chose his strategies with great intuition. We were a team aboard that boat, and handled all the tactics together. In addition to all that, Miguel brought his personality. He's solid, calm, and loyal. A man of few words, though they're always precisely chosen. His personality complemented my own, which was somewhat more restless. I really enjoyed sailing with him.

In preparing for the World Championships, I incorporated some of what I'd learned as a naval architect. I now had a better understanding of the forces that act on a moving vessel, and I made decisions based on that information. I worked the shape of the sails, measuring everything, taking notes and running tests, looking for the best way to configure the Snipe. I designed the daggerboards and the rudders.

My obsessions also included the tactics and statistics involved in competitions. I had a method I used to try and predict the different scenarios the regatta could present. With each of these variables, questions arise. How should we position ourselves on the course? What will the opponents be doing? When you're on the water, you don't go in a straight line. Each team much choose which side to take, and only at the end of the race do all the ships converge on the buoy marking the finish line. Whoever charts the best course—even if it's a slower one—can get there first. There have been a few times when we had a hunch that a particular angle would be the most favorable one to take, and then all of our competitors go in the other direction. When that's the case, we can take more risks. But if our hunch doesn't pay off and everyone else is right, we'll find ourselves at the back of the pack. Those variables—from when to risk it and when to play it safe, to the geometry of the event, to what decisions to make in different instances and in different scenarios—are absolutely essential when it comes to slower boats like the Snipe.

I devoted myself to studying the sport of sailing with the same dedication I applied during my college winters in Southampton. I read everything I could get my hands on. Martín Billoch, who is a more intuitive sailor than I am, was surprised by my development. One morning, at the club, he asked me what had prompted this change. I explained my goals and recommended the book that had become my own personal Bible: *Advanced Racing Tactics* by Stuart H. Walker, a yachtsman and professor of pediatrics at the University of Maryland. A great skipper himself, Walker wrote a number of books in which he systematized different aspects of the theoretical knowledge needed to win races and which included simple yet pleonastic graphics. I read these works—as well as many other writings on the subject—underlining the most important passages and noting my own thoughts in the margins. It was the perfect cross between theory and experience.

Another tradition I adopted around that same time was visualization or guided imagery, as we called it. My mother had passed the technique on to me during my dad's recovery from cancer treatments, and now I could apply it to sailing. When I was competing in the 470 class, I would get angry when something didn't go my way. I would lose focus and stop thinking rationally, which lead to more mistakes. I was entering into a vicious cycle of anger and powerlessness. I started using guided imagery techniques to combat these reactions. Before a competition, I'd hole up in my father's boat where I could calm down and do the exercises properly. I visualized different scenarios in the hopes of improving my performance. It was something very personal, and at first I avoided doing it in front of my friends or fellow competitors. I was ashamed.

As was almost always the case, I was short on funding. With Miguel on board, we had a lot of enthusiasm, but not very much money, and that affected what boat we could purchase for use in competitions. The safest option was to go for one of the plastic Snipes, but they were more expensive, and I wasn't convinced. The alternative were some older wooden boats built in Brazil by Alberto Linenburger. They'd gotten a reputation for being particularly swift thanks to Torben and Lars Grael, two Brazilian brothers who won the 1983 World Championship in Leixões, Portugal, with a Linenburger that was over twenty years old. The Grael brothers had kept the original hull but restored the rest of the ship. This idea of theirs proved successful and Linenburger boats from the 1960 series began to grow in popularity. Each Snipe carries a number on the sail corresponding to the year it was built, and theirs was 12296. The idea, then, was to find one with a number close to that.

One day a Linenburger hull that was even older appeared at the Náutico San Isidro. It bore the number 10863 and it was in rough shape. A Brazilian sailor had lashed it to the roof of his car and drove it there to elude customs officials. He abandoned it there and returned to Brazil with a brand-new plastic Snipe built by an Argentine shipyard. I got the boat as a gift—either that, or I paid something like $300 for it, I can't remember which—and brought it over to my parents' house.

Miguel looked at it in amazement. He couldn't believe I thought we could win a world championship in a boat that looked like that. After restoring it, and in homage to the state in which we found it, we baptized it Pijocho, a slang term for something in bad shape. Pato Forester, an artist friend of mine who now lives in England, painted the name in black cursive letters on the side of the white hull.

Almost the entire fleet of Snipes from Buenos Aires was there at the Yacht Club Olivos. And the sailors were bigger and more experienced than we. They all trained together and shared an intense social life of barbecues and outings. The logical thing for any first timers to the class would be to join this group, but Miguel and I decided to isolate ourselves at his club, Náutico San Isidro. There we could be alone and calm.

The actual course where the regatta would be run was about six miles away, but we took advantage of that distance and trained. We spent more time sailing than any of our competitors, always focused and aware of the fact that we needed to improve. Even if we won a heat, we'd stay out late on the water, after everyone else had returned to the club, if we thought there was something we could do better at. We also did a lot of physical training. There was a 10K loop in Bajo de San Isidro which we ran three times a week, and we worked out at a gym called Mr. Mundo. Miguel and I were two skinny young guys mixed in with the regulars, who were mostly body builders and rugby players. We never wasted a second. We'd start the timer when we got to the club after sailing and turn it off when we were ready to go. We challenged ourselves every day to get quicker and quicker at breaking down the ship and changing our gear. Our record was five minutes flat. We were striving for efficiency when it came to our procedures, taking advantage of what little free time we had. Miguel was still in school and had a bit of freedom, but I was working for Germán Frers' Naval Architecture and Design firm at the time.

The Frers dynasty in Argentina began with Johan Gotthilf Hermann Frers, who arrived in Buenos Aires from Denmark on December 10, 1843. Johan adopted the name Germán and established the tradition of giving that name to the firstborn son. The third generation Germán went on to become a successful naval architect and sailor. His son, also named Germán, learned to design boats with his father before going on to perfect his skills at Sparkman & Stephens, a large naval architecture and yacht brokerage firm in the United States, before continuing on with the family business. In 1984, when I started working for the Frers, their brand was one of the most renowned in the world.

Their studio was located at 1926 Guido Street, just a block from the Recoleta Cemetery, in a distinguished Buenos Aires neighborhood. With hardwood floors, high ceilings, and old wrought iron elevators, the building had quite an elegant feel to it. Germán did as well. I remember his system for staying clean during a long race from Buenos Aires to Rio de Janeiro in which we competed with his boat: he brought with him a collection of identical white shirts so he could change as soon as one got dirty.

The studio was open from nine to six. To get there I took the train from my parents' house in San Isidro, which is where I had been living since returning from England. But in order to more fully prepare for the World Championships, there were some days when I would bike to work, using the commute as a way to get in some exercise. I dressed in a casual style—a collared shirt but no tie and a pair of trousers—but I was always neat. Edu Galofré, who had moved there from Spain and married an Argentine woman by the name of Bárbara Romero, and Martín Billoch, my two great companions from Southampton, also worked for the firm. The stately atmosphere was the complete opposite of the houses we used to live in in England.

This was my first formal job, and I learned a lot. I'd spend long periods of time contemplating the pictures that covered the walls of actual ships that had been designed on the very drafting boards we were now using. Architects like the Frers designed racing sailboats that went on to win major regattas. This generated prestige and attracted top tier clients and shipyards who would purchase the designs in order to mass produce boats suitable for casual weekend sailors.

Germán managed to take an Argentine design studio and make it into one of the world's best. And he did so with style. There are other designers who care more about performance and speed. They create sailboats that may well be winners, but they aren't beautiful works of art. Germán, on the other hand, takes great pride in his aesthetics. His ships aren't just fast. When you watch them sail, you can't help but notice how balanced their lines are. They hold their harmonic forms and dimensions from every angle. I learned a lot just from being surrounded by a culture of excellence. I admire his work to this day, as well as everything he did for the sport of sailing and the shipbuilding industry in our country.

Frers has natural talent. He draws freehand with the precision of an artist. Back then, there wasn't much in the way of computer-aided design software, and we did everything in pencil. Like the other draftsmen at the studio, I worked standing at an elevated desk on a large roll of transparent paper. It was common for Germán to stop by your workstation and, while you were in the middle of a correction, he'd draw out one of the pieces you were working on. He was so meticulous with his strokes that, later, when you did the calculations, the proportions would coincide almost exactly with the drawing he'd just done by hand.

But there was something else that hung over the good environment like a shadow: the particular coldness that Germán could exert. Martín is critical of this aspect of his personality. I'm not quite as blunt, but still, while I recognize his enormous merits, I must admit I never quite felt entirely comfortable with him. He is a great designer and ambassador for Argentina on the world's stage, but as a young man I found it hard to relax when I was standing next to him. There was just a hint of tension between us. Over time, that began to dissipate. And many years later, when I was in another phase of my career as an athlete and designer, we would work together again.

During the preparations for the Snipe World Championships, we spent a lot of time with Miguel at his family's home in Bajo de San Isidro. There are nine Saubidets, nearly all great sailors in their own right who stood at the forefront of the sport, testing new, fast, and physically demanding spinoffs like windsurfing. I always enjoyed being around them, and their house was the obligatory stop we made on our way home from the club.

Silvina, the oldest, would occasionally glance at us without paying much attention to our conversations. I knew and liked her, but I figured she was operating on a different frequency. Even though we were the same age, I always imagined her dating older guys. A brunette who, like all the Saubidets had Asian-looking eyes, taught aerobics, along with both classical and contemporary dance. She had a strong and determined personality which came from being the first-born child in a large family.

I was in one of my phases of being absolutely focused on sailing, and the chances that I would have taken the first step—that is, asking her out on a date—were slim at best. At the time, it was almost inconceivable that a woman would make the first move, but one day she mentioned something to Miguel and, to cut a long story short, one night I pulled up to the Saubidet house in my mother's Renault 4... only this time I wasn't looking for my crewmate but for his sister. We went to a bar and the connection was instantaneous. I had spent the better part of the day on the water and was very tired, but Chivi kept me alive and alert.

I had always avoided formal relationships. My years in England and my fascination with the wind had made me disinclined to form ties. I avoided emotional commitments at all costs. But it was different with Chivi. I fell intensely in love with her from the very first moment.

Despite being surrounded by sailors, Chivi was oblivious to the world of sailing. I once tried to open her up to it, but it ended in failure. Martín had to take his Basilisco, a boat he had designed, from Buenos Aires to Punta del Este, and he invited me to join him. We'd arranged to leave as soon as we got a good weather report; one day I was awoken at four in the morning by a call from him. A pampero—a strong, cold wind blowing up from the south, which was advantageous when sailing to Uruguay—was coming, and we had to set sail as soon as possible. Chivi had a wedding to attend in Punta del Este, and I convinced her to join us on the voyage.

We set out at high speed, scudding across the surface of the waves. Martín and I happily took turns at the helm, checking the clock and wondering whether we could break the record for sailing between Buenos Aires and Punta del Este. Chivi started out enthusiastically enough, but around midmorning a strong gust of wind knocked the boat on her side. It took us awhile to get her upright and stabilized again. When we finally succeeded and resumed the trip, the look on Silvina's face had changed significantly.

The Basilisco was a small vessel, just over seven meters in length, and very light. It had a small cabin below deck, but in those weather conditions, she was a real shaker, and Chivi got a little seasick. She begged us to turn back, but we convinced her to continue on to Montevideo. If she could make it there, we'd keep going. She had no choice but to hold on for dear life and hope that the horror would soon be at an end. Fortunately, it was a swift crossing. After less than twenty hours, the ship's bow entered the port of Punta del Este. Martín and I were elated: we'd broken the record. But Chivi was cross for quite some time.

My passion for sailing soon began causing disagreements between us. From Monday through Friday I'd work at the Frers studio and found time to train with Miguel. When the weekend came around, I'd do quite a bit of sailing while Silvina wanted to spend more time together. We had recurring arguments, and eventually, roughly a year after we started dating, our situation got so stressed that we broke up. Far from bringing a sense of relief to my professional and athletic routines, I felt Chivi's absence in my life. I desperately missed her, and soon enough we were back together. She started bringing up the idea of marriage. I didn't share that dream, but I didn't object either. I was in love. Our problems, which were due to the lack of time we spent together, hadn't been resolved, but they were diluted a bit by how near I was to my athletic goal: the Snipe World Championship.

In the preparatory races, Miguel and I stood out from the rest of the competition. There were other highly skilled sailors in the category, but we started winning races right from the start. We came up with new strategies and developed our own training system. Those first few victories came in calm winds. We were both light—Miguel weighed about 140 pounds while I came in around 155—which gave us an advantage when we didn't have to go by ourselves out over the water to counteract the force of the wind. To that, we added our natural ability to maximize speed on the course with the sheets let out and the wind propelling us from behind.

Under certain conditions, the Snipe's V-shaped hull allows you to plane across the crests of the waves, which greatly increases speed. We were able to maintain that effect longer than the rest. We were zigzagging, leaping from one wave to the next, passing competitor after competitor. Like a couple of dance partners, we shifted our body weight in a coordinated manner, riding across the smallish waves of the Río de la Plata. We'd often reach the first buoy far back from the lead pack, but would pull out a victory in the end thanks to a couple of sharp cuts across the crests of the waves that frustrated the competition and put us in front. Having that extra bit of speed gave us tremendous confidence in our ability to recover.

When the winds were stronger, we had to work harder to keep up. In addition to hitting the gym for strength and running to build up endurance, we'd put on soaking wet sweaters to add a few pounds. This way, we were able to stay competitive in these conditions as well. We were beginning to dominate the rest of the Argentine fleet, but we had no room to spare. We fought for each and every race.

Our primary rivals included Torkel Borgström, who was running with Juan José Grande. Julio Labandeira was also competing: a very tough opponent with whom we didn't even exchange glances when we crossed paths in the middle of a race. Our biggest challenger was Johnny Mac Call, who was racing with Sergio Ripoll, my former Cadet crew member. Johnny was a couple of years older than I, and on land we got along really well. On water, however, we were fierce competitors.

The weekend regattas brought together some forty boats. They were run by Pedro Sisti, also known as Nucho, a great sailor in his own right who collaborated with the World Championship organization and supported the Argentine team. At the time, the Snipe was the class to be in, the one with the highest local interest and involvement. The competition between the Olivos fleet and us—the newcomers from Náutico— was intense. Some old river wolves were really gnashing their teeth at seeing our good results.

I was obsessed. While on the train to my job at Frers studio, I was thinking of alternative ways of assembling the boat to gain speed. I kept meticulous records of every Snipe configuration and the results earned in the various preparatory races. I wrote everything down, from wind conditions to our successes and mistakes, the course, my and Miguel's weights, whether or not we were well rested, and even our attitudes going into the competition. On the back side of that sheet I'd write up an elaborate analysis of the race and opportunities for improvement. In other words, a significant amount of methodology and work had to be added to the foundation of inspiration and skill.

In 1985, that same year as the World Championships, we won both the Argentine national championship and South American title, which was held in Punta del Este just a few days after my father passed away. We also prevailed in most of the tune-up regattas before the championship event. My record for that season stood at twenty-eight wins. Six times I was the runner-up, once I came in third, and four times I finished fourth. There was a process for choosing the three crews that would represent the nation at the World Championships, and we were selected first.

But the fact remained that we had never competed in a Snipe World Championship before, and we didn't know what level our foreign competition would be at. The only information available to us was that, in the previous championship, Johnny and Labandeira had finished fifth and eleventh respectively. Our goal was to at least finish ahead of them, especially since we had the advantage of being locals who had a solid understanding of the conditions that the course might have to offer. Because of that, we believed we should be competitive. But those were simply our speculations. Either way, the 1985 World Championships would be our debut against international competition.

As the first few teams began arriving in Argentina, the differences in funding between us became quite evident. The Japanese disembarked at Náutico with a shipping container containing their pristine white plastic Snipe. Our boat, on the other hand, had already been in use for over a year since we fixed it up. In some parts of the hull, underneath the peeling paint, the old, original wood would appear as a result of the aggressive pounding and jostling that was common among the Río de la Plata fleet. And besides that, she was nearly eighteen pounds heavier than the new Snipes. Florin, the club pro who had been watching us train tirelessly for months, now looked at us with astonishment and some disbelief. He couldn't understand how we intended to defeat the latest technology with no other weapon than our battered and beloved Pijocho.

I looked to Torben Grael, who had won the previous World Championship with a restored Linenburger. He was fresh off the Los Angeles Olympics, having returned home to his native Brazil with a silver medal around his neck. I had a poster of him in my room: he was my inspiration and the reason I bet on El Pijocho. Every morning, as soon as I opened my eyes, I'd look at the picture of Grael's victorious Snipe. I admired his style and the beautiful way in which his boat rode atop the waves. Then I'd remind myself that the goal was to defeat him, to take his place among the world kings of the class.

Meanwhile, the Náutico San Isidro was preparing for the big event. We were there for Miguel—the Saubidets had always been club members—but still I felt very comfortable there. Silvina was also a member. Plus, the club was close to home—I'd ride there on a woman's bike with only three gears—as well as the race course. There was a relaxed atmosphere there, one that included children and families. What was missing was the reverential respect for customs and mores that often times weighed rather heavily on me at the club where I grew up, where I put down roots, and which I recognized as my own. El Náutico, my adoptive club, offered other social and athletic activities, including a gym, swimming pool, golf course, squash and tennis courts, volleyball, and soccer.

It was still rare for a top-tier sailing competition to be taking place in Argentina, and the overall excitement was felt in the cheers of encouragement we received from members and employees alike. On Saturday, November 23rd, 1985, a good many of them gathered in the club's park overlooking the river for the opening ceremonies. There was a parade for the delegations, flags were raised, and military band played the Argentine national anthem. The next day would be a practice run, with the official championships starting on Monday.

On the first day of competition, we won both our heats, establishing ourselves as legitimate candidates. Speed on the open course was an important advantage, and in both races we overtook several other boats when we had the wind at our back. In the second of the two, we left several foreign teams flummoxed when we went from eighth to first, turning one of the buoys along the course with agility and skill. That night we went to bed with the satisfaction of a job well done—we were among the fastest in the fleet—but still I was somewhat restless. I didn't have much of an appetite, which was normal for me during a competition. Miguel, on the other hand, was sleeping like a baby. His calmness was one of the pillars that supported our team. With second and third place finishes, Johnny and Sergio had showed themselves to be our closest rivals.

The championship regatta involved seven races over five days, and we were holding on to first place. Besides Johnny's crew, the third team from Argentina, Gonzalo and Francisco Campero, two brothers who had started sailing Snipes just a few months before, were showing great potential and really pushing us. When it came to foreign competition, the most dangerous crew were the Japanese. The helmsman, Miyuki Kai, had been world champion in the

470 class. Torben Grael, the defending champion, was launching a boat of his own design—he had stopped sailing on the Linenburger—but he was far from the lead pack.

We had the day off on Thursday, and the Club Náutico organized a tour of the delta. There was a pickup game of soccer, a barbecue enlivened by songs sung by the Norwegians, and I had the pleasure of getting a picture taken arm-in-arm with Alberto Linenburger, the Brazilian who had built Pijocho almost 30 years ago. It would be the last break in the action until the competition was over.

Saturday, November 30th, dawned with a warm breeze coming in from the northwest. It was the final day of competition, and the river was filled with boats that had come out to support us. Silvina, my mother, and a number of my siblings were there as well. Sebastián started the now-longstanding tradition of joining me for major championships. And he wasn't alone: he'd brought several of his rugby friends, along with a big bass drum and an Argentine flag with the words PIJOCHO CORAZÓN emblazoned across it. They didn't fully understand the rules of the competition, but they drank beer, swam in the river, and cheered loudly. We narrowly avoided a dangerous accident when one of Sebastián's friends fell out of a boat and the propellor ripped off his shirt.

We were still in first place and well-positioned to win the championship. The only ones who had a shot at overtaking us were Johnny and Sergio, but in order for that to happen they would have to win the final race and hope we finished no higher than fourth. There were other combinations that could result in us losing the title even if Johnny didn't come in first, but in order for any of those to happen, we'd have to finish very badly indeed.

The championship final became a duel between our two teams. Johnny adopted an aggressive style right from the start, trying to force us into making a mistake. We held our own, but they got themselves in a better position early in the race. After the first downwind stretch, which is where we would usually pass several boats, we found ourselves worse off than when we started. Johnny passed that mark in third place while we were nineteenth. If those positions didn't change, the championship would be lost. But Miguel and I didn't give up. The wind wasn't steady that day, meaning there would be plenty of opportunities for those crews who were able to properly read the changes in direction and intensity. Through patience and good execution, we crossed the finish line in seventh place, one spot behind them. There was a roar of honking, drums, and cheering. We were world champions! Miguel and I embraced one another. I had a few seconds of peace before boats loaded with friends and family pulled up alongside us and the celebration began. I looked up at the sky and thought about my dad. It had only been a few months since his passing, and I remembered the words of encouragement he gave me during one of my last visits to the clinic: "Keep going, no matter what happens. Just keep going," he said to me, his voice weak. "This one's for you, Dad," I managed to whisper just before the festivities broke out.

Sebastián's rugby friends were in charge of tossing us overboard: the first of the day's many celebratory plunges. We were towed back to the club with an escort of dozens of boats cheering us on. Chivi joined us on board and gave us the Argentine flag she'd flown throughout the entire regatta.

Back on land, I hugged my mother. Torkel carried Miguel off on his shoulders and my brother Martín did the same with me. Together we made the rounds of the club's park, which was filled with members celebrating our victory.

At dusk, when the wind had already turned southeast and a pleasant breeze swept in, there was a ceremony. Miguel and I had donned suits and ties to receive our trophy, but—once again—we would end up getting tossed into the waters of the Río de la Plata.

"This is your house," said Jorge Salas, president of the Club Náutico San Isidro, said to me as he presented me with my award.

I smiled gratefully. That's exactly what it felt like to me.

Chapter Five

Industry Dreams

"Just another fish." That's how my son Theo once described me in an interview. "My dad is a son of the sea. He's all about the water. It's like he's just another fish," he said. With his immense sensitivity, Theo needed only a few words to sum up my fascination with water. I've always lived near a river or the sea. Whenever I visit a costal city, I like to take a walk along the shore, I enjoy getting to know the port. If it's up to me to pick a spot for lunch, we'll most likely end up at a restaurant overlooking the water. Whether it's sailing, surfing, paddle boarding, there's nothing about the water I don't like. It's where I find tranquility, peace of mind.

But I need stimuli from other sources as well. Looking back over my story, I realize how I've often engaged in demanding activities and interacted with intense personalities that obliged me to step away from the water and from boating. These activities and relationships never extinguished the powerful call of the sea, but they did cause me to return to port every so often and connect with what I want and value on land. Without that balance, my life would never be complete.

This tension between water and land accompanied me throughout the years. Resolving the struggle between my penchant for boating and the demands of family and social life has never been easy. At the highest level, which is where I chose to practice it, sailing requires a lot of time and extended trips. There were phases when it was hard to reconcile the number of hours I devoted to the sport instead of my other occupations and concerns. At one point I even thought I'd retire from sailing if my marriage and my family depended on it. But in the end, I decided to remain true to myself. Today, I would like this choice of freedom—together with the commitment it implies—to be one of the primary lessons I leave for my children.

I can come to such conclusions now, at fifty-eight years of age, but I didn't see things quite so clearly when I was twenty-seven or twenty-eight and trying to juggle all of my obligations. The amount of time I devoted to the sporting life was always a source of dispute with Silvina. But at the same time, the determination of her spirit was one of the things that attracted me to her, and I did manage to step away, even if for a little while, from the boats. During my years in the Snipe, it was customary to join in barbecues and nights out with the other sailors. I barely ever participated in such things because Chivi wasn't interested in them. I may have complained at times, but the truth of the matter is that, ironically, this restriction helped me to broaden my horizons. Not everything revolved around competitions and training. With Silvina, my worldview was enriched.

In time, our four children arrived, making my life so much fuller than it ever would have been if I had devoted myself solely to sailing. They drastically altered the priorities I had up to that point in life and presented me with a new and enormous challenge. The greatest. The satisfaction of raising them as children, and to spend time with them now, as adults, leaves all the other challenges of my sailing career in the background.

Silvina and I got married on a Saturday in the spring of 1986. The religious ceremony was held at the Catedral de San Isidro, a church with a medieval feel and an atrium overlooking a tree-lined square. I knew it well because it was directly across from my school, and I frequented it often during a bit of religious fervor that I had at the end of my elementary school years. At sunset, after exchanging rings, we walked a few blocks along the cobblestone streets of our neighborhood's historic center to Chivi's grandmother's house, a beautiful colonial structure which we filled with family and friends.

We had a limited number of guests. Instead of sending out invitations, I preferred to call friends and hope that the festive spirit would make up for my lack of organization. Fernando García Guevara, a friend I had made out on the river and with whom I'd become quite close, worked for a company that exported meat, and I worked with him to stock the grill. We added music and not much else was needed. It was a great party.

Miguel and I had had to compete that morning, and we arrived just in time. The absence of the bride's brother would have been a shock. Lack of a groom, however, would have been a scandal. Luckily, Chivi was busy with the preparations and didn't mind my absence. She did get a bit upset, though, when she saw my windsurfing board—my new hobby—strapped to the roof of the car we drove to Cariló, on Argentina's Atlantic coast, where we spent our honeymoon.

When we returned, we moved into an apartment in the heart of San Isidro. I'd been searching for a more secluded alternative and of course I focused on the waterfront. During my forays into windsurfing, I'd fallen in love with a makeshift farmhouse on the river. I liked homes constructed on stilts, which protected them from floods, but I just couldn't convince my brand-new wife. Years later we bought a little house in Bajo de San Isidro, next to my brother

Sebastián. Silvina's family, especially her father, Raúl, were a tremendous help when it came to renovating it. I had a studio where I spent my nights designing the PK22, a sailboat nearly twenty-three feet in length.

El Bajo (as it's known) had something of a bohemian village feel to it, which was very different from the rest of San Isidro. A steep ravine and a set of train tracks mark the border of where this particular neighborhood begins. Its proximity to the river, along with an irregular coastline populated by reeds, lends it a lethargic rhythm, one in tune with the slow flow of the waters. I have fond memories of La Luna, a restaurant we frequented. The owner, an artist, had decorated it with his own paintings. Around that same time, a squash court opened up nearby, and I became a fanatic. I still practice this anaerobic sport, which pushes your heart rate to the maximum. It's a great complement to my physical training and helps me maintain mental agility and focus when competing in regattas.

Our idyllic little El Bajo was shattered one night when the river rose much more than normal and flooded the house. We desperately hauled our furniture over to my brother's place and began planning to move. But the next day I was to fly to Holland, and I didn't suspend the trip. To this day I still blame myself for that decision. I should have stayed with Silvina and Yago, who was just a few months old at the time.

Like many of the important decisions in my life, becoming a parent was something we hoped for, though it wasn't exactly planned. When Chivi got pregnant we started thinking of baby names. She wanted something short and original. Yago, a variation on Santiago, was one we both liked. He was born on March 22nd, 1988. I was in the delivery room holding Chivi's hand. All of a sudden, we became a family. I was overjoyed. I was, among so many other things, only too happy to spend many late nights changing diapers.

We'd read a book about the benefits of teaching newborn children to swim. The premise was that, after nine months in the womb, water was the newborn's natural environment. Since the same was true for me, this idea made perfect sense. Yago wasn't even six months old before we got in a pool with him. Following the book's directions and with the guidance of an instructor, we released him slowly and smoothly. I still remember the smile he flashed us when he found himself floating there, along, underneath the water.

Chivi and I did our best to maintain a routine, and Yago adapted to it without any problems. We brought him with us in a stroller whenever we went out to dinner with friends or to family cookouts. When I had to travel to a training session in Rio de Janeiro, Yago became famous among the sailors at the club for the ease with which he would nap on a makeshift bed of two chairs.

Besides being a father, husband, and sailor, that was around the time when I became a nautical entrepreneur. The opportunity arose in 1985 with an invitation from my friend Gabriel Mariani and his older brother, Guillermo, with whom I'd competed in Cadet series events. They were going to start building Optimists and they wanted me to design them.

"That sounds great," I said. "But instead of paying me for designs, I'd like to join as a partner," I proposed.

They accepted. I left the Frers studio to embark on a business venture with the Mariani brothers, leaving the stable income and prestige of the firm in favor of the challenge of establishing something of my own. I also swapped out the sophistication of Germán's downtown office for a warehouse in Ciudadela, a manufacturing area west of Buenos Aires, where we opened the shipyard. I did this all without hesitation, excited about the possibility of working together with two great friends on a common project: manufacturing boats in Argentina that would win championships and be sold around the world. Gabi, who grew up in a tougher neighborhood than I did, was amused by my sudden transformation. "Did you need a passport to go this far west of San Isidro?" he joked. The one thing I didn't change was my preferred method of transportation: my bicycle. Getting to Ciudadela involved a stretch of a busy highway, General Paz, where I'd grab hold of a truck's bumper and catch a ride to save me the effort of pedaling.

The Mariani brothers had some experience when it came to business ventures. They lived in Ramos Mejía, an area far from the river, but a mutual friend had introduced them to the sport of sailing, and after that the whole family was hooked. I got along great with Guillermo, their father, who was known as Tatín. I always admired him for his playfulness and creativity. He played a number of different instruments and was a serial entrepreneur. When he started doing well, he bought a boat, but then the economic tides turned and he had a hard time making ends meet. He was trying to reinvent himself through different business ideas until one day it occurred to him to copy the pulleys and other nautical hardware that was being manufactured by Harken, a company based in Wisconsin in the United States. He moved the washing machine he had on his patio and set up his machinery right there. It was going so well that he decided to legalize his relationship with Harken. Without speaking a word of English, he traveled to their corporate headquarters and convinced them to give him the rights to sell the brand in South America.

His greatest self-reinvention came at the age of fifty-seven, when he decided to retire. Gabi and Guille, his two oldest children, were already working for him. At a family dinner one night, he announced that he was going to build a boat and that he and Norma—his wife and the mother of his children—would be going sailing. He was leaving the company to them. All he asked was that his credit card be paid off, which was all they would need to live on board the vessel. Tatín fulfilled his dream and, over the next few decades, he crossed the Atlantic no fewer than ten times. On his final cruise, he took a tour of Scottish distilleries. He was ninety years old.

The Mariani brothers decided they wanted to build a shipyard, and they thought of the Optimist, which was, and still is, the world's best-selling boat. Winner, a Danish brand which was licensed to manufacture the boat in Argentina, dominated the market. This was the plan that Gabi and Guille presented to me, and immediately I got on board.

With just $4,000—all the capital they had raised—we launched our ambitious plan to design, build, and sell the very best Optimist. We were convinced this could be done from Argentina, which was still on outer edges of the nautical world. We were three friends between twenty-three and twenty-six years old with a dream and a tremendous capacity for work, plus the energy generated by our commitment to pursue our own project.

The first task, which was designing an Optimist that would outperform Winner's version, fell to me. It had to be fast, but it also had to have sleek lines: something I'd learned from my time at the Frers studio. And the Marianis also had a soft spot for design. The class regulations established minimums and maximums for the boat's measurements, but I could operate within that scale. In order to examine the Winners in the greatest detail possible, I not only applied the technical knowledge I'd learned in college, I added my experience of having sailed the ship—I still remembered how it felt from all the many years I spent in Optimists myself—and coaching the Argentine national team. As such, I was able to identify weaknesses in the design and wrote down ten basic ideas that, if incorporated, would add up to better performance and aesthetics.

Generally speaking, what we did was a more efficient distribution of the ship's bulk. We wanted it to be more buoyant, which would make it easier to glide across the surface of the waves. In order to achieve this, we built a more curved bottom. We also modified the edges; that is, where the bottom of the hull connects with the sides. While the edges on the Winner were all straight, we designed ours to be well-rounded at the front and sharper in the back in order to generate better hydrodynamics. That, along with a few other changes, had us convinced that our Optimist would be a success.

I spent two months at the drafting table conceiving the boat. Despite being only 2.36 meters long and 1.12 meters wide, there were numerous possible variations. And I knew that the sum of all the minute details would result in a significant difference. I set up a workspace in a room on the top floor of Chivi's parents' house overlooking the cobblestone street that leads down to the river. Cristóbal, one of the youngest of the Saubidets, watched with awe as I hashed out sketches. Tobal, as we called him, was sailing in an Optimist himself and growing in talent. Besides being fast and aggressive, he was a budding leader in the class. I suggested he test the prototype as soon as we had it ready, and he readily accepted, confident the results he achieved would be the best possible publicity.

When the blueprints were finally ready, we began to build our Optimist. Each of the business partners had a specialized role to play. In addition to being the designer, I was responsible for being the public face of the company. The idea was to utilize my contacts as a marketing tool. Guille had studied engineering and was in charge of envisioning and setting up the whole industrial process. He spent many hours rummaging through his university library, searching for information with which to solve the problems we were encountering. Gabi had a business administration degree and was in charge of orchestrating the company. He was also quick to help with any manual labor that was needed. But when it came to the Optimist itself—from its aesthetics to the construction techniques—the decisions were made between all three of us. On top of all that, we had Tatín's contributions as well.

We set Argentina's 1986 Optimist National Championship as our goal. We wanted our boat to make her debut in front of the entire local fleet on that date, but despite the progress we were making, we began to realize that there just weren't enough hours in the day to reach it at our current pace. Needing an extra sets of hands, we hired the crew of street sweepers who worked the block where the Mariani house was located. Fat Raúl was a real go-getter with quite a diverse set of skills. He painted, he cut the grass, he knew about electricity... basically, he did whatever Norma, the boys' mother, needed. He recruited Beto and Quico, his two assistants, and one day the three of them arrived at the warehouse in a 1950 Mercedes Benz with a hole in the floorboard.

During the final stages of development, finding ourselves increasingly pressed for time, we starting pulling overnight shifts. We took short breaks in turn using the one available table. The work was intense, but we had a good time doing it. One day, overwhelmed by the chaos that had enveloped our workshop, I bought some filing cabinets and ordered the paperwork. At once proud and surprised by how well my initiative was received, I told the Marianis that they should start calling me "The German Lange" as a tribute to my father, who was always methodical. It's what some of his friends called him.

We first made a wooden mold followed by a fiberglass cast. Then we laminated the Optimist. The whole process took around a hundred days. We chose the name Lange by Harken, but before long, only the Lange was left. Identifying the boat with my last name was something I would later regret, but at the time it worked. It was white and we glued red racing stripes to the stern: a basic design which we associated with Harken. The Marianis designed the logo. It was quite a difficult task, but in the end, we had our prototype ready to go.

Eager to take her out for a test, we took the boat to the club and gave it to Tobal so he could take her for a spin.

"She's a real firecracker," he said as he traced the boat's lines.

My brother-in-law's inklings confirmed my calculations: this boat was faster than any Winner. Armed with this new Optimist Lange, Tobal started making real strides in the tune-up competitions prior to Argentina's Optimist National Championship. He'd already been one of the top sailors in his old boat, but with the new one he was winning by wider and wider margins. He even took it upon himself to drop hints among his sailing friends that this new Optimist cut through the water faster thanks to the rounded edges and the redesigned gunwales that were better for hiking out his body when negotiating the waves. We watched, expectantly, from a motorboat as Tobal first showed his Lange to the other competitors, all of whom smiled when they saw that what their friend had been telling them was all true.

The only people who weren't quite so happy were those who owned Winner Optimists, and who started snooping around for what they believed would be supposed violations with our boat. Despite being a youth class, Optimist sailors can be quite competitive. A skeptical rival filed a protest, arguing that Tobal's boat was in violation of the rules. An official verified that one of our measurements exceeded the limits by a hair's width. This error in construction didn't give us any advantage over anyone, but it was enough for them to strip Tobal of the trophies he won with the new boat.

He wasn't discouraged and neither were we. We knew that the Santi (which is what Tobal had dubbed the first boat we gave him) was a prototype. We took it back to our workshop to make the alterations and, with the information we gathered, we began to build our second Optimist. The Argentine National Championships were fast approaching, and we wanted to have two of our boats in the fleet. We asked Tobal to suggest someone, and he put us in touch with Santiago Doval, a friend of his who was also a top competitor.

The championships took place in the city of La Plata. The Marianis and I went every day to follow the races. We were nervous. We knew the initial fate of the company lay in the young hands of Tobal and Santiago. There was no doubt that our new boats were faster, but everything depended on the boys sailing well, measurements being correct, and—above all—on nothing breaking. The boat we were most worried about was Tobal's. The conditions were very windy, which would expose any structural flaws, and all the alterations we'd made had weakened its framework. It was the first boat we had built, and we had only time to make corrections on the second one for Santiago.

This was unfortunate, because Tobal was sailing at an expert level, and he was considered one of the favorites. He ended up finishing fourth, which was a great result considering he had two forced retirements due to equipment failure. The second Optimist, however, was perfect, and Santiago Doval became the Argentine national champion. Guille, Gabi and I celebrated with the boys. During the awards ceremony, parents began coming up to us and asking about prices. We were on our way to conquering the local market.

In order to succeed outside of Argentina, we'd have to put on a shining display for the biggest stage of all—the World Championships—where every year the top five Optimist sailors from each country come together to compete. We became the official supplier to the Argentine team for international competitions, but it took us a couple of years to start getting really good results. The boats were great, but we also had to think about the talent level of the boys sailing them. With that in mind, I convinced the national federation to hire Miguel Saubidet as coach.

Our boats and Miguel's demanding training regimen were combined with a talented gang of sailors. Progress came quickly. Gabi and I traveled to all the races and we really enjoyed seeing how young Argentine sailors were becoming the dominant kings of the youth class: a rite of passage for just about every star of the sailing world. But it wasn't easy. We were constantly being harassed by the official measurer, and there were business conflicts as well. Winner, which had a near monopoly on the world's supply of Optimists, didn't like the fact that an audacious group of South Americans were snatching the market from them.

In addition, a fundamental problem arose. The international association wanted all the boats to be identical, so that the only variable was the quality of the helmsman. But as builders, we were looking for just the opposite. We wanted our boats to the sleekest, fastest, most beautifully designed Optimists in the fleet. The dispute centered on the measurements that had to be taken of every boat before they were cleared to compete in a World Championship event. Our Optimists were within the regulations, but just barely, because we were looking to push the limits of everything when it came to improving performance. This left us vulnerable to construction errors, and the official measurer knew that. He was a Frenchman who didn't much care for us and went to great lengths to find any little detail that could potentially disqualify us. The guy was an absolute stickler and we didn't trust him.

The biggest conflict occurred during the taking of measurements before the 1990 World Championships in Portugal. In addition to building some truly stunning boats for the Argentine team, painted with the sky blue and white of the national flag, we'd reached an agreement to become the official suppliers to the international association. Gabi and I were happily unloading a truck loaded with seventy brand new Optimists to deliver to various teams, but the official measurer insisted yet again on complicating things for us. Interpreting the rules in his own way, he identified an alleged deviation in the construction that would rule all of our boats out of the competition. The error he was accusing us of had no effect on the boats' performance, but the Frenchman was adamant. After his judgement, we had just a matter of hours to make them all compliant. Otherwise, not a single Optimist Lange would be eligible to compete in the World Championships.

This was a disaster. The crew chiefs and parents of the seventy competitors for whom we had chartered the boats were growing restless and rightfully pressuring us to come up with a solution. Our international reputation was on the line, and Gabi and I worked all night. Exhausted from not having slept, we finally managed to get the measurer's stamp of approval on all of our boats. After that, it was even more rewarding to see the boys from Argentina sweep all the top spots. The other crews competing in our boats also performed quite well.

That World Championship was the beginning of Argentina's supremacy in the category. Martín di Pinto was crowned champion and Agustín Krevisky came in second. Argentina also won the team title. The following year, in Greece, we repeated with Krevisky as the victor and Asdrúbal García Guevara finishing runner-up. I was especially thrilled to see Asdru, the son of my dear friend Ferdi, earn silver. An efficient method began to show its value: there is no better way to teach a boy how to become a champion than showing him how his own teammate is able to do it.

Our dominance was absolute in 1992, when Ramón Oliden was crowned world champion in Mar del Plata, a city on the Argentine coast. Ramón won all but two of the races, and in those he finished second... an unprecedented achievement. I attended the championships with Yago, who gave him a cap with the Optimist Lange logo. During one of the first races it blew off into the water. Ramón was so far out ahead of the rest of the field that he was able to stop and grab it and still come out the victor. He was an incredible talent and I'll never forget his name.

That stretch of results was an important boost for our fledgling shipyard. "Lange Boats Have Won the Last Three World Championships" read the commercial brochures we printed out during those years of growth. All of a sudden, we had forty employees spread across two locations. We were producing three boats a day, totaling 600 in a year, and we exported seventy percent of that production to forty countries around the world. And that was just what we were turning out in Argentina. We'd created a schematic for the entire production process and put together a book detailing every step along the way. This allowed to maintain a level of excellence while expanding and selling licenses in Spain, Denmark, and the United States.

We were also coming up with innovative aesthetic options for the boats: personalized designs and logos which Ramiro Señorans, a cousin of Chivi's, would paint with an airbrush. We handled all the company's marketing, which was a central part of the operation, from our Department of Art, Development and Productive

Revolution. The name, as ridiculous as it is bombastic, was an ironic reference to the rambling lines often uttered by Carlos Menem, then president of Argentina. It expressed our ambition but also the playful spirit with which we approached our work.

The person in charge of maintaining the festive mood was Ferdi, a tireless jokester who had recently joined the company. Every once in a while, his antics made us a bit uncomfortable. One of his classics was, when we went out to lunch, to stutter so badly that he exasperated the server. Other times, he'd enter a building or location pretending to be a hunchback. Miguel Saubidet also joined the team, and gave presentations at yacht clubs around the world to which we were pitching our boats. It was a perfect combination: we weren't just selling the boat itself, but also an introduction to the coaching method that was producing so many champions.

It should all have been wildly successful, but conditions in Argentina conspired against our prosperity. The country went through two peaks of hyperinflation that disrupted the economy. We were primarily constructing our boats from imported materials, and prices skyrocketed. Furthermore, the government's measures to control the value of the dollar were hurting us. The crisis—just one more example of how ungrateful Argentina tends to be with its entrepreneurs—liquefied the dividends that we were planning to distribute among the partners towards the end of those years, but the company managed to survive.

The golden years of our shipyard coincided with the dominance of Argentine Optimists on the international stage. It was a great time in our history, one which—to this day—has yet to be repeated. Miguel, one of those who trained that generation of champions, still remembers the pressure he imposed on his athletes as coach. Today, though, he takes a more critical look at training requirements.

Recently, a parent at the Náutico asked him what they could do to replicate the past success. He replied that the intensity was neither necessary nor good, that if a young boy or girl has the heart of a champion in them, then they could engage in the training methods with however much passion and devotion they bring to the table. But for everyone else, sailing an Optimist should be more recreational: a space for learning, making friends, and gaining independence by connecting with nature.

Miguel walked away from sailing and coaching for many years. He was a young father and decided that sailing wasn't going to allow him to support a family. Nor was he willing to make the sacrifices of constant traveling and prolonged absences. He left the world of boating to work for a multinational corporation. It was a great loss for the sport, but I understand his decision. After all, the same dilemma presented itself to me when my own family began to grow. "You loved it more than I did," Miguel told me once when we were reminiscing over our athletic careers. It's probably true.

I was willing to give up a lot in order to pursue competitive sailing. Even the shipyard we'd worked hard to build from the ground up. In 1991 I accepted an offer to move to Cádiz, in southern Spain, along with Chivi and Yago. I'd been hired by the municipal government with the idea of developing the sailing and shipbuilding industry in the region. But the plan never quite got off the ground, and a few months after we settled in Europe, I was off sailing professionally on large boats, which is what I was really looking to do after leaving Argentina.

I maintained some of my functions with the shipyard from Spain, but I had stepped aside from daily management. When I returned to Argentina, Guille and Gabi and I no longer had the same drive as when we were first starting out. To make matters worse, yet another national financial crisis was underway, and the company needed a large injection of capital in order to stay afloat. My brothers Sebastián and Martín were doing quite well for themselves working for a bank, and they bought the Mariani's share of the business. The Lange brothers took over as owners, but years later we sold it.

That was the end of a business venture started by three daring friends. The legacy of our Optimists remains, as I occasionally come across one at a yacht club during my travels. So too does the great privilege of having partnered with the Mariani brothers. They took it upon themselves to expand upon their tradition of manufacturing excellence. From those humble beginnings on the patio of their home, when Gabi envisioned a factory, the Marianis built an empire. They went on to found King Marine, a renowned racing sailboat shipyard. But perhaps their greatest achievement was born in response to a situation that seemed all but insurmountable.

In 2008, the global financial crisis paralyzed the shipbuilding industry. The Marianis had to decide what to do with their two plants, one of which was located in Argentina with the other in Spain. They did their research and uncovered an opportunity in agriculture—an industry they knew nothing about—and used their knowledge of carbon fiber to construct the arms of the sprayers used in fumigation. Their success was almost instantaneous, and the John Deere corporation bought the rights to it from them.

I'm proud of my two friends, who on several occasions offered me other opportunities to partner with them. I love seeing them every time they invite me to celebrate one of their tremendous industrial achievements. And Gabi and I have even become family, now that my son Yago is engaged to his daughter Martina. They're living together in Barcelona. When they first started dating, Gabi sent me a message that read, "We've been friends, partners, and now we're in-laws. I hope that doesn't mean we'll also be grandparents too soon!"

Chapter Six

The Olympic Flame Has Been Lit

One morning in early 1988, I opened my door to find Pedro Ferrero and Raúl Lena standing there. Toto and Tati, which is how they were known, had come to propose something to me.

"What do you think about taking the helm of our boat at the trials for the Seoul Olympic Games?" Toto asked.

Like track and field, Olympic sailing is a sport with many different subcategories. It includes roughly ten different disciplines, each with its own class of sailing. This provides for sailors with many different talents and body types. Some boats are ideal for taller and heavier sailors, while in others a more stylized physique is preferable.

The Soling is a sailboat that weighs in at over a ton. It was designed in Norway to stand up to the strong winds of that particular region. And it takes a crew of three to sail it. Toto, who owned the vessel, was an experienced sailor. Forty-nine years old, he'd competed in three Olympic Games in the class. Tati was thirty-eight, ten years older than me, and the strongest among us. He had a real affinity for the gym. Both were good friends and dominated competitions in Argentina. They were looking for a new helmsman, and had first solicited the talents of Miguel Saubidet, who left the crew when his wife got pregnant. That's when they called on me. I was taken by surprise, but I accepted.

They had the boat in perfect condition and would do all the hard work. All I had to do was steer. We went out for a few training runs, and it was enough for us to win the Olympic trials against twenty other crews. The Argentine federation announced that it would finance at least part of the trip to Seoul, and we began our preparations. The funds they awarded us weren't enough to cover the entire campaign, and all three of us had demanding jobs: Toto worked in a sail shop, Tati in a candied fruit factory, and I was with the shipyard. We were still several months away from the Games, but we had no other option than to train on weekends and, when we could, after work.

We kept the ship at the YCA headquarters in the port of Buenos Aires, and I was able to slip away from the shipyard to get in a few hours of training in before sunset. Toto and Tati would be waiting for me with the ship ready to sail. During the winter, it would occasionally be dark by the time we docked back at the club. Exhausted, I faced the long trek back home, where Chivi was waiting for me with a newborn Yago.

Besides the lack of time, there was also the problem of weight. None of us was much more than 150 pounds, which was very light compared to the demands of the ship. In windy conditions, heavier crews had an advantage over us. Tati had the idea of using overalls, and his mother sewed us some uncomfortable brown suits that contained four layers of absorbent fabric. Before races, we'd jump in the water to add some water weight. It was cold in the winter, but the padded overalls allowed us to add around a dozen pounds per person, which was still well within the regulations.

Shortly before the Games we managed to get some time off work, and we spent a week in Rio training with the Brazilian national team. We slept in the club's storage spaces. Except for an accident involving Tati—he hit his head and needed five stitches—we had a great time. We were also able to run the North American Championship course in the waters of Lake Michigan while crashing in the basement of a friend's house in Chicago. Before flying to South Korea, I passed through San Diego, where I picked up some sails that Vince Brun, the Brazilian owner of a shop called North Sails, had lent us. Meanwhile, Toto and Tati flew directly to Seoul to prepare the boat we had rented, which also happened to be the UK's backup vessel. That's how precarious our organization was.

The sailing hub was located in Busan, a port city on the southeastern edge of the Korean peninsula. On clear days, you can see Japan from the coast. We complained about all the kimchi, a spicy preparation of fermented vegetables, and the organization made an allowance for international dishes. Toto and Tati bunked together while I shared a room with my friend Ferdi, who had qualified, along with Diego Miguens, as an Argentine representative in the Tornado class.

Ferdi's presence lent a festive air to our stay in South Korea, especially after he was literally knocked out of the Games after breaking the hull of his boat in a collision with another sailor. Unable to compete, Ferdi dedicated himself to finding some entertaining nightlife in what was, at the time, a rather dull Seoul. I still remember the eventful early morning return to the Olympic village from a neighborhood on the outskirts of the city where nobody spoke a word of English.

Busan met us with some of the most unsuitable conditions possible: strong winds and big waves. And to make matters worse, we had to sail for roughly two hours through the frigid Sea of Japan just to get to the race course. Wrapped up in our hideous, makeshift overalls, we were chilled to the bone. After the first few couple of heats, we found ourselves near the back of the pack, but little by little we learned how to manage these extreme conditions and were able to put our skills on display. As was most often the case with the boats in which I raced, we were among the fastest in the fleet when it came to planning across the water. Sometimes we were the fastest of all. It's how we took advantage of our relatively low weight when forced to sail into a headwind.

In the third heat we got out to a good start and found ourselves in sixth place coming into the final stretch. As we neared the finish line, we rode a couple of waves and picked up some speed. The top crews, who had been competing in this class for years, watched in surprise as we flew by them. We came in first and gave each other a clumsy embrace, as we were limited in our mobility by our thick, padded overalls. That was where I first experienced the intoxicating sensation of winning a race at the Olympic Games. It was unlike anything I'd ever felt before.

At one point in the competition, we were in a position to make the podium. We ended up finishing ninth, which we still considered a success. We weren't a seasoned team, and nobody considered us much of a threat to win a medal, but we were still able to finish ahead of traditional boating powers with much larger budgets than ours. A number of the pre-Olympic favorites could tell they were falling far short of their goal and ended up throwing in the towel. We, on the other hand, running with borrowed sails and a rented boat with just a few months of preparation, were more relaxed, which helped. The pressure to win a medal can undermine your performance: a lesson I'd apply years later when the roles were reversed and I was among the favorites.

The Seoul games first sparked my Olympic passion. I can even point to the specific date when that love was born: September 17th, 1988. That was the day we flew from Busan to Seoul to attend the

Opening Ceremony. Before heading to the stadium, we passed through the Olympic Village, and I was impressed by the tremendous global community of athletes. We walked past gymnasts and boxers. We saw Carl Lewis, the American sprinter, who was at the peak of his career and won two golds in South Korea. I admired the seriousness with which he prepared, and I understood this was the only way to achieve what, from that point onward, was my goal: a medal.

From Argentina, the Games had represented something distant, but all of that changed after Seoul. I realized I had talent, potential, and most of all, I had desire. What I was lacking was a good preparation involving time and international competition… and the money to make it happen. I promised myself I'd try again, but with a better foundatin. To that end, I would dedicate a significant amount of my efforts over the next thirty years. The next Olympics would be in Barcelona, in 1992, and since I was living relatively close at the time, I was looking forward to competing again.

Cabrera de Mar is a small Spanish town that lies in a small mountain range that runs parallel to the Mediterranean. It has a mere 4,000 inhabitants and a castle that, luckily, doesn't attract hordes of tourists from Barcelona, which is just an hour away by train. In Cabrera, life is lived calmly between the mountains and the sea. In the summer, people head to the beaches. Edu Galofré and his family live there; I'd met him during our time studying together in England. The mild climate there was the perfect refuge for when we wanted to escape the cold rain of Southampton. In 1991, after my job in Cádiz to get the sailing and shipbuilding industry off the ground fell through due to the typical inefficiencies of public administration, Edu convinced me to move there. We rented a house from an elderly Catalan couple, and Chivi, Yago, and I settled in

Cabrera. He helped me find a job working on the big regatta sailboats during the upcoming Spanish season.

The sport of sailing was on the rise in Spain at the time, and with King Juan Carlos and his family being fanatics themselves, it helped spread awareness and attract sponsors. A number of important businesspeople assembled teams and hired sailors to compete in their boats. Edu and I started out on Longitud Cero, Vicente Tirado's sailboat, along with a great group of friends. Vicente, a lawyer from Castellón, was like a father to me during my time in Spain. One of the King's daughters, Infanta Cristina, piloted the Azur de Puig, whose crew was initially made up entirely of women. Later, we were called upon to join the team. Races were intense, and I handled the tactics. The Azur de Puig's philosophy was to be competitive but always keep the atmosphere on board pleasant.

There was an interesting schedule of tournaments. The season began in the spring, and every two or three weeks a new event was held in a coastal city in either Spain or Italy. These were high level regattas and generated a fair amount of tourism from the people who came to admire the sailboats. The culminating event was the Copa del Rey, which was held in Palma de Mallorca. Competitions were held on the weekend, so Edu and I could travel on Thursday and be back home by Sunday night. It was a much more convenient arrangement than what one would have to face if one wanted to be a professional sailor in Argentina.

In Cabrera, Chivi and Yago and I joined the Galofrés on family trips to the mountains or the sea. I tried to recreate the Argentine custom of Sunday afternoon barbecues, but the quality of the beef wasn't quite up to par, so I incorporated grilled chicken: a new specialty of mine that I'd improvised on the beach. Edu and Bárbara had two children: Santiago, the eldest, and Gabriela, who was Yago's age. They all went to the same school, which was five blocks from home. I dropped off Yago there on my bike every morning after breakfast.

Our house had a room which occasionally served as an office. It was there that I handled the business of the shipyard. One of these tasks was to provide support to the Danish gentleman who bought our license. Silvina stayed in Cabrera while I drove to Denmark with Yago. During that, our first great adventure together, we visited Legoland, the amusement part that had fascinated me when I first visited during the 1975 Optimist World Championships.

In the afternoons I'd hop on my bike and ride to the sports complex in Barcelona. The city was preparing for the 1992 Olympic Games, and being in such close proximity put me in a much better position when it came to training than I had been in Seoul. Plus, the Spanish federation was very generous and opened many doors for me. I trained with them as if I was part of their own team.

During the time we lived in Spain, Chivi became pregnant with twins. There were some difficulties that arose during the pregnancy, and our initial joy quickly became a complicated emotional process. We flew back to Argentina anticipating a difficult delivery, and that's exactly what happened. On November 21st, 1991, Ferdi drove us to the hospital where Theo and Borja were born. They were born at seven months and each weighed less than two pounds. The prognosis from the doctors during those first few hours wasn't encouraging. The twins were literally fighting for their lives. We spent many agonizing days in the neonatal intensive care unit, hanging on to the doctors' every word and commiserating with other parents there in similar situations.

The twins' condition eventually stabilized, but it was all quite difficult. The emotional gut punch at seeing them so vulnerable was compounded by harsh economic realities. They wanted to cut off care because of some perverse clause in our insurance policy. We started crunching the numbers only to realize that, in order to cover future hospital bills, we'd have to sell the house. I spent days filling out paperwork and rushing from office to office, fighting the bureaucratic system holding us hostage. My friends and family members were a fundamental source of support. Martín and Sebastián consulted Carlos Aleman, a lawyer for the family who suggested I threaten to take the story of what was happening to us to the media. In fact, I had just been a guest on the TV program hosted by Bernardo Neustadt, a popular journalist, to talk about the shipyard. The tactic proved effective. The insurance company and hospital conceded, and we were able to afford the treatment without having to give up our home.

The twins were released from the hospital, but the consultations and care would go on. Especially when it came to Theo. We took him to the best specialists we could find, but we weren't quite satisfied with any of them. In the end, we were able to come up with the proper diagnosis. The treatments would be a little harder on him, but he'd get through it. My uncle Wolfgang helped us understand the situation a bit better. Ultimately, Chivi and I decided not to continue spending money we didn't have on doctors, and instead we took it upon ourselves to do some physical therapy to boost and encourage his development. This turned out to be the right decision. During those early years, Theo always went above and beyond, which shows in the fierce personality he has today.

Once the twins were out of danger, we returned to Spain. There, our life in the village came to be defined by our medical needs. In San Isidro, our two extended families—which amounted to an army of aunts, uncles, and grandparents—were there to help us out, but in Cabrera it was just us and the Galofrés.

As an athlete, I experienced one of the greatest disappointments of my life: not being able to participate in the 1992 Barcelona Games. My plan was to compete in Soling again, and I'd been training with the Spanish team. I had been in contact with the Argentine federation to guarantee my eligibility, but at some point they seemed to be impeding things. I was insistent, both with phone calls and letters. I explained that I didn't necessarily need their financial support—that what I really wanted was for them to allow me to register—but it was all to no avail. Ultimately, they gave me the authorization, but it was a mere six weeks before the Games began, and on top of that they gave notice that there would be no Soling crew among the Argentine delegation. By that point, it was already too late. There was no time to prepare for anything else. I said no.

I watched the Opening Ceremonies at home on TV. When I saw Luis Doreste, a Spanish sailor and one of my contemporaries, reciting the Athlete's Oath, I started to cry out of anger and frustration. I couldn't understand whether being virtually boycotted by the Argentine federation was out of ineffectiveness or jealousy. Either way, it didn't matter. The only certainty was that I hadn't been given a chance to compete. Not the way I wanted, anyway. It's true that I could have accepted that last minute authorization. Being at the Olympics is such a valuable experience that, to this day, I still wonder if it was wrong of me to turn it down. Accepting it, though, would have meant compromising my principles.

The lack of respect I was shown by the Argentine federation contrasted sharply with the support offered to me by the Spaniards. After the Barcelona Games, they suggested I become a naturalized Spaniard and start racing with them: a very tempting potentially career-altering proposition. The conditions were ideal, and finally I would have the means to compete in international prep events. Plus, in Cabrera, I was just a bike ride away from the high-performance center where the sailing team was based. It had easy access to the sea, a large boathouse for storing the vessels, a gym, locker room, and the best coaches and trainers. The decision was difficult for me because I'm a proud Argentine—I get excited every time I see the sky blue and white flag stamped on my sails—but my federation's attitude, coupled with the lack of economic resources with which to compete against the international powerhouses, left me no other options. It's a sacrifice I'd have to make if I wanted to achieve my goal of not only appearing in the Olympics but being seriously prepared to win. So great was my desire that I decided to compete for Spain.

Just as I was getting my papers in order, I received a call. Surprised by our good performance in Seoul, Ferdi and Diego had caught the attention of Carlos Miguens, a businessman who then owned Quilmes, the largest brewery in Argentina. Miguens tends to keep a low profile and had asked me not to mention him by name—it was only a few years ago that I was finally able to thank him publicly—but his company was willing to become our sponsor and finance our campaign for the 1996 Games in Atlanta. This news was a dream come true: I'd be able to train properly and represent Argentina to the best of my ability. It was also good news for Chivi, who'd been wanting to return to San Isidro. The excitement of launching an Olympic campaign, complete with time and money, led me to make a rushed decision when it came to the class in which I would compete. That mistake would end up costing me dearly.

Chapter Seven

A New Method

With the omniscience of his nineteen years, Carlos Mauricio Espínola listened undaunted to the first orders from his new coach, whom he'd only just met: "Do a warm-up jog to the High Performance Center and we'll get started there." He and Gastón Camaño, the friend with whom he shared a back room where they fell asleep to the sound of the train, complied with the directive. When they reached the facility's track, they received new orders: keep running.

Daniel Bambicha, the man giving the instructions, checked his stopwatch and unveiled the workout: "Okay, five sets of two laps all out with a one lap recovery." The sponsor of the windsurfing boards they competed with had hired Bambicha, and this was their first training session. Neither Carlos nor Gastón knew how long it would last, but eventually they realized there was no set ending. Bambicha was testing their limits. Their resilience. He was looking to see where one of them would break, where they would surrender.

Hours went by and Carlos held his own. The heavy heat of that December morning in Buenos Aires was almost pleasant when compared to the hellish summers in Corrientes, the coastal city where he was born. Gastón, on the other hand, was drenched in sweat and his tongue was hanging out. He couldn't keep up with his friend any longer.

"I can't take it anymore," he announced.

"Okay, that's enough for today. Stretch it out. See you tomorrow at the same time," Bambicha said, finally ending the introduction to his rigorous training methods.

The powerful bond Camau and Bambi would form triggered a sequence of very successful events for Argentine sailing. They started a tradition of bringing home medals from every Olympic competition. Camau won silver at the 1996 Atlanta Games, and also made the podium in the three that followed. Along with field hockey star Luciana Aymar, who also has four medals, he is the most decorated Argentine Olympic athlete. After Atlanta, Argentine sailors reached the podium eight more times: a record for a nation like ours. In the past, sailors—even those of us who had competed in the Olympics—were forced to juggle international competitions with work and family life. Camau and Bambi professionalized the discipline.

I joined up with this pair of fanatics when I was thirty-three years old with three kids and a shipyard. The chemistry was immediate. I quickly tuned in to Bambi's discipline, I followed Camau's relentless pace, and I contributed my technical knowledge of sailing and my analytical drive. Together we developed the KGB, our training method, and developed the system we still use to this day and which has brought so much success to Argentine athletics.

The name is a lighthearted reference to the Soviet security agency, and it was our way of laughing in the face of our limitations, though we did use certain espionage techniques on some of our rivals. If we saw them in the water, we'd take photos to gauge how their boat was riding, and we'd go to the marina at night to get a look at their set-up. Such was the level of our insanity.

Camau didn't come from a family of sailors. One summer, while vacationing in Florianópolis, in southern Brazil, he and his sister, María Inés, were fascinated to see people windsurfing. On their way back to Argentina, their father bought them a surfboard. The Paraná river's current flows quite powerfully by their home town, but they were able to find a more suitable location just over twenty miles away in the Totora lagoon. That's where they began to learn. Every morning, as he ate breakfast before heading to school, Camau would look up at the treetops to see if there was enough of a breeze to surf.

In those days, windsurfing was all the rage in the country. Camau had what it took and began to stand out. His desire to measure himself against the very best led him to compete in Buenos Aires. He was in his final year of night school; in the mornings he worked in the fields with his brother, in the afternoons he trained, and at night he studied. He financed his first trip to Europe by harvesting cotton. Both he and his sister qualified for the '92 Barcelona Games, where he finished twenty-fourth. He vowed to be better prepared by the time the next Olympics came around.

El Mencho, which is what I occasionally call him, referring to the tough countrymen from his region, is a reserved, calm, and meticulous young man who keeps his focus on his family and the things around him. Bambi, a former sprinter well versed in Soviet stringency, saw in him the traits that make up a great athlete and molded him into a racing machine.

I first learned about this duo when I returned to Argentina after the frustration of not having been able to compete in the Barcelona Games. I called Bambi on the phone and we met at Tarek, a Vicente López gym, on the north side of Buenos Aires. It was a popular spot frequented by rugby and soccer players who played for the national teams. I biked there from my house, went up to the second floor, and there, sitting in an armchair next to the stairs, was Bambi. He got right to the point.

"What's your goal?"

"I want to win an Olympic medal."

"Alright. I can help you get there, but it'll be tough."

"That's okay. I'm ready."

He introduced me to Camau, whom I'd only known by name. I knew my way around a gym, but this was another level entirely. Bambi had been known to kick athletes out of his team if they didn't show the commitment he demanded.

"I finished," I said after completing the exercises he'd given me for that day. "What's next?"

We were off to a good start. Maintaining this relationship with Bambi would be essential, even as I was about to make one of the biggest mistakes of my career: competing in a Laser.

The Laser was designed by a Canadian by the name of Bruce Kirby, whose goal was to create something affordable that could be transported on the roof of a car. In 1970 he won a contest to build a boat that would retail for under $1,000. What he ended up with was a small, simple sailboat. She weighs in at just over 130 pounds, measures just under fourteen feet bow to stern, and sails with a crew of one. The class doesn't allow for modifications that improve performance. All Lasers are identical, putting everyone on equal footing. The best sailor wins. It was added as an Olympic event for Atlanta, and since cost wasn't nearly as much of an issue, I'd be able to compete evenly with those from the great powers of the sailing world. I'd tried it out in a few competitions when I was still living in Spain and got some good results. So I decided this was the category in which I would attempt to qualify for my second Olympic Games.

Later, during a week of storms coming out of the southeast, I realized I'd made a mistake. I'd done well in competitions when the wind was low and my lean frame was an advantage, but the Laser is a boat best handled by a sailor who stands around six feet tall and weighs around 180 pounds. It requires a great deal of athleticism and exceptional physical preparation to drive it over the waves. I'm tall, but I'm also skinny. On my first windy outing, I hiked myself out over the water on the windward hull, but the boat simply didn't respond to my 160 pounds of body weight. Losing speed, the bow plunged and the boat took on water, slowing it even more. It felt rough and slow, as if I were on board a submarine: the complete opposite of the sense of pleasure that I get from a boat that glides easily across the surface of the water. After two more days of rough weather, I decided to return to the club, my legs feeling heavy and leaden. It was one of the few times in my life where I cut a workout short.

As I showered, I realized I had a major problem. The regulations for this particular category didn't allow for any modifications or customizations, to achieve a faster configuration, which is one of the aspects of sailing that I most enjoy. With the Laser, I'd gotten myself carried away with good early results and my eagerness to get started on the campaign. I became acutely aware that, in order to overcome the challenges this particular boat presented to me, physical preparation would be essential.

I'd never considered physical fitness to be one of my strong points. Bambi, to whom I'd committed myself, showed me how to build up the strength that the Laser required. It was a significant challenge and time was short. We decided to hit the gym even though the preparatory races were going on. This often hampered my performance, because I was racing with exhausted muscles, but it also presented us with the best chance at achieving our goal of winning a medal.

My alarm clock would go off at 6:30. I'd eat breakfast and bike to Tarek. If it was raining, I'd hitch a ride. Chivi had the car, and I hate driving in city traffic. Bambicha would be waiting for me there at 7:30. We'd warm up a bit before starting our weight routine. The primary goal was to strengthen my legs so I could hike better in the harness off the side of the boat. The workouts were so intense that often times I'd get up from the machines dizzy from the effort. Around eleven, when I was finished with my routine, I'd shower up and head for the shipyard. I took care of any pending business, have lunch, and around three or four in the afternoon I'd head to the Náutico, where I'd spend a couple more hours sailing alone, though occasionally I'd train with Cristian Herman, a Chilean who also sailed in a Laser. Finally, around seven in the evening, I'd return home where Chivi was waiting for me with the boys. Together we got them fed and into bed.

Dinner was key because I needed to gain some weight. I knew that reaching 180 was almost impossible, but I could at least put on ten or twelve more pounds. I consulted with a nutritionist who gave me a list of foods and told me to cross out the things I didn't like. The only item I marked off the list was dietetic gelatin. The problem was that, during championship competitions, my stomach would shrink up and my appetite vanished. I couldn't even have breakfast the morning of a race. Bambi had to sit next to me and help me through the tortuous task of getting some food down my gullet. We tried smoothies and they seemed to work well enough, but they weren't getting me all the calories I needed. I found the solution in a type of liquid supplement that's given to sick people. They were expensive, but I contacted the manufacturer and we were able to reach an agreement. The company provided them to me free of charge, and in exchange I brought them on board as a sponsor. My obsession with gaining muscle mass was such that I set an alarm to go off every morning at dawn to remind me to go down to the kitchen and eat a few slices of round steak that I'd prepared.

I wore a weighted vest while sailing, which was not only permitted but in fact common practice among sailors. I added about seven pounds, but it came with a physical cost. My back was being pushed to the breaking point. During that time when I was sailing Lasers, I had to have the meniscus repaired in both of my knees. I chose to have as little anesthesia as possible, which would shorten my recovery period. Obviously, my body wasn't prepared for what my mind had set out to achieve.

Racing in the wind was a challenge for me. I just couldn't keep up with the strongest and heaviest sailors in the fleet. Words like "Strength" and "Spirit" appeared often in the motivational quotes I carried around with me at the time. "Demand more from your training" and "Gain the strength to impel the boat" were two of the goals I'd set for myself heading into the 1995 World Championships in Tenerife. By that point, fatigue was beginning to have an effect on my focus, which frustrated me. "Enjoy every workout, have fun, and stay excited," I wrote.

It was a tough time, and the bond I'd forged with my teammates, Bambi and Camau, helped me endure the intensity of those years. I'd never have been able to hang in there without them. Camau and I were both competing in very demanding classes. In my case, the critical points were the legs and abs. Camau, on the other hand, had to focus more on his upper body in order to take advantage of a new rule. When the breezes died down, windsurfers were allowed to quickly flex the boom back and forth, almost as if they were rowing with the sail. This enabled them to keep going, but it required a tremendous amount of athleticism. And Camau was one of the strongest in the entire fleet. I, on the other hand, was suffering. Even as I managed to gain some muscle mass, I wasn't able to transfer that improvement to actual racing. In fact, I seemed to be getting worse. That's when a new team member, Daniel Espina, who is still with us to this day, joined the crew.

I met Yogui, one of the many nicknames we have for Dani, in a yoga class he was leading at the Center for High Performance Sports, or CENARD. I'd started attending in hopes of improving my flexibility, and after class one day I asked him about his story. In those days, yoga wasn't commonly implemented into the training regimen for competitive athletes. Dani was born in Patagonia, in southern Argentina, and lived in Chascomús, a town about seventy-five miles south of Buenos Aires. As a child, he suffered from seizures that left him shaken and upset. Looking for alternative treatments, he turned to yoga. While on a training retreat in India, a yoga master talked to him about ways for athletes to bring the discipline inherent in yoga to their respective sports. He found this interesting, he said, and began specializing in it, which is what eventually brought him to CENARD.

I sensed that his calm attitude and his small-town humbleness concealed a wealth of wisdom. Bambi agreed with me, and Dani joined our team. We invited him to a pre-Olympic regatta in Savannah, Georgia, which would be hosting the sailing competitions at the Atlanta Games. As was the case with Bambi early on, Dani didn't know much about our sport. In fact, he didn't even know how to swim.

When we started working together, we quickly realized what was the problem: I'd focused so much on building muscle that I'd lost sensitivity. I was hanging better on the hiking strap, but the strength that I'd gained was working against the soft touch I needed in order to steer. The challenge was to generate power while simultaneously being able to maintain a feel of the boat and pick up on what the rudder was transmitting to me. Dani, Bambi, and I started looking for ways to marry the body's tension with the hand's subtlety. Bambi worked on the physical aspects while Dani focused on the mental, and we quickly realized that it would be impossible to separate one from the other.

Through posture, breathing techniques, and stories told at a leisurely pace, Yogui taught us to silence our minds. "There's a difference between silent and silence," he said. "Often times we're silent, and yet that little voice inside your head just keeps on talking." The idea is to exist in the present in order to achieve an absolute presence in both time and place. That way we're better able to maintain focus, which is an essential tool in any competition, allowing us to make split-second decisions while avoiding fears and illusions.

Camau had a hard time accepting these unconventional methods. He's a practical man who believes in what his eyes can see. He's naturally more predisposed to Bambi's coaching style. But he agreed to incorporate yoga as a means of stretching, and he gradually became fascinated by the benefits of visualization.

There was a final preparatory race shortly before the Games and I came in third. Camau didn't fare well at all, even losing to Marcos Galván, his Argentine sparring partner. "We're here to win a medal, not this warmup event that nobody cares about," Bambi said, reassuring him. Training sessions in the gym were reaching their peak, and Camau was finding it difficult to apply the more subtle techniques that make all the difference when it comes to speed on the board. That was the reason he was getting beaten by windsurfers who weren't at the same skill level as he was. But he believed in Bambi's training regimen and arrived at the threshold of the Olympics with his spirit intact. For me, trained in the old school of always playing to win, this was an important lesson on how to prepare for a campaign.

The Atlanta Games was where we started the tradition of spending a lot of time getting to know the race course and, if possible, living somewhere other than the Olympic Village. It was our way of becoming locals. Camau, Bambi, Dani, and I moved into a rented house along with our respective coaches: Hernán Vila with Camau, and Maciel Cicchetti, or Cicho, with me. The competition area was at the mouth of a river. We could drive there, but it was quicker to go by water, and we invested $1,500 in a pair of old boats. One day we accidently left Yogui on a deserted island where we often left the boats. When we went back several hours later, he was meditating quietly without showing the slightest sign of concern, proving to us once and for all that he truly did live according to his mantra.

Our water taxis were the envy of all the other teams. But one afternoon we were on our way back from sailing when one of the boats began to take on water. The wind had picked up and the old hull couldn't withstand the pounding waves. Dani, who still hadn't learned how to swim, turned as pale as a sheet as he clung to his life preserver. We veered towards the coast and managed to make it to ground, where the owner of a nearby house took pity on us. He ushered us inside and called for a proper taxi.

On July 22nd, 1996, we ran the first two heats of the Atlanta Games. I came in fourth in the first and won the second, giving me a good boost of confidence. It had been a windy race, under the same sort of conditions that I struggled with the most back when I had started with the Laser. Back at the marina, I hugged Bambi. The sacrifices had finally paid off. However, there was an unpleasant surprise waiting for me: when I looked at the results sheet, I found I had been disqualified for an alleged premature start.

Starts are always complicated. All the sailors are trying to position themselves in the right place at maximum speed when the horn blasts and we can cross the imaginary line between two boats that marks the starting point. Crossing that line too early is one of the risks we take, but I knew in my heart that this time I wasn't guilty of the infraction. On the contrary, I got off to a difficult start, and was back in the second pack of boats. I filed an appeal to have the decision reviewed. Witnesses were called in, and the commission gave me back the victory. Finally, I was able to go to bed, late and tired.

The next day my results weren't quite as good, though I was still in third place overall. The problem, though, was that the judge who had originally disqualified me appealed my appeal and asked for the case to be reopened. Once again, I had to deal with a long night of hearings, which didn't go in my favor. The following day it was my turn to ask for the ruling to be reviewed, and after a tense and grueling process, I was awarded the victory for the second time. But the stress had caused me to lose my focus. I wasn't sleeping well and I wasn't following my diet. After spending so much effort proving my innocence, my results took a nosedive. In the eighth heat, I was disqualified again for an early start, which this time was justified. A medal was now out of reach.

On one of those afternoons I went shopping with Dani. I needed to get out of the house, to distract myself. I was beaten. I'd put all the time and professionalism I had into my preparations, but I didn't get the result I wanted. Yogui didn't say much and instead listened to my rehashed theories before agreeing that the appeals and protests had thrown me off my game. In the end, I finished ninth, the same result I had when racing with Toto and Tati in the Soling. The difference was that we had gone into Seoul with no expectations and ended up celebrating a much better result than we had anticipated. In Atlanta, however, I took the loss hard.

But there would be joy for Camau. As my chances went up in smoke, he established himself as one of the strongest competitors in the class. Except for one heat in which he was disqualified for an early start (it was his "discard," the worst of his twelve races that wouldn't count towards his final results), he always finished in the top six. He came into the final day of competition second overall. He didn't have a path to win the gold, but there were two rivals trying to catch him from behind. Camau stood up to the pressure and held on for the silver. It had been thirty-six years since an Argentine sailor had stood on the podium at the Olympics. I was happy for my friend and for the entire team. His success was a vindication of our training methods.

Towards the end of the games, Chivi came with Yago for a visit, and we took a vacation to Disney. But by the second day I was already fed up, so we drove south to Key West, where we bought masks, snorkels, and fins and enjoyed the wonders of the seabed. Still, though, my spirits weren't much improved. I was still exhausted and dejected.

When we returned to Buenos Aires, I came down with a very bad case of hepatitis. I was completely bedridden. I didn't even have the strength to get up and walk to the door when the doorbell rang. Was this my body's revenge for the battles I'd put it through over the past few years? No, it was more mental, it was a consequence of the frustration the Atlanta Games had left in me. During those days of recuperation, I had plenty of time to think about all the effort I had put into sailing the wrong ship. Another campaign in the Laser for the Sydney 2000 Games, when I would be thirty-nine years old, was out of the question. It would have been crazy. Physically impossible. Having come to the realization that you only reach your peak level of performance in a particular class during your second Olympic cycle, the impossibility of returning to the Games in a Laser made me realize how big of a mistake I'd made.

On the other hand, Silvina had left things quite clear. Her patience reached only as far as Atlanta. Our marriage, as I understood it, wasn't going to endure another four years of what we'd just gone through. Our fourth child, Klaus, had been born on June 13th of the previous year, and she was feeling overwhelmed. My traveling was the primary reason for our recurring arguments. At the time, I didn't have an international schedule that was quite as intense as the one I do now, when I'm away from home anywhere from seven to nine months out of the year, but I was still on the road quite a bit.

Nomadic life was commonplace among my European sailing friends, but I was based in Argentina and the distance made everything more difficult. The other drawback was more cultural: Chivi and I grew up in an environment of large, close-knit families with a dynamic of family barbecues, birthday parties, and other social gatherings which she was often forced to attend by herself. Another Olympic campaign would mean another four years of the same, and she wasn't willing to do that. I decided to step away from the boats for a while and get a taste of life on land.

A business group that had sponsored me during my Laser campaign was setting up a frozen product distribution service and they offered to bring me on to help get it up and running. It would be up to me to hire the team, analyze the competition, determine the cost structures, meet with potential clients, and handle all the other tasks that come with starting a business. The manufacturing experience I'd gained from working at the shipyard was helpful, but this was still the first time I'd be working on something completely unrelated to boats. My break with the nautical universe was swift and complete. I didn't even go for the occasional weekend sail. Never had I been that disconnected from the water before. I traded in my life jacket for a suit, and my regattas for downtown office buildings. The only remnant of my previous life was my bicycle, which was still my preferred means of transportation.

It was around that time that an opportunity arose to move closer to the coast. I found a house at 33 Orientales, a street in Bajo de San Isidro that runs along a canal and ends at the river. It's a quiet neighborhood with lots of old trees. The only signs of movement are from the parishioners who congregate on Sundays at a small nearby chapel. We invested our savings into buying and renovating the house. I drew up some plans with the help of architect friends and handled many of the details myself, including the heart pine floor, which I reclaimed from a demolition.

There was yet another economic downturn during that time, and the project I was working on lost traction. That gave me an excuse to resign. I could feel my Olympic spirit beginning to reawaken, but Chivi remained adamant. One morning she told me she dreamed that the boat's mast had snapped and I'd given up sailing forever. We were both tired of arguing about the same thing time and time again. I let the comment pass, but that conversation stuck with me. Silvina wanted me to give up the one thing I enjoyed most in the world. All day I had the horrible feeling that I was sleeping with the enemy. It was the trigger for our divorce.

In truth, travelling to compete was only part of the problem. It had been over a year since I last got on a plane. Still, though, our relationship was deteriorating. The fact of the matter was that we each wanted different things out of life. We'd fallen in love when we were very young, but now, after more than ten years of marriage and four children, we had become very different people. It was a time of painful conversations and tears, until one night when I left home and biked towards the river.

I slept on Ferdi's boat. I was nearly forty years old, I was away from my children, and I had neither a job nor savings. We'd invested everything we had in the new house, which I had just left with nothing but a bag of clothes and my bicycle. The pitter-patter of the waves lapping against the hull helped me ward off the sadness. Up to that point, my dream had been on the negotiating table. First with my father's mandate, and later with Silvina's vision of a couple and a family. In this next phase of my life, I promised myself, nothing would come between me and my seafaring call.

Chapter Eight

The Happy Image Machine

The divorce was a painful process for the entire family. Yago, who had just turned ten, still remembers the difficult scene in the living room of our house there at 33 Orientales when Silvina and I spoke to the boys. We had only moved in recently, and there wasn't much in the way of furniture. Silvina sat down on one of the kitchen chairs, and I on another. From an armchair, along with his three brothers, our oldest looked on with a fear in his eyes, sensing that what his mother and I were about to tell them would not be good news. Borja was holding on to a memory of dinner at the neighborhood grill. We all hugged each other silently, trying to hold back tears. That weekend he devoted himself to searching for four-leaf clovers on the Náutico's grounds. "May my parents get back together," he repeated, his eyes closed as if in prayer, every time he found one.

The boys were the main reason we put off the decision. We had always looked for ways to keep them from suffering. My attempt to quit sailing and work for the food distributor was a last-ditch effort to save our marriage. It didn't work. Boats or not, our relationship was broken beyond repair. We'd been taught, both at home and in school, that marriage was an everlasting commitment. A union for life. But that concept left us despondent and depressed. I had to contradict the values I learned growing up and separate myself. I did this because, among many other reasons, I didn't want my children think it was okay to compromise and accept the hypocrisy of staying married just to keep the family under one roof. Instead, I chose to let them understand, sooner or later, that it's better to fight for what one wants.

Those first few months away from home were truly difficult. I was miserable and I missed the boys dearly. And I felt guilty. I spent most of my time alone. Recovering from a divorce and getting on with your life is, as I tell my friends a process that takes time. It's a wound that never fully heals.

Six months later, Ferdi's relationship also came to an end. He left home and moved into the boat with me. Together, we dealt with the emotional shock as best we could. Ferdi slept in the aft cabin and was in charge of fixing breakfast, while I, in the bow, was responsible for dinner. That coexistence was the first step for me on the path to healing. I'd sit there on the deck and spend the afternoon contemplating the course of the river. Accompanied by music and a traditional Argentine tea known as mate, I was amazed at how, little by little, we were transforming a painful situation into a new opportunity.

It was impossible to be bored with Ferdi around, and together we began to live our lives as single men. We went tango and milonga dancing at the clubs on the south side of the city. I remember having breakfast on board the Sueño de Amor—the Dream of Love, which was the suggestive name we gave to our floating home—where we celebrated an epic night with scrambled eggs.

Life on the boat was so convenient that I decided to buy one of my own. I borrowed a motorboat and visited the piers of all the yacht clubs in the area. I spoke with the sailors, expressing my interest and leaving my phone number. One day I received a call about a boat that had been in a fire. I went to check it out. The engine was gone, but with a little work the hull and interior could be restored. Despite the superficial burns, the old wooden structure, solid and elegant, had held up with dignity. The owner would let me have it for $10,000.

We towed the Toi et Moi—that was the name of the boat—to the Náutico, and anchored it in a hidden marina. There, secluded from the other vessels, I would have a bit of privacy and could avoid what I assumed would be the eventual complaints from club members who didn't like the fact that two bachelors had moored their houseboats at a yacht club. Nevertheless, I hired some help and got to work on the restoration. We cleaned her up and painted her white with varnished details. I didn't have the money to replace the engine, but that wasn't a concern. This would be my home, not a means of transportation.

The boat was just a temporary solution. I still needed to generate some income. Up until that point, money had never been a priority in my life. But all that changed with the divorce. To begin with, I had to find a way to support my four children. And looking for a job that kept me out of the water was out of the question... though there was more to it than that. I was determined to pursue my calling as a sailor. I knew that resuming my career as a professional boater in Europe would mean long periods of time away from my boys, but it was the path I wanted to take. My mother was absolutely essential during this stage of my life. She filled in for my absence and helped raise the boys. She organized activities for them, she took them to the doctor, but above all she gave them lots of grandmotherly love. She enjoyed looking after them so much that my travels gave her a secret joy: the chance for her grandsons to sleep over at her house.

The days before that taxi ride to the airport and my imminent departure were tortuous. When I was diagnosed with cancer, I began to wonder if the disease hadn't started to incubate during that sad ride to Ezeiza Airport. The notion came to me after consulting a specialist in nontraditional Chinese medicine. "A diseased lung is a sign of grief," he told me. As I look back over my life, I still can't find a more bitter fortune than that. When I arrived in Europe, I got so deeply involved in my work that the pain began to dissipate, but I still remember the hurt in me left by the divorce. It was hard on the boys as well, and each of them was processing it in his own way.

Because he was the oldest, Yago had the worst of it. During one Christmas celebration, my sister Inés found him outside crying in a corner of the yard: it was time for the family photo, and yet his dad wasn't there. He was also hurt by the fact that I wasn't at his First Communion. During his teenage years he went through periods of great anger. One night he got into a fight with Chivi and stormed out of the house to wander aimlessly between the boat and his grandmother's house.

Klaus was still just a boy when we separated. He has no clear memories of those days, but my travels affected him nonetheless. One morning, as they were getting ready for school, he asked Borja if I didn't love them: the only explanation he could think of for my absence.

The twins also suffered. For years they didn't really know what I was doing. They watched the final race at one of the Olympic Games when it was shown on TV, but they weren't interested in the sport. Theo says he never answered anyone at school when they asked what his father did or what awards he'd won. Maybe that was his way of protecting himself. Borja only got hooked on sailing when I started competing in open ocean races. He was more interested in the adventure of sailing around the globe, not in a game of racing between buoys.

Our family is one of intense bonds and emotions. Although we spend a lot of time apart, I like to think the distance never threatened our love for one another. We celebrated each and every occasion we had to see each other. The union is strong and its foundations were only strengthened during those years of separation when it came to the life that my children and I shared on the boat and on the river.

The Toi et Moi lacked a shower, a motor, and decent heating, but it had the best garden in all of Buenos Aires, complete with a golf course, squash and tennis courts, and a wharf, all right there on the river. On the weekends, the Náutico is filled with families, but when the sun goes down on Sunday, the club is empty. The clamor dies down and is replaced by the songs of the birds. From Monday to Friday, all forty-nine hectares of that island, accessible by a bridge that spanned a channel, became a playground for my four boys.

"Do we own the Náutico?" Klaus asked me one afternoon when we entered the club without showing our membership cards and greeting the sailor guarding the entrance by name. I told him yes. That's how we felt.

Since my job forced me to spent long periods of time away from my children, I wanted to make the most of the moments we did have together. Whenever I returned to Buenos Aires, they stayed with me all the time, which meant that, for a few days at least, I had the same relationship with my kids as any other separated father. At other times, the distance prevented us from living a normal daily life, and kept me from responding to any potential emergency. The boys could sense these things missing from their relationship with their father, and I went to great lengths to make up for that.

The Toi et Moi didn't have a phone and we barely ever invited anyone else aboard. The boat was our lair. Living there might not have been ideal, but it was wonderful.

Sometimes the five of us would all bike to school together. Yago had his own bike, and I carried the other three with me. Theo was strapped to my back, Borja would sit on the frame, and Klaus was on the handlebars. It made for some good exercise to kick-start my morning gym routine. Around noon I'd pick them up and go for hot dogs at Coquito, a tiny little convenience store just a block from the train station. It's run by two families, the Grandinettis and the Rubinis. I brought them cans of Coke from my travels to add to the collection they had on display behind the counter. To this day, the employees at Coquito still recognize us when we drop by.

In the afternoons the boys would hop on their bikes and roam around the grounds. They built ramps, splashed along the river bank, paddled around the island on surfboards, went hunting for toads, patrolled the golf course, and fed the otters. Four untamed cubs who knew every square inch of the Náutico. The sailors all looked after them. Their adventures were updated versions of those that, three decades earlier, I shared with Martín at the Yacht Club.

To escape the throngs of members who flooded the club on the weekends, we'd head out for even more rugged territory. In the delta, about an hour down the El Durazno branch of the river, we built a cabin. The adventures began as soon as we got on the board the launch. On the way home, we'd often stop at El Pajarito, a pizzeria, also located there in the delta. One morning we ran out of gas and had to improvise a sail using our tent in order to navigate back to the bank of the river. Another time I had to dive down under the muddy waters to remove a line that had gotten tangled up in the propeller. When I popped back up again, I could see the panic in my sons' eyes. I've always been able to hold my breath for long periods of time, and the boys had been frightened by how long I'd been gone underwater.

The cabin was really a fully functioning house. It had a living room that opened into the kitchen, a bathroom, and three bedrooms. Just what we needed. But the most interesting things happened outside. The geography of the delta region—a giant group of islands separated by winding waterways—creates a very unique local culture. Inhabitants live in relative isolation, traveling by boat to get supplies, visit the doctor, or take their children to school. The people there are used to life amidst the forces of nature, and we were part of that dynamic.

The boys would dive off the dock into the river, fish by tying a line with a hook to a plastic bottle which served as a float, and take the motorboat out on their own, going on expeditions all throughout the wetlands. We had a vegetable garden. Hogs, chickens, and cows were our neighbors. But the biggest attraction that came to the island were the horses. Escopeta and Pepo had gotten loose and quickly returned to their feral state. Neither my kids nor I had any sort of experience with livestock, and yet we managed to get them bridled and ride them. We even got them into the river. When they let them, the boys would bathe them and trim their manes and tails. They also adopted the caretaker Celso's dog. Rambo would leap into the water to greet us every time he heard the sound of our boat, and wouldn't leave the boys' side throughout the entire weekend.

One morning, when the four of them bolted off on one of their adventures, I sat there by myself and realized just how lucky I was. The divorce had taken a toll, but we were still spending the happiest years of our lives together. The tight quarters there in the small cabin in the delta—and, above all, the boat—brought us even closer together. In time, each of them would go off on his own path, and never again would I have the great joy of seeing the four of them running free across an island.

The boys always played a lot of sports. And it was around that time that they got hooked on tennis. During the week, the club's courts were empty and available. Theo became fanatical with the rebound wall. He didn't much like to compete against others, but he'd spend hours at that wall hitting the ball over and over again. It was his way of unloading. We had to buy him new sneakers every couple of months because he was wearing them out so fast. Theo always reminded me of a bull: when he gets something in his head, he goes after it and doesn't stop. He suffered the usual bullying from some of his classmates in school, Borja often stuck up for him, but not always. To this day he still blames himself for the few times he didn't show solidarity with his brother.

Clashes on the tennis court between Borja and Klaus were classic. Despite their difference in age, they played even matches. Borja was more tactical and experienced, but his younger brother made up for that with sheer physical power. Klaus is tall, strong, and talented. He skates, surfs, plays roller hockey, soccer, rugby... if you name a sport, he played it, and he excelled in all of them. He always wanted to become a professional athlete and became a fan of David Nalbandian, an Argentine tennis star who was once ranked as high as third in the world, dreaming of one day following in his footsteps. At first, he had no interest in sailing whatsoever.

Yago started taking lessons in the Optimist at the age of six, two years before the standard age, and began competing very early on. It was a mistake. He was just too young. He lost his early enthusiasm and stopped sailing altogether. Still, though, he's always loved sports. He was an excellent runner and attended CENARD with Bambicha to train in track and field. Years later, he'd return to the boating world. And even without a foundation in the youth classes, he quickly became a talented helmsman.

Borja and Theo were also initiated in the Optimist at the Náutico, but they didn't care for it either and moved on quickly. Klaus wanted to be with them. He never finished the official training and instead learned to sail on his own, just as Martín and I had. I just handed him a boat, gave him a few basic safety lessons, and let him go out and play. I had a feeling he'd be able to figure out from which direction the wind was coming and how to adjust the sails. I was right. At that age, learning is pure intuition.

Some years later he ran into his friend Fidel García Guevara, Ferdi's son, who was going to compete in some regattas. Ferdi offered to bring him on board, an offer that fascinated Klaus. At eleven years of age, he'd only recently started competing. But he learned quickly and soon caught up with his peers, all of whom had been sailing since they were much younger. At the end of his Optimist years, he was among the best in Argentina, but he was also too heavy for the boat and never managed to qualify for a World Championship. He did stand out in the 29er, another youth category, alongside Mateo Majdalani. From there, he jumped to the 49er, an Olympic-class ship which he still sails to this day with Yago.

During the time the boys and I lived on the boat, we showered in the club locker room and kept our clothes in the trunk of an old Volvo. For dinner, my specialty was noodles—always the same brand, Don Vicente—with butter and cheese. We'd mix things up a bit and have rice with tuna and vegetables, as well as the occasional roast. We had a small television connected to a VHS player and two movies, The Mask of Zorro and Braveheart. The boys could recite all the lines from memory. There were also some CDs of rock in Spanish—Andrés Calamaro, Jarabe de Palo, Fito Páez, Charly García, and Luis

Alberto Spinetta—along with some jazz and Brazilian music. One day I bought a PlayStation, but that turned out to be a rather fleeting fling. It would only work if we connected it to one of the club's TVs, and the boys soon gave up on it. Instead, the boys preferred using the leftover noodles as bait: they'd cast a line out through one of the portholes and fall asleep clinging to the fishing pole. Once, they woke up to the bite of a catfish.

For her part, Silvana set about creating a home and setting guidelines and boundaries. And she did so very well. We argued a fair amount after the divorce, but we always agreed on the freedom with which we chose to raise our children. At the time she was teaching barre à terre, a type of dance. She also worked with students to improve their physical posture. She has a very spiritual, very holistic view of life. Borja remembers when he came home crying because of a sore throat. Instead of taking him to the doctor, she explained that this pain could be related to an emotional obstacle. She was going to get him a book on the topic, he said. At the time, Borja didn't understand why she wasn't reacting like a traditional mother, but today he appreciates the open-mindedness that radiated through her home.

All five of us agreed that the divorce, and my travels even more so, were difficult, but the free and simple life at the club and at the cabin was a wealth of joy. It was something we clung to in order to make the time until our next encounter more bearable. When my imminent departure clouded our spirits, I would tell them the time we spent together was magical even if it couldn't last forever. According to Borja, those days served as a machine churning out happy images that he could turn to whenever he missed me at night. He would close his eyes, reminisce over some adventure we'd all experienced together, and that would help him fall into a deep, peaceful sleep.

Chapter Nine

Catching the Wind

"So, Lange, was I right or what?" With this single cunning question, Ferdi García Guevara shatters the idyllic mood I'd found myself in for the past few minutes after he handed over the helm to me and I felt the excitement that rushes over you just before confidence settles in. We are off the coast of San Isidro and the Tornado is pure adrenaline. The sheer power of this vessel that flies along at breakneck speed while balancing on one of its twin hulls is something I have never before experienced. All the information I've gathered during my hours and hours of training simply vanishes with every wave we effortlessly surge across. The Tornado has sails—it's propelled by the wind and it floats—but that's about all it has in common with the other ships I'd come to know up to that point. There's so much I'll have to relearn, so many antiquated concepts I'll have to revise, but I don't care. In a matter of minutes, we've covered more distance than I would ever have thought possible. It's as if the Río de la Plata had suddenly shrunk in size. In the midst of this discovery, a question comes to mind: why did I wait so long for this?

There's a world of difference between monohull sailboats and those with multiple hulls, also known as catamarans. Until Ferdi convinced me otherwise, I'd always raced in traditional, single-hulled boats. The Optimist, the Cadet, the 470, and the Snipe were all constructed of one solid hull and they have a similar ride and feel to them. Catamarans, on the other hand, have two thin hulls connected by beams with a net known as a trampoline in between them. This setup alters the physics of the boat and changes the way it moves. The Tornado and the Nacra, the two Olympic catamarans I later raced on, are much faster than the classes I was familiar with up to that point. "Stop dragging yourself along in those slow old boats and live in the now!" Ferdi yelled. I laughed, but other than that, I ignored him.

The Tornado was conceived as a way of adding a fast, modern category to Olympic sailing competitions, and first debuted at the Montreal Games in 1976. Ferdi was on his way back from a regatta with his Snipe when he caught sight of one of the first catamarans to hit the water in Buenos Aires. The image of a Tornado raising one hull up out of the water to generate unprecedented speed, with the crew members hanging out over the water in the trapeze, struck him. He found out who the owner was, asked if he could try it out, and never set foot on board a Snipe again. "The Tornado was my cocaine," Ferdi says, flashing his Joker-like smile as he recalls his early days in the new category.

I didn't have quite the audacity of my friend, and it took me the better part of a decade to realize that catamarans were the right class for me. Unlike the normal trajectory of an athlete who bursts onto the scene as a relative youngster before gradually fading into a retirement which, in most sports, happens well before the age of forty, my career unfolded in quite the opposite way. I went into my first Olympics, Seoul '88, with barely any training and using a boat I hardly knew. For my second time around, Atlanta '96, I went in well-prepared but competing in the wrong class. It wasn't until the Sydney 2000 Games that I found, in the Tornado, a category where I could put my abilities on full display. On top of which, the catamaran's arrival coincided with my divorce. My determination to pursue my wish of being a professional sailor, along with an exceedingly fast ship that allowed me to sail in a completely unprecedented way, resulted in a newfound sense of freedom.

Cole Parada immediately accepted my proposal to try and qualify for the 2000 Sydney Games in the Tornado class. We've known each other since 1983, when I was his coach for the Cadet World Championships in Holland, which he won as his brother Guillermo's crewmate. In addition to being a great athlete, he's a generous and intelligent fellow. Together we won the 1993 and 1995 Snipe World Championships. For the former, which was held in calm weather, he lost over twenty pounds. For the latter, where the winds were much stronger, he put them back on. That was the kind of commitment we were going to need.

In a Tornado, Cole's short stature presented a problem. During windy conditions, one of the crewmember's tasks is to hike him- or herself out over the water in the trapeze to keep the boat from capsizing. Teams with taller crew members would have an advantage over us. Also, we were learning how to sail a completely new vessel while on a limited budged in a short amount of time. There again, we were already used to getting by with the bare minimum. When we competed in the Snipe, we stayed in an hourly rate motel on the road outside Porto Alegre, or we crashed in the van which was parked on board a Spanish ferry.

The Tornado is a highly technical boat, and during those early days we made hundreds of mistakes. Once the mast fell off because we hadn't put it together correctly. Unable to afford a traditional coach, we were deeply gratified to accept the help of Vladimir Bolotnikov, a Ukrainian who'd followed his wife to Argentina in search of a new life, and who graciously volunteered his knowledge and expertise. He brought experience from Olympic sailing crews in his native country and was ready to work in a new one. The Yachting Federation of Argentina called me up one day and told me about him, so I gave him a call and we decided to meet. Using basic signs and elementary Spanish, we explained to him that we had no funding but would be happy to accept his help. We borrowed a Zodiac so Vladi could follow us around while we trained. When gasoline was running low, he'd drop anchor at the mouth of the canal and wait for us so he could tow us back to the ramp at the end of the day. Little gestures like that proved his loyalty and dedication. Vladi had fled his homeland at the height of the crisis unleashed by the fall of the Soviet Union and was grateful for the opportunity. Eventually we were able to convince the Náutico to hire him, and he did a wonderful job teaching the youth categories.

We did a brief tour of Europe and, once again, we received the support of the Spanish federation and coaches. In order to get the boat from one competition to another, we looked for space in the bigger teams' trailers. The Spaniards shipped the hulls for us, and the French transported the mast.

Adapting to the catamaran wasn't easy. In fact, I was quite frustrated at first. Faster boats are much more sensitive to the intensity of the wind, and this creates wide variations in speed. It's all but impossible to strategically defend your position. Races are up for grabs until the very end. During that first year, I often found myself irritated when what I considered luck ended up determining the results. Over time, though, I came to accept this new way of confronting the competition, and even came to enjoy it. I owe this in no small part to great sailors like Roman Hagara and Darren Bundock who dominated the class. What they had wasn't luck. They knew something that I didn't. And that's when I understood: before, it was important to know the fleet. Now, the key lay in being able to read the wind.

There's a profound difference between these two priorities, one tied to the very different mechanisms that influence decision-making. On slower boats, you can map out your moves and those of your opponents. But in catamarans, you have to transform your mind, to become something of an artist able to perceive the vicissitudes of the wind and go grab it before anyone else can. Tactics and strategy, my old strengths, were suddenly less relevant than the feeling, the sensitivity needed to go fast and to the right side. Intuition has to be added to reason. Heart must be included alongside an agile mind. Of course, intuition isn't triggered in a vacuum. It's brought about by hours of training and a wealth of acquired knowledge.

Unlike tactical planning, the art of reading the wind is something that fascinates me more and more. It's part of the awareness that we train for during our visualizations with Dani Espina. Nothing makes me happier than a boat that sails well. When that happens, I shut my mind off. I feel so connected that time stands still. Bending to the will of the wind and the movements of the sea is what keeps me hanging from the trapeze of a Nacra at fifty-eight years of age.

In the beginning, Klaus asked me a lot about tactics. That was when I realized that too much information has the potential to be counterproductive. I was running the risk of turning him into a theorist and killing his creativity. I explained him that you don't need to study in order to be a good sailor, you need to trust your instincts and spend hours upon hours out on the water developing it. There would be time for the rest later. I've become convinced that this is the best learning method... and not just for nautical purposes.

In January of 2000, the same year as the Olympics, we finished thirteenth in the World Championships held in Sydney, thus qualifying for the Games. We were far from the front of the pack, but on one particularly windy day we got very good results—starting fifth and finishing second—and we were excited.

Unlike the thorough and conscientious preparations we went through for the previous Games, we ran a relatively short campaign leading up to Sydney. Even though we couldn't organize joint sessions in the gym due to differing schedules, Camau helped us both out. His silver medal from Atlanta had made him a star of the Argentine sporting world—he was our flag bearer during the Opening Ceremonies in Sydney—and it enabled him to support the team and bring on sponsors. He was always very generous and shared his organizational scheme with us.

Camau tracked down the house that would serve as our bunker during the last few months of training up to and including the week-long competition. We settled in there along with Eduardo García Velasco, his coach and sparring partner, Dani, Bambi, Cole, and Galarza.

Galarza was in charge of the kitchen and, as one would expect, he was convinced that Australian seasonings had no flavor. So he flew there with bags full of Argentine spices, which resulted in him spending a few hours trying to explain, in his broken English, why the airport's detection dogs were alerted to his luggage. This setback went on to become part of the repertoire of stories with which we entertained ourselves every night. I approached him once when I was thinking about getting away from it all for a couple of days.

"I'm burned out, Galarza. I need to reboot," I told him.

"Let's go fishing for a couple of days," he suggested.

We settled in a little town on the coast, and while we didn't catch anything, we did talk a lot. I told him about my divorce and the sadness I felt about being away from my children. We became very close friends during that period of time. Galarza would prove to be of fundamental help when it came to taking care of family matters over the next few years. He always checked in with Chivi and our kids when I was traveling to or from competitions.

We were out training with Cole, so Galarza went to Sydney Airport to pick up Yago after his long flight from Buenos Aires. He stayed with us in the house. Together we watched the women's 100 meter final won by Marion Jones. Several years later, the International Olympic Committee would formally strip her of that and her four other medals and wipe her name from the record books after she admitted having taken steroids. We also attended a women's field hockey game. Las Leonas, or The Lionesses, as the Argentine women had dubbed themselves, won silver and began a stretch of great results for the team and the nation. Yago was mesmerized by all the athletes and had a loop around the Olympic marina that he circumnavigated on his skateboard. He asked Galarza to time his laps and he worked to lower his splits. He wanted to be an Olympian too one day, he told me.

On September 17th, 2000, we ran in the first heat of the Sydney Games. We got off to a good start and reached the buoy among the top three boats, but fell off the pace in the final stretch with the wind at our backs. This course, by design, requires a very particular way of sailing the Tornado. The Australians have developed a technique they call The Wild Thing, which consists of using the crew members' own weight to tilt the boat and lift one of the hulls completely out of the water. With less surface area submerged in the water, resistance is lessened and speed increased. It's an effective method, but extremely difficult as well. We rehearsed it during the brief training period we had before the Games and were able to master it, but we weren't performing so well when both hulls were in the water. It was harder for me to decide which bow to ride the waves with at any given moment. It was tough being overtaken on the homestretch, which is where we were used to being the ones making up ground. We tried to stay positive, but there were times when I took out my frustrations on Cole.

Reaching the winner's podium was a fleeting dream at best. In none of our previous events did we have a result that would have encouraged such hope. But then, halfway through the competition, we found ourselves among the teams still in contention. But that dream vanished on the next to last day: we had two bad results, including a disqualification for an early start. Cole says that as soon as the race began, he heard the race official call out a warning that we were over the line. We could turn around and start again, which would vacate the penalty, but it would leave us at the back of the fleet. According to Cole, I told him we hadn't crossed the line early and that we would continue on.

We finished in tenth place overall. A fair result. This was my third Olympic Games, and the podium was still very much in the distance, but this time I didn't fall apart.

After the Sydney Games, Camau, who had just won his second silver medal, said he wanted to retire from windsurfing. Changing to a different category was a big gamble on his part. The two medals would have assured him the support of both sponsors and the federation if he wanted to embark on another Olympic campaign, but it wasn't clear whether they would back him on a new and risky gambit. We had always dreamed about the possibility of competing together, and decided to finally give it a try.

When I spoke with Cole in Buenos Aires to announce my alliance with Camau, I assumed he had no interest in pursuing another campaign. And while we remained great friends, we never touched on the subject again until now, more than fifteen years later, when I called him up to talk about the idea of reconstructing our story together for this book. I was surprised to learn his take on how our team came to an end.

During this recent conversation, Cole told me that after Sydney, he believed the plan was to continue on the same course and prepare to be at our peak performance level for the next Olympics. What I had communicated to him that day, he explained, disappointed him. He was surprised by the news, which reminded me that our relationship had somewhat cooled for a period of time after that. I'd been so engrossed in my new project with Camau that I never even realized what pain I'd caused my friend. In fact, I was so oblivious that I offered him to be our coach for Athens 2004, and only now do I understand why he didn't accept.

Cole told me that he was happy to have won a medal in Athens with Camau, but the one he truly celebrated—according to him—was the one in Beijing in 2008. We gradually became close again and worked together on a number of projects. For the 2016 Rio Games, he came on board as a coach. We shared countless hours sailing and biking, enjoying each other's company. During our talk, I was able to once again confirm his generosity. "With time, I was able to heal the wound," he told me. "I understood your rationale and I didn't disagree with it. You took the jump you needed to take." Cole was graceful enough to let me go after my Olympic obsession. After all, he knew just how much I wanted that medal.

Where it all began: being five or six at the wheel with my dad.
(family archive)

First times: Sailing with Martin Billoch and friends. (family archive)

Playing with Martin Billoch in a cadet. (family archive)

My great aunts Fanchi and Polú: They taught me a lot. (family archive)

College times: with my fellow-students Martin Billoch and Edu Galofré in Southampton, Great Britain. (family archive)

My brothers and parents. (family archive)

On the *Toi et moi* after the separation:
The kids loved the adventurous life on the water. (family archive)

Days on the beach when the kids were young. (family archive)

Training on the laser in Mar del Plata, preparing for the Olympic Games in Atlanta, 1996. (Gustavo Fazio)

Our team at the Olympics in Athens (2004):
Ramón Oliden, Daniel Bambicha, ich, Camau Espinola, Dani Espina and Mariano Galarza (family archive)

Tornado-training with Camau for the World Championship, 2006, in San Isidro. (Gustavo Cherro)

Camau Espínola and I, celebrating Athens (2004) with our fantastic training companions Roman Hagara and Hans-Peter Steinacher.

On the podium with Camau at the Olympic Games, Beijing 2008.
(Carlo Borlenghi)

In a 29er with my son Klaus, fifteen years of age at that time.
(Matías Capizzano)

Around the world in the *Telefonica Black*, October of 2008.
(Sailingshots by María Muiña)

Silvina, myself and our children. (family archive)

Class-reunion: 2009 with friends from school in Yacanto, Córdoba. (family archive)

Post-surgery-training: cycling with Borja and Theo in Cabrera de Mar.
(family archive)

Opening ceremony of the Olympic Games at Rio de Janeiro.
In the company of Cecilia, Klaus and Yago. (family archive)

Bear hug from my sons in celebration of the triumph. (Matìas Capizzano)

Chapter Ten

Why Didn't We Win in Athens?

"That's it, guys. There's no sense in carrying on. Let's head back," Galarza pleads.

It's six in the afternoon and it's been thirty hours since we left the port of Buenos Aires in hopes of breaking the sailing record to Mar del Plata, but it's already clear to us that we're not going to achieve that. The Tornado wasn't prepared for the crossing, and last night we were hit by a storm with winds of nearly thirty miles per hour. We'd really taken a pounding, but even worse is the fact we still had one more night to get through before we'd arrive.

We're due east of the Cariló spa, still over sixty miles outside Mar del Plata. Mariano has come out in a Zodiac to intercept our course. He's brought us water, aspirin, chocolate, sodas, and cereal bars. But mostly he is here to convince us to give it up. He says we've already been featured in all the major newspapers in the country, and that yesterday a number of TV stations covered us from a helicopter as we embarked on this adventure. We'd already achieved our goal of capturing the media's interest. Why keep going?

"They don't know how rough you look," he says to us. "You're pale and shivering with cold. Be reasonable. Head for the coastline, leave the Tornado on the beach, and spend the night in Cariló."

"What do you think, Camau?" I ask my partner with a wink.

"Should we listen to your brother-in-law?"

"Stop pussyfooting around, Galarza," Camau replies.

"You heard it, Mariano. This team doesn't quit. Wait for us in Mar del Plata with a nice hot meal," I say before letting go of the Zodiac and unfurling the Tornado's sails.

February 2nd, 2001, the scheduled date for the start of our attempt, dawned under a bad omen. A pampero was in the forecast, but we couldn't postpone the challenge. We'd chosen the day specifically to coincide with the start of the Buenos Aires-Mar del Plata regatta, which is one of the primary events on the Argentine ocean sailing circuit.

It was a promotional event, but also an adventure. The kind of crazy thing I love to do. And Camau as well. Back when he was windsurfing, he was determined to attempt a crossing from Puerto Deseado, in Patagonia, to the Falkland Islands, but a Navy captain with whom he was consulting ordered him to give up the idea. It was just too dangerous.

Before shoving off, we'd only had time for a couple days of preparation in Buenos Aires. Camau was just getting to know the Tornado. I had my experience from Sydney, but the boat had been upgraded and modernized, and we were still adjusting to the new configuration. We had to prepare the catamaran for a trip which, according to our calculations, would take at least twenty-four hours, given that the record we wanted to break was thirty-one. We improvised some watertight spaces to carry food, protection from the elements, a pair of GPS devices, a satellite phone, and spare parts. We also installed a positioning and status tracking system provided by Hawk, the vehicle location company which had joined us as a sponsor. And there was yet another problem: I hadn't yet had surgery on my eyes, and my vision was far from good. If Camau fell overboard at night, I was going to have a very tough time finding him. And Camau hadn't mastered the ship yet, so if it was me who fell, we weren't sure if he'd be able to rescue me. So we devised a safety system that would keep us tethered to the boat at all times. It was one of the few precautions we took.

We left the port of Buenos Aires at noon and started off well, but the pampero hit so hard that we were forced to lower the mainsail. Just before six in the afternoon we saw an Argentine Naval Prefecture helicopter carrying photojournalists hoping to get aerial shots of us for the papers. To the south, however, dark, foreboding clouds heralded a sudestada—a climate phenomenon bringing rotating winds, heavy rain, and rough seas from the southeast—which would be unleashed with the setting of the sun.

The gale churned up great waves. The ship was heavy with provisions and not riding well. We were afraid the structure wouldn't hold up to the storm with so much weight, so we decided to jettison part of our water reserves. The GPS units got wet and were unusable. We tried to navigate by the stars, but neither of us had much experience with ocean-going sailing. We saw some lights in the distance and called Galarza on the satellite phone so he could use his positioning systems to tell us where we were.

"Near Montevideo," he said, alarmed. "What are you doing there? You're going the wrong way!"

We were exhausted, having spent over ten hours hanging from the trapeze, but still in good spirits. We marveled at the phosphorescent trail the Tornado left in her wake: an effect caused by noctiluca (silicans), a type of plankton that shine in the sea. Despite the risk and fatigue, we were having fun: sailing through the night, in the middle of the ocean, far from shore, which is a very rare experience with these Olympic-class ships.

With the sunrise came a sense of calm. The sea had lost her fury and was now a glassy mirror. Our backs stiff and sore, we lay down to doze. After we had warmed up a bit, we took off our wet neoprene suits. A boat from the Prefecture came alongside us to see if we needed anything. We told them we were fine, and they accompanied us for a while blaring some cumbia through their speakers.

Our second night in the Tornado was a long and cold one. Galarza was in Mar de Plata, waiting for us, unable to sleep. He checked our position every ten minutes to confirm we were making progress. If our signal stopped moving, it could be a sign that we'd capsized. Yago was also there with him during that sleepless night. In the end, forty hours after having set sail, frozen half to death and with our faces crusted in salt, we finally arrived. We weren't even close to the record, but the voyage had sealed our alliance. It was confirmation that we both had the same sense of determination and the capacity to deliver.

At first, nobody believed in our project but ourselves. Windsurfing doesn't have the same level of complexity, it doesn't require the same technical skillset as a boat like the Tornado, and there were plenty of sailors who doubted Camau's abilities. During one of our first regattas together, I realized that my friend didn't have a full grasp of all the terminology. "Raise the daggerboards before we get hooked on something," I said, but instead Camau shot off to take the helm. We both laughed at the mistake. Our sport is riddled with jargon. Some terms can be justified by their specificity, but many other words have no real meaning other than to show that you belong. We weren't interested in belonging. What mattered to us was performing to the best of our ability, and if there was anything Camau had shown was that he knew how to hang medals around his neck.

In recognition of the fact that my partner's Olympic successes had given him a much larger reputation than I had, the team was called Camau-Lange. Tradition holds that the helmsman leads the pairing, but we decided to reverse the formula. This order was not, however, an indication of leadership. As in most of the classes I competed in, I was at the helm. Camau, with his physical strength and athleticism from windsurfing, was comfortable being a crewmember. Each of us had our own specialties and fulfilled different roles, but at the same time we were peers and shared responsibilities and decisions. The trick was learning how to combine our different experiences and skill sets. In doing so, the respect and friendship that we'd forged became fundamental. Before entering a regatta, we'd work out our strategy together. There were days where one of us was more inspired than the other, and on those days, that person's opinions prevailed. Oftentimes, that depended on wind conditions.

One of the functions a crewmember serves on a catamaran is to stabilize the boat by shifting his or her weight from side to side across the netting between the two hulls. Camau patrolled that wet, unstable surface with the dexterity of a cat. And he could do that without hooking up his harness: a skill that requires incredible balance. All those years of standing on a windsurfing board had given him a high level of sensitivity. The speed of the boat, which I can feel from the helm, is picked up by Camau through his feet. He was able to make smooth, calm adjustments when the Tornado glided across the face of a wave. On top of all that, he was strong. We had to reinforce the ship's gears so they wouldn't snap while maneuvering. Other crew members had to bend at the knees to be able to pull the line that controls the sail, but Camau could do it with his body extended, allowing him to hike out fully on the trapeze and keep the boat upright.

Another of his virtues was his meticulousness. He took great care of the Tornado's setup and spent many hours at the marina working out the details. Each rope had to be the correct color and length. Even the wetsuits we wore while competing were impeccable. When I look back at pictures from the Athens days, I'm still amazed by how perfectly they fit, having been custom-tailored and made from a special type of lycra. When they were ready, Galarza, who was in charge of the gear, tried them on first and sent us a photo showing his 220-pound frame absolutely spilling out of the wetsuits, which had clearly been designed for our body types, which were much more slender than his.

Scheduling was Camau's responsibility. After consulting with me and the rest of the team, he put together the training and racing calendar, which was designed to put us in peak physical condition for the Games. Not the week before, nor the week after. This way we avoided unnecessary wear and tear. This method required a lot of trust. Everyone on the team had to understand and accept the fact that a poor showing in a tune-up competition was no cause for alarm. On the contrary, allowing yourself the occasional defeat brings with it the freedom to try new things and to learn from them. When it comes to preparation, the method is more important than the result. Improvements, advances, and even consequences always appear in the long term.

One of my jobs was competitive modifications. The Tornado is one of those classes where each crew can make certain adjustments to their equipment as long as they remain within the parameters set by the governing body. This leaves a lot of room for tweaking designs. And our crew paid special attention to the sails.

Our team had remained basically the same since the Atlanta Games, but we needed to add a coach. We didn't have the budget to hire any of the big names on the circuit, and so I thought instead of Ramón Oliden, the kid who dazzled me when he easily won the Optimist World Championships in 1992. We had been rivals in the Snipe class, which is when I could confirm his great talent for sailing. When I called him up, he was still only twenty-three years old, yet already excelling as a youth class coach. He didn't have any experience with catamarans, but he brought his talent, his youth, and his eagerness to learn. He was excited to join the group.

That was the time when the KGB really began to take shape. For competitions that required extended stays, we all traveled together. A full house made for a more bearable routine. In fact, we had fun. Camau and I are very competitive and we kept making up things to bet on. Anything from a ping pong tournament to a run from the house to the club. One day, when he saw me caught up in a long conversation with Chivi, Ramón joined in the game. "I'll bet you a six-pack that you will get back together." I'm still waiting for Oliden to pay up on that one.

In March of 2001 we entered our first international regattas, and we came out with good results. We were a team of relative newcomers, but the modifications that were made to the Tornado class following the Sydney Games worked to our advantage. The other crews also had to learn how to master the new design, and everyone made plenty of mistakes early on. One of ours was particularly memorable: we set up one of the sails, known as the spinnaker, backwards, and didn't even realize it until we tried to hoist it in the middle of a race. Of course, we had to retire.

At Hyères, one of the traditional spring European regattas, it was a different story. It's usually a rather windy event. One day the fleet decided that conditions were too harsh to compete. It was too dangerous, they argued, and would put undue stress on the equipment. Race officials announced that the competition would continue as scheduled, but the crews revolted and refused to even put their boats in the water. Camau and I ignored the protest and went out anyway. Once we reported for duty, others felt obliged to follow. Some gave us strange looks, but we weren't about to be intimidated. We were there to command respect.

In training, crews are grouped according to certain similarities. They sail together to measure speed and test the equipment, especially the sails. If anyone from outside the group lines up to join in, they have to first turn into the wind and stop to avoid the newcomer. There was one time when Ramón got close to a rival crew in the water, and their coach zipped across his bow in a Zodiac in a threatening manner. It was the only way to protect the information the crew was gathering, though it also served as a show of strength and dominance.

Thanks to our encouraging results and developments, we caught the attention of the Austrian team that had won the gold medal at the previous Olympics. Roman Hagara and Hans-Peter Steinacher figured we could be good training partners. We were fast, but more than that, they trusted our loyalty and appreciated our technical skill. They knew we were on a level that would generate mutual growth and help put us ahead of the rest. From our point of view, the union was pure benefit. Training with the top team in the fleet drastically shortened our learning curve. We agreed to a complete alliance. Not only would we serve as training partners, which was common in these sorts of agreements, but we'd also share notes on all aspects of our boat, from rigging the sails to the fine tuning we did to our navigational techniques.

Hagara and Steinacher had their sails all figured out. Robert Jessing, a man in his seventies who lived in Klagenfurt, an Austrian lake town with a population of around 100,000, designed the setup. As part of the agreement, we'd collaborate on the design and

Jessing would manufacture them. Even a small difference in construction could mean a big difference in speed, but we trusted the Austrians.

It's not very common for elite competitors to form such close relationships with one another, but it makes sense in sailing. Unlike track and field, where you work against the clock, in our sport the only way to improve your speed is to measure yourself in relation to another boat. Plus, there are three medals up for grabs at the Olympics. We were all aiming for the gold, but simply reaching the podium represents a significant achievement.

Working with the Austrians was on my list of responsibilities. Camau didn't like going to meetings. We were four strong personalities in a cooperative agreement, but that doesn't mean it wasn't competitive. At one point, Hagara wanted to pull rank and impose the hierarchy that the gold medal from Sydney had given them, but Camau had a pair of silver medals to his name and wasn't intimidated in the least. When conflicts like this took place, it was my job to step in and get the relationship between our crews back on track. All four of us were open and honest and the alliance prospered. We ended up becoming great friends. We competed with each other to the fullest, never holding anything back, but we also defended one another from third parties. It's always good to have a wingman out there on the water… especially when it's an Olympic champion.

We could sail for hours at a time. The differences between us were minimal, which led to drag races that went so long we'd lose sight of the coast. When one crew managed to build up a big enough lead, we'd adjust, realign our boats, and go at it again. We did this over and over. The French team joined in for a couple of training sessions, but the agreement with them was only on the water: we didn't share any information on any technical matters. We progressed quickly and were close to being on par with the Austrians.

Hagara and Steinacher learned to sail in the lakes of their homeland and were the best in the world in low-wind conditions. When the wind was gusting and the water choppy, we had a slight advantage. We complemented one another, and soon enough we were the two best Tornado teams in the world.

In December of 2001, Argentina was shaken by a new economic and political crisis. We've had plenty of them throughout our nation's history, but that one in particular was quite serious. There was looting, over thirty deaths, and five presidents succeeding one another in a matter of weeks. The recession hit just about everyone, but especially those who lived in poverty, which in Argentina represents a significant part of the population. Those were times of serious anguish and distress, and what was going on in my country hurt me deeply. We empathized with their plight, but at the same time we had to maintain focus, to remain resolute.

The value of the Argentine peso plummeted and we had to rework our Olympic plans. We needed around $180,000 per year to cover our expenses leading up to Athens. This included equipment, travels, and coaches. The problem was that costs were measured in dollars while our income was measured in pesos. Before our currency was devalued, the exchange rate was almost one to one. After the crisis, it was around three pesos to every dollar.

Galarza set up a series of meetings seeking financial support. We appealed to a number of companies, but they were all in the process of cutting costs. Government offices were in a state of chaos, and the documents showing what we paid for travel expenses were misplaced. The people who held the purse strings when it came to sports funding kept being replaced, and we had to explain to each new functionary who Camau and I were. Things weren't going well with the federation, and I left one particular meeting in a daze. I continued on with my contracts as a professional sailor on larger vessels, and I brought Camau along as well. He worked with me for a while because we needed the money, but being accustomed to windsurfing and the Tornado, he just didn't feel comfortable.

We tried what seems like a thousand and one ways to keep moving forward while still maintaining a rigorous training regimen. Those were complicated times. Camau is very fond of folk music, and we listed a lot to one song in particular which would become the team's anthem: "Stone and Road" by Atahualpa Yupanqui, a renowned Argentine folk singer. "At times I am like the river / I arrive singing / And without anyone knowing my life, / I leave weeping..." goes the final verse. Many years later, with Ceci by my side, we baptized the boat in which we were going to compete in Rio as Camino, meaning "The Road" or "The Way." We'd thought about Piedra, meaning "Stone," for the other one, but we didn't want to add any weight to the boat, not even in name. In the end, we christened her Cicatriz, the word for "scar."

Economic limitations prevented us from attending a number of pre-competition gatherings. We also weren't able to invest in developing the sails. Aware of our financial problems, Roman and Hans-Peter offered a solution: Red Bull, the Austrian energy drink maker, who was also their sponsor. The company loved the project and added us to their team. Besides the financial support, Red Bull proved to be an ideal partner in other ways as well. The company had an innovative marketing strategy: building their brand by tying it to artists and athletes with a sense of risk and adventure. Their vision was in tune with our entire philosophy. It's a fascinating company and I've learned quite a lot from them. We never signed a contract, there weren't even any written terms or conditions on how we had to display their logo. The entire relationship was based on trust and the values we shared. Red Bull showed up at a critical moment in my career, and today, twenty years later, we're still working together. Our alliance is unconditional. They even welcomed Yago and Klaus into the team.

With Red Bull and the Austrians as partners, we reached 2004, the year of the Athens Games, in a good state of affairs. We were considered, along with Hagara and Steinacher, favorites to win. But another obstacle appeared on the horizon: the Australian team, Darren Bundock and John Forbes, had recently been unbeatable. They were fast and they had style. It was simply a pleasure to watch them sail. In addition to their sheer talent, I was convinced that one of the keys to their success lay in their sails. To add to the mystery, they stopped sailing whenever Ramón approached them in the Zodiac looking to snap a photo or two.

Earlier that same year, Red Bull had hired a helicopter to get aerial shots of us in competition. Now, we took advantage of it to spy on the Australians from the air. This wasn't exactly customary on the circuit, but we were desperate. We analyzed the photos alongside the Austrians, but we couldn't point to anything that could decisively explain their recent success. Regardless, something had to be done.

"We have to modify our sails," I suggested at a meeting.

Camau and I had discussed this and we were both convinced it was the right thing to do. But Hagara and Steinacher were upset just hearing the proposal. The World Championships, which would be held in Palma de Mallorca, were just weeks away, and our pathway to Athens, they argued, didn't allow for such a drastic change. The calendar had been set months in advance, and the choice of sails had been made. There was no going back now, they said, determinedly.

It was interesting to see how two cultures as different as ours achieved excellence, each in their own way. The Austrians believed in forecasting and foresight to the extreme. But that adherence to preprogrammed strategies often limited their flexibility. When things went the way they predicted, they were simply unbeatable. But when something problematic cropped up, we had the advantage. We were well-versed in improvisation, and we weren't afraid to make decisions on the fly.

"If we don't make a change, we're conceding the point," I pressed. "There's no other way to catch the Australians."

Camau didn't speak up, but I knew he wasn't about to compete while at such an obvious disadvantage. We also believed there was still time to get to Athens ready to race. But the Austrians wouldn't budge. It was a contentious meeting that ended without an agreement. Each crew would do what it believed was best.

We were short on time. I flew out to see the sailmaker, while Camau took care of getting our boat to Palma de Mallorca. Once I arrived in Klagenfurt, I had to convince Jessing to modify our sails. He was an old man who lived above his workshop where his wife worked as the receptionist. Hagara, his friend and confidant, wasn't there, and Jessing hardly spoke a word of English. The first thing he did was resist the idea. He examined the photos we'd taken of the Australian's sails and took a few measurements.

"They're the same," he determined, using the rudimentary language with which we communicated. "If they're faster than you, it's because they're sailing better."

But I knew there had to be something else at play. We continued to study the images, and I came to suspect that the difference might be that the Australians were using more versatile sails. Because of a subtle detail of their design, they automatically adapted to changes in the intensity of the wind and waves. We, on the other hand, had to manually adjust our sails all the time, especially in choppy conditions, making us less efficient. Ultimately, I was able to convince him of this, and together we started designing and constructing our sails. We had just three days to get everything done before I returned to Spain. Jessing designed the new sails in a single day and spent the next two gluing and sewing them. I caught a train to the airport and arrived at my destination with a new set of sails and the phone number of an attractive woman whom I'd met during my trip.

Camau was waiting for me in Palma de Mallorca with the boat all but prepped for the World Championships. We put in some hard training during the last few days leading up to the competition. The Austrians would go on to have a performance to forget. We, on the other hand, with our new sails in place, reached the final race neck and neck with the team from the United States. There was a lot of wind that day, and while they were ahead for most of the course, we passed them in the home stretch on our way to becoming World Champions.

In 2001, when mapping out our long-term campaign, we had circled this date. We were aiming to have one of our defining performances before the Athens Games. This marked the first time an Argentine crew had won a World Championship in an Olympic class. It was absolutely thrilling to see something that was once just a wish on a calendar turn into a dream come true!

We were thrilled with our triumph, but there wasn't much time for celebrating. Ramón and Camau dropped me off at the airport—I was flying back to Austria to continue working on the sails—before continuing on to the next destination in my Volvo. The had the trailer loaded with the Tornado and the Zodiac. They were tired and it was getting dark. Ramón was driving, and his eyes were growing heavy. They closed. It was barely a second. When he opened his eyes again, he overcorrected and the trailer tipped them over. Luckily nobody was coming, but Camau held up his right hand to protect himself and ended up cutting the tendon in his middle finger. What would have been a relatively minor injury for someone else was a serious threat to us. That was the hand Camau used to grip the sheet which controls the Tornado's sail.

Ramón felt guilty and offered to resign, but I wouldn't accept it. It was an accident. He was part of our team: our coach and friend. After two operations—one in Austria and the other in Corrientes—followed by nearly a month of recovery, Camau returned to sailing for a pre-Olympic tune-up race in Holland three months before the Opening Ceremony. We finished first. We were still sharp.

We arrived in Greece among the favorites and immediately put the KGB plan into action: setting up our extended stay headquarters outside the Olympic Village. The entire team—Ramón, Galarza, Bambi and Dani Espina—settled into a house we rented in Glyfada, a suburb in South Athens which was home to the sailing competitions. It was on a hillside just twenty minutes from the Parthenon, but we weren't there to see the sights.

The Austrians had finally convinced themselves of the need to change sails, and were now a bit faster than us. When they took a bit of a break to return to their home country, we changed our mast. By the time they got back, we had the edge on them. We kept making tweaks and adjustments up until the last minute, and the only time we altered our training regimen was to attend the Opening Ceremony, where Camau was, for the second time in a row, the flag bearer for the Argentine delegation.

On Saturday, August 21st of 2004, I woke up ready to begin my quest for Olympic gold. I was better prepared than I had ever been in my life. The team was experienced and we were coming off some great results. We were defending World Champions and the top ranked team in the fleet. Two sentences beginning with But, regardless of all that, I was nervous. On top of the normal pressure you feel at the Olympics, I felt an extra burden. Camau had won two medals in his two previous appearances. But I was carrying not only the weight of earning my first, but also the responsibility of continuing my partner's streak. And, as always, my nerves manifested themselves in my lack of an appetite.

We were performing well, but the results just weren't coming for us. With three races to go, we were sitting in fifth place. We were able to make up a few spots and went into the final day of the competition third overall, with the Australians and the Dutch nipping at our heels. We decided to do everything we could to hold onto that position—first and second were well out of reach at that point—and that strategy worked. We crossed the finish line with our objective accomplished. Still, though, it was tough at first to celebrate the bronze. We'd come to Athens with dreams of gold around our necks. Hagara and Hans-Peter had from the Sydney Games and came over to share the joy with us. All four of us got on their boat, and only then did we begin to loosen up and appreciate what we'd achieved.

That bronze was my first Olympic medal. It was Camau's third: an accomplishment that confirmed his status as a legend among Argentine athletes. To that point, nobody had collected as much hardware as he had. Before stepping up onto the podium, he whispered a bit of advice in my ear: "Don't get distracted, Santi. Savor this moment because it doesn't last long." I tried to follow his advice, but I couldn't help myself as the excitement washed over me. Twenty years had passed since my first attempt to qualify for the Olympics. Many sacrifices had been made over that long period of time. Some were still fresh, like the time I'd spent away from my children. The image of my father flashed through my mind, and I knew he'd have been happy to see me crowned with the olive wreath on my head and holding up the Argentine flag. Red Bull threw a party on the beach. Bambi and I celebrated late into the night and got a bit drunk. My brother Sebastián, who had traveled with us during the last few regattas, joined in the festivities. I hung my credentials around my neck and took my place with the team for the closing Ceremony. I was eager to get back home. My four children all met me at the airport. I handed them the medal and they turned it over in their hands, trying to decipher the ancient Greek inscription on the back.

The bronze brought me a tremendous sense of happiness, but I admit that, during the medal ceremony, in the silence before the Austrian national anthem was played, I would have liked to have been along with my own. We left Athens with the feeling that we were good enough to have brought home the gold. To this day I still don't understand how we didn't win it. I went back over the tapes searching for clues. In the first heat, we had a comfortable lead before a sudden change in the wind slowed us down. And there was another time where a slower competitor prevented us from executing our tactics as planned. Such circumstances are typical of our sport, and you learn to live with the fact that changes in nature herself can alter the final results. In sailing, it's not only your rivals who put you to the test. It's also the wind.

So why didn't we win in Athens? There are no clear answers. Unlike my previous Olympic appearances, there were no mistakes in the selection of the boat, no lack of preparation, no bad calls by the judges. It didn't happen simply because nothing is guaranteed. We did everything we had to do, but perhaps our competitors did it just a little bit better. Medals aren't deserved, they're earned. And sometimes the difference between winning and finishing second or third is all but imperceptible.

Chapter Eleven

A Boat Is a Living Being

"**OK.**" That was Camau's response when I asked him if I could visit him in Corrientes last year. His message on WhatsApp didn't include a "sure" or "of course." Not even an emoji. I chuckled as soon as I saw it. Camau was still Camau.

We trained together for nearly fifteen years and twice teamed up to compete in the Tornado class in the Olympics, but to this day we've never been in frequent contact. It isn't necessary. When we do see each other it's as if time simply hasn't passed. Our relationship is based on a shared history and a deep, mutual sense of acceptance. We know and respect each other. We've been staunch allies and we can count on one another as friends.

Once he considered his windsurfing career to be over, Camau never set foot on a board again. The same was true with the Tornado. We ran the last race of the Beijing Games and he said goodbye to boats forever. His Olympic success made him famous—we paraded through his hometown on the back of a fire engine after the second medal we won together—and he traded sailing for politics. He was elected mayor of his city and was very close to winning the governorship of his province. He served as a senator and as Minister of Tourism and Sports. He offered me a position managing high performance sports in Argentia. It was an interesting prospect, and I thought long and hard about it, but in the end I didn't accept. I wanted to continue with sailing. Camau came to visit while I was training with Ceci for the Rio Games, and hopped on board the Nacra with me. For a few fleeting minutes, we were back to being the team we had been a decade before. He was there with Tobías and Theo, his two children. From the smile on his face, I gathered that he enjoyed that moment.

Today his life consists of family and politics. That much I was able to confirm during the weekend we spent together in Corrientes. We had lunch at his apartment, which was on the tenth floor of a high rise overlooking the river. Cecilia, his wife, had put together a book of photos and memories from his years as an athlete, from the early years of windsurfing to the Beijing medal.

The reason for my visit was to review our adventures before writing this book, but it ended up being more of a tribute to the KBG. Dani Espina overcame his aversion to airplanes and joined us. Galarza, who also lives in Corrientes, hosted a barbecue at his large country home that features a quincho, or a large outdoor cooking area. To this day he's still the best host in the world. I invited Ceci, and she came with her girlfriend Mica. It was such a delight to celebrate the continuing history of a sports team that is also a group of friends.

We retold stories like the one about Omarcito, a homeless man from Uruguay whom we met in Palma de Mallorca. He was cultured and a great conversationalist. A Diogenes of sorts with a unique kind of wisdom. He lived in a shipping container near the port and we spent many hours with him during the days leading up to the Tornado World Championships, which we won in 2004. Bambi was worried he was distracting us, but Camau and I enjoyed talking with him. Years later, he showed up in Corrientes, and Camau got him a job. Then, one day, as suddenly as he appeared, he left without saying goodbye. And then there was Raúl, another vagabond we met in Mar del Plata. He was squatting in a house next to ours that was still under construction. We used to chat with him during breaks in our training. He had a vast repertoire of philosophical aphorisms, one of which seemed particularly suited to us: "You have to plan for the unforseeable," as he put it.

Between cups of mate and small, cheesy rolls known as chipá, we reminisced over how our training system had to be adapted for the 2008 Beijing Games. After Athens, Camau and the Austrians wanted to retire. They were tired of life on the road. I was the only one of the four who wanted to press on. My argument in favor of continuing was that we had already acquired a great wealth of knowledge, materials, and work ethic. Instead of training for four full years, we could get the team together closer to the Olympics. "Let's do a shorter, more intense campaign," I suggested. It was enough to convince them.

The one time I went sailing with Camau in 2005 was an adventure. We wanted to repeat the spirit of our voyage to Mar del Plata. With the support of Red Bull, we organized the Récord del Plata, a competition to see who could cross the mouth of the Río de la Plata the fastest. The starting point was Perú Beach, a windsurfing club on the San Isidro coast of Argentina. The finish line was Colonia, a historic walled Uruguayan city with cobblestone streets.

It was a journey of just over thirty-two miles. According to the rules we established, the crossing could be made at any point during a span of four days. Each team would have two chances, with the idea being that they would watch the weather forecasts and decide for themselves when the conditions were most favorable for them to depart. Around fifty sailors registered for the event with many different types of boats, from catamarans to monohulls and even windsurfing boards. Fans and Olympic medalists alike all joined in.

Although the forecast on the first day of the event was bad, we set out just the same, along with Gonzalo Costa Hoevel, a windsurfer friend of ours. Just over twelve miles outside of Colonia, the river started getting rough. We hadn't gone sailing in quite some time, we were out of shape, and a big wave capsized us. When we finally got the boat upright again, it was out of control and drifting aimlessly. We didn't have the strength to haul ourselves back on board, and were being dragged through the choppy water. Camau couldn't hold on and eventually had to let go. Still clinging to the catamaran, I tried not to lose sight of him, but we were drifting further and further apart. It was getting dark and the situation becoming more tense by the minute. Camau tried to remain calm while treading water, craning his neck above the waves searching for a buoy to grab on to and save energy. Luckily a safety boat soon passed by and rescued us. The next day, with more favorable wind, we made our second attempt and won.

During those years I worked for the America's Cup, the oldest and most prestigious sailing competition in the world, and I reserved the last few months of 2006 for one of my favorite regattas, the Tornado World Championship, which would be held at my very own Club Náutico San Isidro. Having previously hosted the Snipe World Championship, I knew that the club would organize an impeccable event. I feel immensely proud every time I represent Argentina. I also feel the responsibility of serving as a kind of ambassador. It makes me happy when foreigners enjoy this country of mine. Plus, on top of that, I was excited to compete once again in the very same waters where I had first learned to sail.

The KGB settled into San Isidro. All of us except for Ramón, who had resigned in order to go work with the Spanish Olympic team.

We biked to the Náutico and assembled the boat on the same lot that my kids used as a skate park. It was one of the few times we enjoyed the privilege of living and working in the same place together, which is something many families take for granted. And, as always, Galarza hosted the barbecues. Camau invited some friends of his from Corrientes who played chamamé, a type of folk music. Ferdi was there as well, who competed using our backup boat alongside Gustavo Mariani, a friend and younger brother of my partners in the old shipyard business. It was my way of belatedly thanking him for insisting that I make the switch to the Tornado class.

The club was completely transformed. Many club members greeted us, convinced of our imminent triumph. We had won Olympic bronze and these were our waters. "You'll dominate the smaller waves in the river," they said. We smiled uncomfortably at such naivety. We were confident in our abilities, yes, but we were also well aware of the fact that we'd barely competed since Athens. Besides, the championship had drawn the finest sailors from around the world. Forty-eight boats from twenty different countries had converged on the club, ready to compete. Our beloved Río de la Plata was packed with international stars of sailing, including twelve Olympic medalists.

The competition began on Tuesday, December 5th, and we set out prepared for the calm conditions that all the forecasts had predicted. However, with the second race of the day, the sky darkened and a strong, cold wind blew in from the southeast. Hagara and Steinacher looked at me in surprise. I was supposed to know these waters like the back of my hand.

We got off to a good start and settled into third place, but our rustiness became clearly apparent towards the end of the heat when we hooked the sheet around the rudder, dropping us way back. We crossed the finish line in twenty-third place, far from the lead and with no room for another bad race. We were going to have to fight our way out of the middle of the pack.

We spent the rest of the week climbing back up the charts while the Australians and Austrians battled for the lead. During the final days of the championship, the good results we'd been hoping for finally appeared. In the day's first race, we came in second, just behind the Australians. In the latter, our positions were reversed, giving us our first victory of the regatta. It was a hot Saturday afternoon and the river was thronged with boats and launches that had come out en masse to support us. We returned to the club feeling emboldened. With two races left, we were far behind the Australians, who were leading by far, but just six points behind our friends the Austrians.

On Sunday we came out to the very definition of a championship final surrounded by a veritable carnival of boats. Foreign guests were fascinated by the people's enthusiasm. A slight, fluctuating wind blew across the water. The sheer multitude of boats complicated the tacking and jockeying for positions, delaying the race even more. It was already 2:30 by the time the official was able to begin the final countdown. This meant that there would be a single race instead of the customary two, meaning the Australians were completely out of reach. Instead, we would be competing for second place against our Austrian friends and teammates.

We got off to a good start and hounded Hagara and Steinacher relentlessly. Camau says he even felt a bit bad for them when we blew past them, literally taking the wind out of their sails. I don't believe him. He's much too competitive for that sort of emotion, and knows only too well that they would have done the same to us. We ran a masterful final race and reached the final buoy in first place. Our spinnaker was emblazoned with an Argentine flag, and we felt the roar from the crowd as we hoisted it on the home stretch. We crossed the finish line greeted by hundreds of cheering Náutico members who had come out on the club's ferry.

Docking was sheer chaos. The river was churned up by the wakes of all the approaching boats. We tried to avoid them while still waving the Argentine flag. It was one of the greatest moments of my career with Camau, and one of the happiest days I ever spent on board a boat. It also gave us peace of mind when it came to the challenge that lay before us. With less time than a good Olympic prep campaign requires, qualifying for the Beijing Games presented an enormous challenge.

But before that was another important event: the 2007 World Championships. It was held in July in Cascais, Portugal. Rather than defend our runner-up finish in Buenos Aires, our aim was to secure a spot in the Games: a more modest goal to match our limited amount of training. We came in fourteenth, which was just enough to qualify. There was one year left to get ready for Beijing.

The weather reports for Qingdao, where the sailing events would be held, typically called for low winds, so we needed to be lighter rather than stronger. When it came to prioritizing our training, we decided to cut our time in the gym. We had to manage what little time we had as best we could, and opted to spend it on other matters, like designing the sails and putting in more hours on the water. Bambi, who has always been a fitness fanatic, objected. It was the first major disagreement of our professional relationship, and ultimately he wasn't part of the team that traveled to China.

We also needed to replace Ramón, and Matías Bühler was one of the candidates for his position. I took the opportunity to meet him during a trip to Buenos Aires. At twenty-four years of age,

Matías had an outstanding career in the Optimist class, he had just missed out on qualifying for the Beijing Games in the 470, and he didn't know anything about catamarans. In a way, his profile was not unlike Ramón's. The other teammates liked him and I gave him a call to offer him the job. It was February, we were in Auckland, New Zealand, where the 2008 World Championships were to be held, and I told him we needed him right away. Matías was on vacation with his girlfriend at the time, but cut it short and came to be with us.

We finished thirteenth at the World Championships, and we failed to perform well again at the European Championships in the spring. The Olympics were now just five months away and we were still running slow. "Take it easy, Santi, we'll get there," Camau told me after we'd finished near the back of the pack at a regatta in Hyères. I appreciated his confidence, but we had reasons to be concerned. I was nervous.

We arrived in Qingdao roughly two months before the Games to give ourselves time to make whatever final adjustments were needed. We were met there by a surprise that altered our plans. In the first few test runs, crews from the United States and the Netherlands unfurled a daring plan. Secretively, without raising the awareness of any other team, they had developed and implemented a third sail that was entirely different from the setup everyone else used. The spinnaker only unfurls when you're sailing with the wind, but apparently, they had developed one that could be used throughout the competition. We did some test runs with them and they beat us easily. The prospect of losing out on a medal due to a design modification that rendered fighting for position on the water irrelevant was frustrating to say the least. If the projected forecast of calm winds held true, they would be invincible. The risk they were running was that, if the wind were to pick up just a bit, the new sail would become counterproductive. The Americans hadn't been known for sailing fast in low wind conditions, and seemed to be gambling on this strategy.

Our crew had a working dinner with the Austrians to decide what we could do. The chupacabra, which is what we called the new sail, was an extreme play—it was an all or nothing move—and we weren't sure as to whether or not we should adopt it. We spent many nights rereading the regulations and studying photographs of the American and Dutch boats. Jessing had since retired, and we were now working with sails by Juan Garay, who designed everything in Buenos Aires before sending the files to the Austrian federation so they could be manufactured in Europe. We asked Juan to draft a chupacabra for us. Meanwhile, we signed a formal protest filed by the Spanish team. A battle ensued between judges and experts. In the end, we weren't able to get the new sail banned, though they did set certain limitations, thus reducing its effectiveness.

It was a stressful process, but around that same time we experienced a much more dramatic event. With just a few weeks left before the first race of the Games, we were running some speed tests with the Austrians and Italians. The wind was good and steady, and Camau and I were concentrating on the boat. All of a sudden, we felt a strong, sharp blow. Another Zodiac, which we hadn't seen, had broadsided us. It rode up over our hull and came within inches of Camau's head. After a few seconds of confusion, I yelled out:

"What the fuck was that, Angelo?"

My insult was directed at Angelo Glisoni, the Italian team's coach, who was piloting their launch. Without saying a word, Camau shot him a piercing, angry look. Angelo stammered out an apology. Upon further inspection, we discovered the impact had resulted in a large hole in our hull. We were towed back to the marina. Back on land, Angelo accepted his guilt. Contrite, he said he had bent down to look for the camera he used during training and hadn't seen us. By the time he looked up again, it was already too late.

This was a serious problem. We brought two boats to China, but this was the one we'd chosen to compete with. It was a holdover from our previous race in Athens. To protect it, we only used it for major competitions. Our only option was to continue training in our backup boat while our primary craft was repaired. There was less than a month to go, we still hadn't set the sails and our best boat was broken. "At least we know what color the lines are," Camau joked. At least his obsession with tidiness was still intact. In Athens they were blue, but this time they were red.

Neverending days of tension followed. While a technician from Sweden was fixing the boat, we set out in the spare. We woke up at seven and worked until eleven at night. When the Tornado was repaired, we put her back in the water for a test run. We weren't convinced. She wasn't the same boat as before. One side was running better than the other, and we were worried the collision had damaged her alignment. Boats are living things. No two are alike. They may look identical and even have the same exact measurements, but for whatever reason, one of them will be faster than the other. In the end, we chose to go with the backup, though we still had our doubts. On the morning the official measurements would be taken, we convinced the Austrians to go out and test two different masts. One worked quite well, and only then did we feel a bit more comfortable.

Those were exhausting days. We changed boats, we measured our sails, we tested masts. The rest of the Argentine delegation, not to mention our competitors, looked on in astonishment. What we were attempting was crazy. The standard practice among top-tier crews is to plan for about two weeks of intense sailing and then rest. That's how you avoid wear and tear. You shut things down a couple of days before the start of the Games so that your energy levels are full when the racing begins. We, on the other hand, never took our foot off the gas.

In Sydney, as in Athens, we had rented a house outside the Olympic Village where we set up shop. Galarza had his work cut out for him in the kitchen, since he would be feeding us as few calories as possible. Aware of the forecast calling for light winds, Camau and I wanted to be as close to 150 pounds as possible. We ate nothing but vegetables and looked scrawny and rickety. The rest of the team had no choice but to join in... although later Dani Espina and Mati Bühler confessed to me what we'd all suspected: when Camau and I weren't around, they shamelessly stuffed themselves at the Olympic Village buffet. "Galarza, since you're already there, go beat the crap out of that Italian guy," Camau joked at every meal.

When the competition began, on August 15th, 2008, we were coming off just half a day's rest. There was a typhoon circling the area that generated some strange weather. We got off to a bad start, finishing thirteenth out of fifteen crews. The following day we won both our races. We were back in the thick of things.

On the third day we were faced with an unexpected forecast: heavy winds. Better preparation, like we had going into the Athens Games, would have allowed us to take advantage of any scenario, but lack of time had forced us to focus on sailing in calmer conditions, which were what was expected in Qingdao. It was a risk we had chosen to take. When the winds gusted, we were among the slowest in the fleet, but we utilized our skill and endured the siege. We were running in fifth place until, pressured by the Spaniards and exhausted by the effort—Camau's legs were shaking from the strain—we capsized just 300 meters from the finish line. But then fate lent us a bit of a hand and the second race of the day was suspended.

In the eighth race of the Games, we were shining again. We were sailing quite well and reached the penultimate buoy in the lead. All that remained was the final stretch with the wind coming from stern.

"Right or left?" I called out as we approached the marker.

Whenever I felt pressured by doubt, I always appealed to Camau to help decide the right course of action. But this time he wasn't certain either. I looked ahead for gusts of wind across the surface of the water, trying to figure out which way to sail, but it was simply impossible to anticipate which way it might blow. With no time left for debate, I made the call to Camau that we were going to the right. Pure intuition. We expected the rest of the fleet to follow us. It's easier for the leader to track opponents when they line up behind you. But the exact opposite happened. The second-place boat chose to open up the race and went left. Third, fourth, fifth, and sixth did the same, leaving us all alone on our side of the course.

When it came time to converge on arrival, we could see it was going to be close. Since we were separated from the group, our wind conditions were different. A calm patch slowed us down while the others sped on. Our lead was in serious doubt. If we didn't get to the finish soon, a long flotilla of boats was ready to pass us by.

A slight change in nature can overthrow months of preparation. It's not unlike a tennis player who, after having won the first two sets with ease, now finds himself in a fifth set tiebreaker and his serve has just been broken. Although we'd had a great competition up to that point, we were in danger of losing both our lead and our chance at a medal. But we managed to keep calm and maintain our focus, we executed a precise maneuver, and we crossed the line in first place.

We had reached the medal race in third place overall. And it was another blustery day. With a good result, the Germans could have passed us and knocked us off the podium, but they pushed just a bit too hard and ended up capsizing. We almost went down ourselves when I got tripped up and almost went overboard, but Camau grabbed me by the life vest and we were saved.

This time around, unlike Athens, we celebrated the bronze medal with utter exuberance. Four years earlier, we'd had our eyes fixed squarely on the gold. But this time, in 2008, we overcame the challenges posed by a shorter preparation time with experience and creativity. It was a unique event in that we won four races, the exact same number of victories that Fernando Echávarri and Antón Paz, the Spaniards, had totaled in their gold medal run. For us, it was just a couple of subpar results that had kept us from the top.

While neither of us dared to say anything as we returned to the marina, we both knew that these would be our final few minutes of sailing together. Camau had decided to retire. He'd collected a total of four medals: an unprecedented achievement in our country. After eight years as crewmates, having shared joys, frustration, and two Olympic podiums, the curtain was lowered on the Camau-Lange team. On top of that, there were rumors starting to circulate and which would soon be confirmed: going forward, the Tornado would no longer be an Olympic sailing class. At forty-six years of age, and having lost my partner, I too was ready to retire from the Games.

As he did in Athens, my brother Sebastián had been there to support us. He was no longer considered a good luck charm, but rather one of the reasons for our success. He also took it upon himself to serve as director for our awards ceremony. In his opinion, our appearance on the podium came across as soulless. "You barely even waved," he said critically. "The two of you looked almost bitter." This time, he demanded unbridled joy, and even made us rehearse a bit of a choreographed celebration.

The medal ceremony, which was held outdoors in the midst of a gale, turned out to be rather intimate. I thought of my children when they announced our names. Equal parts soaked and excited, Sebastián and Galarza were raving and cheering us on. Camau and I raised our arms, our fists clenched, smiled, and shared a long embrace. It was the end of a beautiful adventure that was missing just one important detail: the gold medal.

Chapter Twelve

He Didn't Leave, He Now Rests in the Sea

We'd already seen each other a couple of times, but Paula de Elía still wasn't quite convinced. Going out for fancy dinners and milonga dancing hadn't done the trick, so I decided to appeal to Toi et Moi. I invited her to have dinner with me on the boat, and while I was focused on serving her the pasta I had ordered from the club's restaurant—my recipe for buttered noodles was way too basic for the occasion—Paula was interested in the details of the restoration work I was doing to the ship. And she laughed when I told her the story about how I used the trunk of a car as my closet and dresser. Later she would confess to me that the combination of obsessing over some things while being entirely absent-minded about others was the very first thing that caught her attention about me.

Paula is an artist and architect. She grew up in the countryside, not far from Mar del Plata, and found sailing rather boring. When I met her, she was dealing with a separation of her own, raising three children, and investing a lot of energy into her studies. She has that strong sort of personality that always seems to seduce me. We started dating while simultaneously juggling our children's schedules, our jobs, and what would become the single biggest deal in our relationship: my travels.

In 2005, between the Athens and Beijing Games, I'd been working with the America's Cup, the Formula 1 of professional sailing, if you will. This competition was first held in 1851 on the Isle of Wight, in England. Since then, it has brought together the best sailors and naval architects from across the sporting and technical spectrum. Some of the wealthiest businessmen in the world—many of whom are sailing enthusiasts themselves—finance the different groups that compete. They're drawn to the America's Cup because of the prestige that comes with it, but also because of the very complex challenge it presents. Teams often exceed a hundred people, and include many different professional profiles. Winning it is an athletic, technological, and managerial feat.

As children, Martín Billoch and I would flip through magazines with photos of the ships that participated, and we followed it from afar as something way beyond our realm of possibilities. Argentina wasn't part of professional sailing's inner circle, and there were rules preventing the hiring of foreigners. Later those norms were relaxed as teams from wealthier nations began seeking out sailors of other nationalities. I was introduced through Germán Frers, who had signed a contract with one of the crews who were preparing for the 2007 America's Cup. I'd returned to work in my studio following the Athens Games, and remained an important link between sailors and naval architects.

The team had been dubbed Victory Challenge, and was financed by the Stenbeck family, one of the wealthiest in all of Sweden. Jan Stenbeck, the founder, passed away in 2002, and his son Hugo, who was barely twenty-five years old at the time, took over the project. We were considered one of the smaller operations, with a budget of around fifty million euros, which was around a third of what the top teams had to work with. In 2005, the situation became critical, and they called a meeting to warn us of the very real possibility that we'd have to drop out due to lack of funds. The appearance of Red Bull as a sponsor came just in the nick of time and saved the program. We were able to finance a training trip to Dubai during the European winter, and although we came to the Cup well behind the leaders, we were on the rise.

It was an incredible professional experience. It was a very collaborative organization, and everyone engaged with one another on an equal level. We maintained the Scandinavian philosophy of cooperation without big egos. I was very attentive and aware of the opportunity experience from the inside how a world-class organization operates. My role gave me privileged access to the decision-making process. All together, we numbered roughly 150 individuals from thirty different nations. There were plenty of twelve-hour days and weeks without rest.

The venue for the competition was Valencia, Spain, and I moved there in mid-2005. Like most of us who settled there for the America's Cup, I rented a modern apartment in one of the newer parts of the city, but I soon felt the neighborhood was rather lifeless, so I found another in the old quarter. It was on the fourth floor of a walkup on Plaza Poeta Llorente street and just a short walk from the Turia riverbed, which has been turned into a central green space for the city. It had a beautiful view of the dome of a church built in the 18th century.

Paula came to visit and helped me decorate. My job was extremely demanding, but we tried to make time to go out for dinner or to browse museums and art galleries. When I couldn't, she would go on walking tours of the city on her own. Sailing was still a foreign concept to her, but she enjoyed exploring the hangars filled with bustling people which the various America's Cup teams had assembled in the harbor. She began to imagine how she might use her design expertise in the boating industry. I told her that I was going to end up cheering for for Luna Rossa, the Italian team whose sponsorship agreement with Prada made them the most elegant in the fleet. One day Germán took her out on a sailboat to see one of my races, and the experience had an impact. Paula likes to be in control of situations and wasn't used to the speed and power of racing boats. It was a nice stage in our relationship. We were getting to know each other, and she laughed when she pointed out that my mood depended upon a particular, highly predictable condition: if I was sailing, I was happy.

Yago was also very much a part of my time in Valencia. In May of 2006, having graduated from high school, he moved in with me and took the exams to begin college in Spain. He studied Business Administration and worked for Victory Challenge. He was the youngest member of the team, paid the least, and did basic tasks like cleaning, buying groceries, and the occasional translation. It was a tough beginning, but he persisted and eventually gained the trust of his superiors. He finished his coursework and, after the America's Cup experience, he continued to be involved with the shore teams of various crews on the European circuit. It was a good job, but he soon found he preferred sailing.

    He bought a Laser, the boat in which I competed at the Atlanta Games, and began training and competing in regattas. He had to remember some basic concepts and techniques he hadn't used since he was young, when he gave up the Optimist, but he made quick progress. A year later he told me he was entering a local tournament and I went to see him race. I was surprised to see the level of skill he had achieved. Yago was starting out on the European circuit, and in 2012 he won the Argentine national championship in the Laser category. I supported him through contacts and underwriting part of his travels. He showed great ability and a willingness to learn. In no time at all, he had carved out his own career as a professional sailor.

On April 16th, the Louis Vuitton Cup began. Eleven teams would compete to select the challenger who would go up against Alinghi, the Swiss team and defending America's Cup champion. The competition involved match racing: a category of sailing in which two boats compete in a series head-to-head events that award points to the winner. Our boat arrived a few days before the competition began and we christened her Järv, the Swedish word for Wolverine, a large member of the weasel family that lives in the forests of the Nordic countries. The järv is famous for its tenacity and its ability to attack animals much larger than itself. It's how we felt about ourselves as a team: small, but daring and powerful.

Magnus Holmberg, the skipper, and Stefan Rahm, the tactician, knew me from the Olympic circuit, and gave me the opportunity to be part of the seventeen-man on board crew. My job, along with three other team members, was to trim the sails and keep the boat balanced. In addition, I had the additional task of climbing the mast and deciding which side of the course was the best on which to sail. The previous candidate for that position had to resign based on his fear of heights, and I understood. Reading the wind is something I've always been passionate about, but I've never done it from thirty-four meters above the surface of the water.

Hanging in a climber's harness and exposed to the pounding waves, I surveyed the seas for signs and clues about the wind. I had to overcome vertigo and train both my body and my mind for this task. The movements of the ship are multiplied when you're sitting atop the mast. I held on tight so I didn't go flying off like a kite, but

I didn't complain. Working the trapeze allowed me to enjoy a privileged experience: high up there, accompanied by only the sound of the wind, I was living the dream of any sailor.

We improved throughout the competition and ended with a streak of four consecutive victories that brought us very close to qualifying for the semifinals. We finished fifth by a hair. It was a tremendous achievement for our humble team and a solid debut for me as an America's Cup sailor. It left me wanting more, but it was time to return to our Tornado campaign with the Beijing Games in the offing.

Those were busy years. A month and a half after reaching the podium in China, I embarked on the Volvo Ocean Race, an around-the-world regatta held in stages. With eight sailboats, each seventy feet in length and designed to be fast if not comfortable, we would circumnavigate the globe while stopping in various ports. We set sail on October 11th, 2008, from Alicante in southern Spain. Our arrival in St. Petersburg, Russia, was scheduled for late June of the following year. In total, we would cover over 31,000 miles.

With the Ocean Race, I completed the triad of great sailing events. The Olympic Games represents the pure essence of the sport. The America's Cup serves as the sport's professional face and puts avant-garde technology on display. And sailing around the world shows its adventurous side.

In 2001 I'd participated in one of the stages that ran from Southampton and Cape Town, but I didn't continue on because I was in the midst of preparing for the Athens Games. Now, on the other hand, I had a more important role aboard Telefónica Black, one of the two Spanish crews. I joined the team in September of 2008, after they had already been training for several months. The scant 155 pounds of weight I brought with me contrasted sharply with the muscular physiques of these high seas sailors who would be my traveling companions.

I arrived alongside Fernando Echávarri, my friend and rival from Beijing. He'd won gold in the Tornado class at the Olympics, he was the star of Spanish sailing, and he was the skipper of the ship. He was the captain of the guard, and I was one of his officers. We were both still exhausted from the Games. I was able to take ten days off in Buenos Aires, but he went straight to Alicante. We didn't have much experience in open ocean sailing, nor were we very familiar with the ship. The one thing I had working in my favor was that I had several friends among the crew with whom I'd sailed on other large vessels. David Vera, a Spaniard born in the Canary Islands, who sported curly blond hair and a great sense of humor, was the soul of the ship. I also liked two other Spaniards, Javier de la Plaza and Gonzalo Araujo, as well as Maciel Cicchetti, or Cicho, who had been my Laser coach for the 1996 Atlanta Games before enjoying a successful career as a professional sailor. The eleven-man crew included seven Spaniards and two Argentines, plus a Swede and a South African who quickly joined in with our Latin hustle and bustle. There was great camaraderie to go with just a bit of chaos. We were Telefónica's B-team—the best prepared boat was dubbed Blue—and the positive atmosphere helped counterbalance our limitations.

Paula wasn't happy at all when, just a few days after returning from my long Olympic tenure in Beijing, I announced my plan to embark on an ocean voyage. We arranged for her to travel to some of the stage ports and do some local sightseeing during the stops. I wasn't quite convinced, but she did travel to Alicante to say goodbye. We had dinner at a restaurant the night before my departure and she confessed to me that she was terrified. The only way to bear the dread of my adventure, she said, was to pull back from our relationship for as long as I was sailing.

The next day the port was abuzz with families and emotions. There was joy at the start of a new competition, but also nerves and a touch of heartache. Many of the sailors had wives and young children whom we wouldn't see again for several long months as we sailed around the world. I thanked Paula for coming to say goodbye. We embraced, and then I got on board.

After the excitement of the sendoff, we settled into the routine of the high seas. We would be out on the ocean for a month before arriving at the first port and everything was on a tight schedule. Crew members alternated between successive shifts of four hours on deck sailing the ship, two hours below deck—though still on call in case we were needed—followed by another two hours of rest, which we mostly used to eat and try to catch a few winks of sleep. Captain Fernando, the Dutch navigator Roger Nilson, and Mikel Pasabant, the journalist we'd brought on board, were the only ones exempt from this regimen.

Barring some welcome tropical rain, grooming depended on our daily ration of three wet wipes: the same kind used to clean babies' bottoms. We took turns napping in the six sleeping bags we shared. The interior of the ship was a humid, stinking, noisy, and crowded space, but we were always exhausted and despite the lack of comforts, we were always ready to crash for the few hours of rest we had. On deck, everything depended on the weather. When the sea was rough, waves crashed across the deck and you had to hold fast in order to not be swept into the sea.

We ate freeze-dried food in high-rimmed bowls. We'd pour hot water over it and up popped various types of carbs and proteins from pasta and rice to beef, chicken, and fish. Also available were cereal bars, dehydrated soup, and muesli. Before setting sail, we had smuggled some serrano ham on board, but that luxury only lasted us a few days.

It was immediately obvious that I didn't have the body type for this sort of competition. David could go days without sleep and eating well. I, on the other hand, had to make a real effort to eat well and get some rest. Otherwise my system would never withstand the rigors to which I was subjecting it. With the help of my friends on board, I was able to adapt, and soon enough I began to enjoy the adventure.

We were isolated, separated from our families, our clothes were always wet, we barely slept, we were always hungry, either scorched by the sun or freezing to death, crowded together and risking our lives in the middle of the sea. And yet I was happy. I enjoyed the feeling of being like a pin dropped into the immensity of the ocean, the sun peeking over the horizon after a tough night, and the show a pod of dolphins put on one afternoon as they played in our ship's wake. I also loved the fact that I was in the midst of an incessant race.

Unlike small class regattas, which only last a couple of hours, with the Volvo Ocean Race we spent weeks trying to outperform our rivals. We never stopped. I would lie down for a nap, dream of the opponent we had in our sights, and when I got up, I'd stick my head out to see if we'd managed to pass them. It was my chance to do what I loved twenty-four hours a day for weeks at a time. There was great camaraderie among everyone on board.

After fifteen days at sea, we crossed paths with a storm and experienced the full power of mother nature. Our ship wasn't prepared for such conditions. It wasn't fast and a number of systems failed, which altered our guard rotation and put extra wear and stress on the equipment. The Telefónica Black had relatively small rudders and was difficult to control when the wind was coming hard astern. She would accelerate coming down the back side of a wave and the concern was that she would sink her bow in the next one coming, which abruptly reduces speed and puts the ship's structure at risk. The key was to time things just right so you could plane the waves without any sudden changes in either speed or direction. I was still struggling with my vision, and since I couldn't read the instrument panel, David was in charge of yelling out the numbers to me.

"Come on you blind bastard! Steer her well or everything's gonna break apart!" he called out in the middle of the storm. His humor served as an antidote to the stressfulness of the situation.

At dawn on October 29th, I took the helm after a long night. Suddenly I lost control of the ship and we found ourselves facing directly into the wind. One of the rudders had split in two. The sails flared with a deafening, terrifying roar. This was a dangerous situation and we had to act quickly before we lost the mast. Cicho came out in his underwear to cut the line that released the sail and, in doing so, he almost got hauled overboard. After twenty vertiginous minutes, we finally managed to get the situation under control only to find that the anchor that held the headsail in place had also been broken. We had avoided a disaster, but nevertheless the ship had sustained damage.

We watched resignedly as our competitors sailed away from us. Instead of a rival crew, we now faced a tedious week of slow sailing to Cape Town. My natural sense of leadership was only increased because Fernando had already been exhausted by the energy he expended in winning Olympic gold in the Tornado, and had spent several days recuperating below deck. Without the adrenaline of competition, the food tasted even more bland and the bunks became even more uncomfortable. Monotony set in. David tried to lift our spirits with stories and songs. One of the few diversions we found during those Doldrum days was attempting to translate the lyrics to "María Isabel," a hit song by the Spanish pop group Los Payos, for our South African mate Mike Pammenter.

That was also when we began talking about what was going on with Fernando. The team was disgruntled and Fernando himself called a meeting before arriving in port. Some of the crew believed he lacked experience and wasn't the right man to lead the voyage. Fernando felt as though the frustrations stemming from their poor performance was being placed on his shoulders.

The conflict put me in a very tenuous position. On critical days, while Fernando was still recovering, I was in charge of the ship. This wasn't a decision—it hadn't even been discussed—but many members of the crew knew me from other competitions and trusted me. Fernando and I had trained together in the Laser class for the Atlanta Games and later in the Tornado for Athens and Beijing. He was the one who had recommended I be a part of the crew aboard the Telefónica. Now, the grumblings about his leadership skills left me in an awkward position. On the evening of November 4th, with all these tensions swirling, we arrived in Cape Town after twenty-five days at sea. As soon as we crossed the line, we hugged one another, relieved to have brought those last few tortuous days to an end.

I took a few days of vacation and Paula and I toured the local vineyards. For once, I tried to stay as far from the sea as possible. We set sail again on November 15th. This time, our destination was Kochi in southern India. We arrived just in time for the New Year celebrations, and I flew to Buenos Aires to spend a few days with Paula and the boys, before heading back to embark on the next leg of the journey.

By the time we docked in Singapore, the conflicts on board had grown. The crew was unmotivated, which increased the chances of an accident. When you're out in the middle of the ocean, it's essential that everyone stay alert in order to identify anything that breaks down and needs repair, which is a frequent occurrence. The strained atmosphere was threatening to undo all of that. The entire crew got together: the situation had become unbearable and I decided to resign. There was no point in risking my life on an endeavor I no longer enjoyed. I pointed to a back injury—which was true, my back was in bad shape at the time—but that wasn't the true reason for leaving the team. With sadness in my heart, I announced that I would not be a part of the competition going forward.

The rest of the crew of the Teléfonica Black continued on with the race. They had a major breakdown that forced them to abandon a later stage, but they had the pleasure of winning the last leg of the race. I was overjoyed. The whole crew deserved that final accolade. When I crossed paths with Fernando again, we were rivals in the Nacra class leading up to the 2016 Rio Games. We're still friends to this day, and it was only recently that we were able to talk about that rugged ocean regatta. I told him how much I admired the courage he displayed in not stepping down as captain, and he thanked me for stepping off the ship so as not to interfere with his command.

Determined to rid myself of the bitter taste left by my abrupt end to the Volvo Ocean Race, I invited my children to Singapore and we flew to Bali, where we spent a great week at the Chill House Surf Resort. We had fresh fruit for breakfast every morning, after which Hanga, a local guide, would take us to different beaches around the island where we could surf.

I had barely finished unpacking after the trip with the boys when I received a proposal from Juan Kouyoumdjian, a talented naval architect and fellow graduate of Southampton, to join his team. Juan K, as he's known in the sailing world, stood out from the crowd at a very young age owing to his fast, innovative designs. His vessels won three consecutive Volvo races. At his company, which at the time was among the very best in the world, Argentines were the majority.

This offer represented a great opportunity. At forty-nine, I figured I was reaching the end of my athletic career. Juan K talked about bringing me on as partner, and I was excited by the prospect of getting back to the work of designing ships. It was something of a retirement plan that would allow me to stay connected to the world of sailing while simultaneously growing as a craftsman. Paula was happy with the change. It meant no more prolonged absences, no oceanic voyages. Plus, we could speak the same language: that of design. However, once again, I would find myself drawn to the siren call of sailing.

An opportunity arose with Team Origin, an America's Cup team that had hired Juan K. The helmsman was Ben Ainslie and the crew included Ian Percy and Andrew Simpson. All three were well-known British sailors. They offered me a chance to be part of their team, and I couldn't resist. A mere six months after announcing my retirement, I was once again hanging in a harness atop a mast trying to gauge the wind while Ainslie, one of the most competitive skippers on the circuit, maneuvered the ship with an aggressive hand. In the end there was a legal dispute and the venture was suspended, but nevertheless it had put further stress on Paula and me as a couple.

The biggest challenge to our relationship was that it coincided with one of the most nomadic periods of my life. During the seven years we were together, I participated in the Beijing Games, the America's Cup, and the Volvo Ocean Race. We survived as a couple because we loved one another and made every effort to sustain that love regardless of the distance, but the constant traveling was taking its toll on the relationship.

A common conflict occurred whenever I was back in Buenos Aires for a few days and I'd try to make what time I had with my children last. They were my priority and Paula understood that, but she wanted to spend some time alone with me as well. Early on in the relationship, I could have dinner with the boys, put them to bed, and go spend the night with Paula before heading back home at seven in the morning to get them up and ready for school. It was a tiring routine. Later on, when our relationship had grown stronger and we were doing things as a family, I tried to convince her to stay with me and the boys. It only happened once. Besides my busy schedule, Paula was upset with the fact that I couldn't always be counted on. I remember one argument in which she reproached me for not even being able to keep a lunch date. I had dreams of a future in which I were retired from competition and we could have a more peaceful life, but we both knew in our hearts that I was getting just so much enjoyment out of what I was doing.

Paula is a very independent woman and our personalities came together to create a passionate relationship. But the conflicts continued to grow. She grew tired of always being the one who made concessions, and told me she wasn't seeing an equal commitment on my part. It was a painful, though civil, separation. We still care for one another and keep in touch. Recently, we even laughed at the ironic turn her career took. She's now one of the most recognized architects of corporate spaces in all of Argentina, and her commitments—as mine once did—now keep her away from Buenos Aires for long periods of time. The nomadic life is a contagious one, indeed.

In 2012, without Paula, I moved to Oakland, California, to work on a new America's Cup project. Juan K's design studio had been hired by Artemis Racing, a Swedish professional sailing team. I rented a house in a hilly residential neighborhood, and the twins moved in with me for the next seven months. My days were long and often began with a phone call that would wake the boys, who would otherwise be sleeping in like normal teenagers. They often visited an old, nearby arthouse theater. Borja checked out the various music venues in the area, and Theo showed a great flair for languages in an accelerated English course he took. On weekends we'd go for a bike ride on a rugged trail a little over two miles from the house.

Yago and Klaus arrived in March of 2013, after the twins had already returned to Buenos Aires. The purpose of their trip was athletic: they wanted to try sailing together in a 49er, one of the most competitive Olympic class sailboats. Their incipient alliance surprised me. They had both sailed, but on different boats. Yago was seeing good results in his Laser, while Klaus had enjoyed a very successful youth career and had bought himself a 49er with his sights set on the 2016 Rio Games. His teammate ended up having a change of heart and Klaus called me, desperate and suggesting that we sail together. The precedent for this was when we raced together in a 29er—a smaller version of the 49er—at the 2011 World Championships in Mar del Plata. We made a great team, and the idea was certainly tempting, but I didn't feel capable of handling a 49er, which is a boat more suited to pure athletes who can perform real balancing acts on the trapeze.

A few days later, Klaus called me again. This time Yago was with him. They announced that they had decided to give it a shot as a duo. I told them I loved the idea and would support them wholeheartedly, but I also warned them about how stressful the process would be and that they had to prepare themselves in case it didn't work out. I was afraid that, as brothers with two very different personalities, the road ahead of them would be even more challenging. I didn't want some potential athletic conflict to damage their relationship as siblings. After this warning, I invited them to the bay area to begin their training.

Klaus had more experience in faster boats and my opinion was that he should take the helm. They, however, disagreed: Yago would be the helmsman and Klaus the crew member. I helped them out by buying them a boat and connecting them with the Artemis team. My only condition was that they fully commit to training.

They immediately demonstrated how serious they were about the task at hand, hitting the gym bright and early every morning. Klaus had to put on some muscle mass in order to handle the tremendous physical stress that a 49er will put on you. Yago was rather stiff coming off his Laser campaign and had to improve his agility. They'd spend around five hours out at sea, learning to navigate the 49er in the cold waters of the Pacific. Klaus was patient and gave his older brother time to adjust. The 49er is much faster than the Laser and Yago liked the speed, but it took him awhile to master the boat. After four months of apprenticeship and plenty of setbacks, they left for Europe to enter their first international championships.

The 2013 America's Cup in the San Francisco Bay was a revolution in the sailing world. The old image of the sport as one of gentlemen in elegant ships had been transformed into a modern spectacle. This had been the vision of Larry Ellison, the tech mogul who poured millions of dollars into recasting the sport. His idea was to turn it into a show of speed and technology, and in order to do that he wanted fast boats along with an attractive and easy-to-understand broadcasting system for races.

New regulation established that one-on-one matchups would be run between massive catamarans over seventy feet in length with masts rising over 130 feet into the sky. But beyond their sheer size, the biggest development was that, instead of a traditional sail, the boat would be propelled by rigid wings, like those of an airplane. The AC72s, as the new ships were called, were powerful and efficient machines capable of sailing at nearly fifty miles per hour. They were also expensive and dangerous. The designers were entering uncharted territory in the world of naval architecture, and they didn't know what limitations there were.

The Artemis team already had experience in professional sailing, but this would be their debut as a contender for the America's Cup. The owner is Torbjörn Törnqvist, a Swedish sailor and billionaire with investments in the oil industry. Our operating budget was around 140 million dollars, and among us were some of the great figures from the nautical world. It was a much bigger and more ambitious operation than Victory Challenge. I was to act as a link between the designers and the sailors. I wasn't expected to actually join the crew during the competition. I would only sail with the team in training.

The design challenges of this new class were enormous. The stiff wingsail generated a lot of power and was difficult to control. Like a race car that has its engine modified to increase horsepower, we were fast, but we also ran the risk of getting off track. The critical moment came when the catamarans would change course and start sailing downwind. During the execution of this maneuver, there were a few seconds where the tensile forces reached their maximum strength. In the "death zone," which is what we called this transition, it was absolutely necessary to act quickly and in a coordinated manner. A crewmember's mistake or a ship failure could be lethal.

That was what happened on May 9th, 2013, the most tragic day I've experienced as a sailor. I was in one of the launches and the team was training with good winds out on the San Francisco Bay. The day was coming to an end when we watched in horror as our boat flipped over in a somersaulting fashion in the middle of a tack. We raced in at full speed to activate the security protocol. When we finished rescuing the crew, we did a quick head count and there were only ten. One crewmember was missing. The bow beam connecting the two hulls of the catamaran had snapped and the boat had folded in on itself. The divers continued to scour the debris from the carbon fiber frame. After fifteen minutes, which seemed like an eternity, they found Andrew Simpson, the Englishman whom I knew from our time together on Team Origin. They immediately started CPR, but it was all to no avail.

The death of Bart, as he was known, struck a very hard blow. He was thirty-six years old and had two young children. He was sensitive, charismatic, and loved by all: one of those people who by his mere presence changes the mood around him. He had grown fond of Klaus and treated him like a godson, which made Klaus feel like a real part of the Artemis team. Just a few weeks before the tragic accident, the three of us had participated in a sixty-mile bike race through Napa Valley. Bart was big and strong. He pedaled in high gear with the ease and tranquility of someone out for a Sunday walk in the park.

On May 31st, I and much of the Artemis team attended Bart's funeral at the old Sherborne Abbey in Dorset, where he was from. There was a reception at the local castle. The Star, the boat with which Bart had won two Olympic medals, was anchored in the park's lagoon. A video montage was played and we toasted with beer. It was a true celebration of his life and showed me a less tearful way of saying goodbye to a loved one. "He didn't leave," whispered one of Bart's old sailing friends. "He rests now in the sea."

Ian Percy, Bart's Olympic teammate, recalled his generosity and announced plans to establish a foundation in his name. The Andrew Simpson Foundation promotes boating programs for kids who wouldn't otherwise have access to the sport. Ben Ainslie, a great friend of Bart's and winner of four consecutive gold medals, read a Charles Henry Brent poem as a final farewell:

> What is dying?
> I am standing on the seashore.
> A ship sails to the morning breeze and starts for the ocean.
> She is an object and I stand watching her
> till at last she fades from the horizon,
> and someone at my side says, "She is gone!" Gone where?
> Gone from my sight, that is all.
> She is just as large in the masts, hull and spars as she was
> when I saw her.
> And just as able to bear her load of living freight to its
> destination.
> The diminished size and total loss of sight is in me, not in her.
> And just at the moment when someone at my side says
> "She is gone",
> there are others who are watching her coming,
> and other voices take up a glad shout,
> "There she comes" –and that is dying.

Back in San Francisco, our America's Cup campaign found itself in crisis mode. On top of the grief we were feeling, there was also fear. Some of the sailors didn't want to set foot on the catamaran again. There was a meeting with Törnqvist, the owner, who insisted on the need to carry on. Several other crewmembers agreed. The sport's governing body updated safety protocols for all the boats and we decided to compete. There was a lot of catching up to do and the process was fraught with problems. We were unable to qualify for the final. Despite the bitterness of defeat, we were glad we were able to compete. It was a fitting tribute to Bart.

Chapter Thirteen

What If We Try Sailing Together?

The sun set and the wind went with it. There we were, floating in the middle of the river with no way to get back to the club.

"Hey, Santi, I figure someone at the Náutico will realize we never came back and they'll send out a launch to look for us," Ceci tells me.

"That's crazy," I replied. "Nobody's worried about us. We'd better start rowing... otherwise we'll be sleeping out here."

We're alone. There's no wind, and we're floating in a seventeen-foot boat. It's our first outing on the Nacra 17, the mixed catamaran that will debut as a class at the next Olympic Games. I close my eyes and smile. This rough start is, I think, a sign. A good sign. Throughout my career, obstacles have always been the prelude to a happy ending. I'm excited for whatever's coming my way. I'm sure it'll be good.

I've made up my mind. Five years after my retirement following the Beijing Games, I'm going back to competing on the Olympic circuit. Neither my age, my knees, nor my ignorance of this new boat will stop me. Any doubts I might have had about the process, the teamwork, or about my own motivations for submitting myself to the rigors of one more campaign vanished when the Nacra nosed her way out of the access channel at the Náutico San Isidro. Once again, I was experiencing what I love: the boat's responses to my adjustments to the sails, wave after wave, were all different. At the helm, in that moment when the wind filled the sails and raised up the hull, I once again felt pressure and excitement running through my veins. I knew I was on my way. It was a message from the boat as it began to react, to shake off its drowsiness and come to life. The same was happening with every fiber of my being as an Olympic sailor.

It all started a few months before in my house in San Francisco. One morning I opened up my email to find a message from Cecilia Carranza: *Hi Santi, hope you're doing well. Will you be in Buenos Aires anytime soon? I'd love to talk with you and get your advice on the Nacra campaign.*

Ceci and I had met during the Beijing Games. She competed in the Laser, the same individual class I ran with in Atlanta '96, and we would go for runs together around the marina. Ceci says she admired the work we put in on the Tornado that had been broken in the crash. While I was bidding my farewell to the Olympics, she was just beginning. Only twenty-one years of age, she finished twelfth, a very good result for her Olympic debut. She also raced in the following Games, in London, in 2012.

In Rosario, her hometown, she became friends with another sailor, Esteban Blando, who owned a Tornado. One day he invited her to try it out and she was hooked. Like the Nacra and other catamarans, the Tornado is more technologically developed and much faster than a single hull dinghy like the Laser.

Ceci had decided that the London Games would be her last in the Laser. She wanted to keep racing, but she felt like she needed a change. She was looking to learn to work as a team and master a more complex ship. When the International Olympic Committee announced that the Nacra would be introduced as a new class for the Rio Games, and that it would be a mixed category, Ceci and Esteban saw their opportunity. They bought a Nacra and started competing on the international circuit.

We set up a meeting for late November of 2013. That day, I opened the door to my house in San Isidro to find her standing there alone.

"Where's Esteban?" I asked.

As we shared a cup of mate, Ceci explained to me that the two of them weren't working well together and things had reached a crisis point. She even went back to the Laser—she had just been crowned women's champion at the latest Argentine national regatta—but she still wanted to make the jump to the Nacra. I listened to her and tried to understand what the problem had been with Esteban, to see what lessons might be learned from it... until, without even thinking about it, a question occurred to me:

"Why don't we try sailing together?"

It was a spur of the moment idea. I just blurted it out as quickly as it had flashed in my mind. In fact, my proposal was so surprising and so completely unexpected that Ceci was left speechless. She said nothing. Not even a "yes" or a "no." To her, as it was with everyone else in the world of competitive sailing, I was a former Olympian who was now working as a professional on large sailboat design projects.

We continued to discuss this, but a certain perplexity began to crop up inside me. "What's with this brash little kid? Does she think I'm too old to sail with her?" I wondered. But, as she confessed to me later, Ceci wasn't being disparaging of me. Quite the opposite. It was true that, to her, I was a retired athlete old enough to have been her father. But that wasn't what had prevented her from answering me. It was out of respect. She just couldn't accept the possibility that I was being serious, that I really wanted us to sail together.

My proposal wasn't resolved during that initial conversation. After that meeting, Ceci said goodbye and went on her way. I was left alone with the realization that I couldn't get the idea out of my head. On the contrary, it grew as the hours went by. Just when I least expected it, my Olympic spirit emerged from its slumber and was claiming me once again. A few days later I sent her an email: "So, Ceci, what do you think about my proposal?" In the end she said yes and we agreed on a time to go for a sail. I couldn't wait for the moment to come. I was going to test the madness of wanting to return to the sport. Would it still feel the same?

Olympic Committee rules state that the Nacra crew must be mixed, but they do not specify who should be the helmsman und who should be the crewmember. That decision is left up to the team. Each position has its own intricacies, and the crewmember in particular needs to have a tremendous amount of physical stamina. Ceci was at the helm when she raced with her former partner, but in our case, it would be the other way around for a number of reasons. The first was that I'd been at the helm of every boat I competed with at the Olympics. It's my natural position. But on top of that, because of my age, I didn't have the endurance to do the hard work of the crewmember. Ceci agreed and took it upon herself to adapt to the demanding requirements of her new position. She was coming from a very physical class, but she still needed to learn how to respond to the specific requirements of the Nacra.

Those first days we sailed out from the Club Náutico San Isidro were supposed to be nothing more than an exploratory venture—a trial run to see how we felt together aboard the boat—but my competitive edge got the best of me and I started trying some speed jibing, a maneuver that requires a lot of coordination. In just a few minutes she was adding a sense of pace to what had become a real training session, as if the start of the Games was imminent. Hiked out on the trapeze, Ceci would turn and look at me in amazement with every signal or command I gave.

The adventure we had embarked on seemed unbelievable to my sailing friends and coaches. They all told me it was crazy to try and recapture my Olympic days at this point in my life. They asked if I was sure I really wanted to travel thousands of miles between dozens of competitions while training constantly and the entire time are pleonastic, one or the other.

Plus, I myself had been critical of the International Sailing Federation's decision to include a mixed class at the Rio Games. The move was in response to the International Olympic Committee's goal of achieving equal representation between men and women, but I felt this could be achieved through sports separated by sex. There was no need to mix genders. After all, it was the path most sports had long since adopted. In soccer and rugby, for example, women's teams were highly promoted. Our federation, on the other hand, was one of the few that chose to put together a mixed competition.

Now, looking back on those days, I understand that the challenge posed by the two-person mixed event was actually one of the great motivations I had during the campaign. I had come out of retirement to take on an aggressive boat, one designed for athletes much younger than myself, in which I was also going to have to learn how to team up with a woman: something I had never done before in all my years of sailing on high performance boats.

Ceci and I were satisfied with our first few test runs on the river and we decided to enter a few international regattas the following year, 2014. We sat down with a calendar laid out before us and marked out around fifty days of sailing, split between training and competing. I was trying not to be overly ambitious, to keep things within the boundaries of what my schedule would allow me to do. But as the season went on, we got more and more enthusiastic, and we ended up sailing somewhere between 120 and 130 days that year. In order to do so, I had to cancel several contracts I had for large sailboats.

The first training session of the 2014 season began in Barcelona in the European spring. Then we ran in the Hyères Olympic Week in France: the very same regatta in which Camau and I had gone to sail while the rest of the fleet remained behind, fearing the strong winds. It was a great learning period. In our search for speed, we tried new and risky moves. And we stumbled at first. When the wind was blowing from astern the boat was very unstable. The Nacra is an unstable beast, and we were trying to tame it.

 Ceci and I were still getting to know each other, and the first thing that surprised me was her truly great level of commitment. Early on, I was still juggling my professional obligations, and I lacked the energy for the hard work our campaign involved. Ceci handled a myriad tasks, including buying the boat, transporting it to events, assembling the control systems, and renting trucks, houses, Zodiacs, and cars. As if that wasn't enough, she was also learning how to handle a catamaran. She watched everything and took it all in. That's the mentality she had as we approached this first phase of our preparations. As she later confided to me, she saw it as a great opportunity to gain knowledge and to grow as an athlete and sailor.

 During that European season, we shared a house with Yago and Klaus, who were starting their own campaign in the 49er class. The possibility of all of us qualifying for the Olympics and marching in the Opening Ceremonies as a family was incredibly exciting. I still look back on those days of living together with great affection: a twenty-seven year old woman, two boys who were nineteen and twenty-six, and me, at fifty-two years of age. That was how season 2014 of the Big Brother Náutica House version of the popular TV show was formed.

Living with a group of young people was a privilege. It filled me with vitality and it presented a wonderful opportunity for us all to get to know one another better. It also offered me a new way of interacting with my children. At night, after a long day on the water, we'd have some great conversations. We talked a lot about the progress we were all making in our training. Just like Ceci and I, Yago and Klaus were trying to master a newer, faster boat. But we also talked about soccer and other sports, we told old stories from the past, shared life experiences, whatever came up. By that point, Ceci was a member of the family.

One of the topics of conversation had to do with relationships between men and women. Why is it that, in the world of sports, women have less visibility than men? Was it a physical issue? Something related to experience? Or do the paradigms of success and attractiveness that are applied differently to men and women have something to do with it? Ceci and my two young sons believed they had fewer opportunities than people of my generation did. Some very interesting debates were taking place there in that house.

We also discussed sexuality. Ceci had a girlfriend, Ana, who traveled with her to some of the competitions. She told us that her family had known about her sexual orientation since she was seventeen, but she still felt stifled. It was hard enough for her to outwardly project this relationship, to say nothing of getting married, having kids, and starting a family. These were all completely unfettered conversations. Yago and Klaus were engaged participants, and I appreciated the fact that my sons had the opportunity to educate themselves with an open mind. Ceci is the same. She's an independent woman who lives her life without asking anyone else for their permission. It's quite likely that someone in that house, myself included, made some macho joke or some off-color reference. Ceci chose to pay them no heed. It was her way of preserving the good climate that enveloped our intense coexistence.

Another issue had to do with modesty. Supposedly there are certain activities that one can do in front of a man but not a woman. I lack those inhibitions. My sport takes place outdoors and I do what I have to do without hiding from anyone. When you're living on board a vessel that's sailing around the world, or when you just have a minute before the start of a race at the Olympic Games, it's impractical to seek privacy to change or relieve your bladder. I always did both in front of my crewmates and coaches, and that wasn't going to change now just because Ceci was there. It's all part of the trust that makes for good teams.

In other mixed crews, when someone needs to urinate, the men will conceal themselves and the women will jump into the water. But once it's soaked, a wetsuit becomes heavier, more uncomfortable, and much more inefficient. I drink a lot of water to stay hydrated, and I have to relieve myself several times a day. Trying to cover it up every time would be all but impossible. Instead of looking a privacy that doesn't exist out on the water, we used that down time to discuss any details that we might have to adjust. You can relieve yourself and get back to a race almost immediately. I understand that's not the most civilized image, and when there are cameras nearby, we try our best to avoid them, but that's just our style. Ceci is a bit more modest when it comes to this lack of inhibitions.

"If you want to put on some underwear, I won't be offended," she told me the time I absentmindedly opened the door to her quarters naked because I couldn't find my towel.

Our first major goal during this Nacra campaign was to qualify for the Olympics. Only twenty teams can compete at the Games. The spots are awarded based on the results in a series of preliminary competitions. The first of these qualifiers was the World Cup, which was held in September in Santander in northern Spain. Our objective was to earn one of those spots, for doing so would allow us to better plan for Rio 2016. I needed to put together a solid schedule so we would be physically ready, and this early event was key. I still had a few commitments on bigger ships, so Ceci took over a lot of the organizational work, including (among many other things) towing the Nacra in my old BMW. She drove by herself without air conditioning through the hot Spanish steppe in the middle of the summer. Her only relief were the bottles of ice-cold water she would pour over her head.

In Santander, Mateo Majdalani, who was just twenty years old at the time, joined the team with the idea of helping Ceci with the logistics while also serving as coach. It was another bet on young Argentine talent, like the one I made with Ramón Oliden and Matías Bühler. Ceci definitely needed a hand, but at first she balked at Mateo's youth. She barely knew him by name, but it was my decision to make. Later, after Mateo had become an integral part of our team, she confessed her initial doubts to me. "I need someone to help me out, not a son," she once told a friend of hers over the phone.

We arrived in Santander with plenty of time, ready to put in some solid training. I had an important work contract on the same exact date as the race, and we decided to leave the decision to compete until the very last minute. If we were in a good position to possibly qualify for the Olympics, I'd suspend my contract and we'd compete in the World Cup. If we felt we weren't quite up to the challenge just yet, we'd use that time to train instead of compete, and I'd fulfill my professional commitment. There would be other opportunities to qualify later in the season.

It was then, when we were really hitting the gas, that Ceci found her body was nearing its limits. The crewmember's job is very demanding, and the physical training was different from what she was accustomed to with the Laser. Her former boat required lower body strength, while the Nacra was all about the upper body. Since our decision to embark on an Olympic campaign had been a sudden one, and we had focused on the more pressing issues like solving operational issues and learning to sail the boat, Ceci hadn't been able to spend enough time in the gym.

One day her forearms just gave out. We got to the club after a workout and she could barely grip anything. This was just a short time before the start of the World Cup, and it was clear to me that we hadn't reached the point in our training we'd been hoping for. That night I went to bed anxious and stressed. I tossed and turned, wondering how I was going to break the news to Ceci that I'd decided not to compete and would instead be fulfilling my professional contract.

Bambi, Dani, and I had a training regimen dating back to 1993. Ceci was coming from a different routine, and we were looking for her to integrate herself into our system. Also, I was used to sailing with Camau, who was a very well-rounded athlete, and much stronger than either Ceci or me. With that history in the back of my head, I realized I'd been expecting her to respond in a way she just wasn't ready for. Sometimes I'd use Camau as an example when I wanted to explain something to her: In this maneuver, Camau would do such and such, I'd say. Understanding that Ceci was going to make tremendous strides, while simultaneously not comparing her to Camau in the prime of his career, would prove to be one of the biggest challenges we'd face in our campaign.

The next morning Bambi presented us with a recovery plan for Ceci's arms that would get us to the Cup. With renewed hopes, we asked the Spanish team's kinesiologist for help, and I called Eduardo Souza Ramos, the owner of the boat that was waiting for me in Ibiza ready for professional competition. A former Olympic sailor himself, Eduardo understood the situation. I decided to stay on and attempt to qualify.

It was a tough competition with fluctuating winds that we knew how to take advantage of. We were newcomers to this class, while most of the other teams had been sailing Nacras for a couple of years. We weren't setting any speed records, but previous experience with catamarans prepared us for this challenge. Ceci was holding up really well. After the final race on a particularly windy day she was so exhausted that he had to be carried back to the club in the Zodiac while Mateo and I brought in the boat. We reached the last day of competition tied for fifth place, just a few points out of second. If we could just put together one solid race in the finals, where scores were doubled, we'd qualify for the Games.

That morning an unexpected problem arose. Yago and Klaus were also in Santander competing in the 49er World Cup, and they weren't doing well. The tension between them had been growing until the day of the finals when it exploded. They fought and things were said. They decided they didn't want to sail together anymore. With just a few hours before our own final race was to be run, I called them both in for a meeting. I would work a bit as a coach and a lot as a father.

I told them they were making a mistake and that no decisions should be made in the heat of the moment. I warned them against rushing to judgement, and to avoid any further conflicts, I suggested they take separate flights back to Buenos Aires. I got them to agree and then, with little time left to spare, we threw the boat in the water and prepared for the decisive race. My heart was hurting. I couldn't believe what had just happened. During those weeks of living together I'd been excited about the possibility of going to Rio together with Yago and Klaus, but this conflict between the two of them brought all of that excitement tumbling down. But, as was so often the case, the problem disappeared as soon as I got on board the boat. Once I was in the water, my focus was all about doing what I needed to do in that exact moment.

The day of the championship final was one of flat water and variable winds. The course was marked out in the Bay of Santander near the coast. We could hear the cheers from the crowd in the grandstands. Even before the start, the World Cup had been decided: the French team made up of Billy Besson and Marie Riou had had a spectacular week and their lead heading into the final race was mathematically insurmountable. Throughout the entire season, they had proved to be head and shoulders above the rest of the fleet. Second and third place, however, were still up for grabs between ourselves, Australia, Great Britain, and New Zealand. Our strategy was to be aggressive right from the start, either win the race outright or finish as close to the top as possible, and then find out whether it had been enough.

We tore off the line in the middle of the fleet, headed to the left side of the course, and reached the first buoy in second place. In first was Mati Bühler, who was competing for the Swiss alongside Nathalie Brugger. His paternal grandfather is Swiss and he has dual citizenship. He chose to accept the offer to compete for another nation after being tempted by the financial support they had offered him. It hurt to see him in Swiss colors, but we understood his decision.

Mati was no longer the young man who needed an explanation as to how a catamaran worked when he first starting training with Camau and me. Now, at thirty-one years of age, he'd become one of the best helmsmen in the fleet. I was very happy to have him as a rival upon my return to the racing circuit. We were old friends, but Mati and I didn't pull any punches during that last race. I wanted to maintain the hierarchy that had been granted by the years, and the race became a clash between two generations of sailors raised along the banks of the Río de la Plata.

Ceci and I won the first tactical battle. As soon as we passed the buoy, with the wind at our backs, we changed course and headed towards the left side of the course. Mati went the other way. He didn't cover us and we were able to pass him. Several of the other teams got caught up behind a collision at the marker and were delayed.

We held the lead until the very end when Mati passed us. The boat with the Swiss flag crossed the finish line ten seconds before ours did. But there were plenty of reasons to celebrate. Second place in the finals ensured us the silver medal at the World Cup and a place in the Olympic Games. My hunch—the question I blurted out to that girl who'd come to my house seeking advice—was starting to make sense. A year ago I had been retired from Olympic competition, and here we were, runners-up at the World Championships. And, most importantly, we had punched our tickets to Rio de Janeiro.

The next day I turned fifty-three. The joy of my birthday and having qualified for Rio was clouded by the fight between Yago and Klaus. The fact that this could mean the end of my children as teammates weighed heavily on my spirit. But regardless we all went out for dinner. Klaus needed to relax after the fight and sought refuge in Mateo, his childhood friend. The hit the bars that night, and from what I gather, there was some heavy drinking involved. The next day Mateo was supposed to take turns with Ceci driving the BMW back to Barcelona with the Nacra in tow, but he was in no condition to drive. Ceci grumbled a bit but played the role of the big sister and took the wheel. From the passenger seat, every so often, Mateo showed signs of life.

I always like to analyze victories with the same precision as I do defeats. If you don't let yourself get dazzled by the results, success can yield valuable lessons. That's what we did as a team as soon as the championships ended. We'd performed much better than expected, but we weren't about to be lulled into a sense of complacency. We'd had an inspired week, but we were not the second-best team in the world. Far from it. Our skill had masked our shortcomings in both speed and maneuverability, among many other things, but what we lacked most was the necessary foundations for sustained quality performances. The other lesson we learned from Santander was that we would have to modify our training regimen in order to meet the needs of both Ceci and I. If we didn't, we'd be running the risk of injury.

We had finished the European in the best possible fashion. Ahead of us was the long summer in the southern hemisphere. We had to use this momentum to train hard and reach the level we wanted to be at. Out of those conversations came a document that I would share with the team: "How to Win in Rio."

Chapter Fourteen

An Unexpected Wind

My cell phone rings and the name appearing on the caller ID gives me a start. I decide to stop the car so I can speak calmly. I pull into a gas station in Olivos, near my house in Buenos Aires, and answer. It's Friday afternoon and people are fleeing their jobs, ready to kick off the weekend.

After the usual greetings, the doctor gets straight to the point.
"The results of the biopsy came back, and they're not good. We have to operate."
"When?" I ask.
"It's urgent. The sooner the better. Can you do Monday?"
"I guess so."
"Good. Come in at seven in the morning on an empty stomach. I'll wait for you in my office after you've completed the pre-surgical procedures." I hang up and collapse on top of the steering wheel. All of a sudden, I start crying. Why me? Why? The question repeats itself time and again in my head. I've never smoked and I've been active in sports since I was six years old. I've lived a healthy life. Why is this happening to me? I have no answers, and that leaves me feeling vulnerable. After venting, I try to put myself back together. I start the car back up and head for home.

After our great World Cup in Santander, we abandoned the cold that was already beginning to creep across Europe to seek refuge in the heat of Brazil. Our destination was Buzios, a town located at the tip of a small peninsula extending out into the Atlantic Ocean, about two and a half hours from Rio de Janeiro. Because of its beauty, it's a highly popular destination for tourists, and it's a true training paradise. We always stop at Casa dos Ventos, which is on the beach, next to the Buzios Vela Club, which is ideal for what we need. It belongs to an old friend and rival of mine in the Laser, Pedro Bulhões. His son João is als a sailor in the Nacra class, and was one of our training partners. To share with a child the same passion that I shared over twenty years earlier with his father was a unique feeling.

That summer we trained with Mati Bühler, the Brazilian team, the Danes, and the Dutch. The days were intense and productive, but they were also tough on Ceci. A physical problem had cropped up: as was the case in Santander, her forearms were subject to fatigue. But at a high level of performance, it's common to train through discomfort, and we decided to press on. We were developing a strong rhythm together. As with any pre-season training, there was a lot of work to be done, and we were running four shifts a day. Ceci was physically exhausted. When she came back from sailing she'd plunge her arms in an ice bath seeking relief. One day she was just too tired to go out on the water, so I took advantage of the fact that Klaus was visiting, and I went sailing with him.

Ceci brought in Laura Cuello, her kinesiologist from Rosario, to see if she could help. But it wasn't enough. The three of us had a meeting and the atmosphere grew tense. Ceci wanted time to recover and felt that I wasn't listening. I explained my rationale, and the fact that I felt it necessary to do everything we could to build a strong foundation for our team. But we weren't on the same wavelength, and soon it became clear to me that the discussion wasn't really about her forearms. What she wanted was for me to understand her point of view. Maybe I needed to put the asymmetry of our relationship on hold, if only for a short amount of time. We were a team, but my dual status as partner and virtual coach brought complications.

To me, it was ultimately a question of philosophy. You have to push beyond fatigue, which is inevitable. What we had to change went deeper than that. It was tied to our attitude towards training, to the excellence we had to aspire to if we were to reach the level we needed to be at for the Olympics. This included physical preparations, but there were other issues which, at the outset, might have seemed irrelevant. Details were an important part of our system, and we went through the sequences with the colors of the ropes, the tidiness of our wetsuits, even the way we covered the boat with the tarp. I'm convinced that, through these minor things, a strong work ethic is built, leading to good techniques which consequently produce results.

We also had different ways of handling pressure. At this stage, we needed to be looking for intensity and rhythm, which was occasionally a source of tension between us. It's true that, when things aren't going well, I can lose my temper and yell out into the sky. It does push us forward, though. Ceci, who has a different sort of temperament, was bothered by my anger. She took it as criticism, and felt that such outbursts generated bad energy within the team.

When it is channeled properly, my obsession is a my obsession can be a great tool for training. But I also know it can be difficult to handle. When the enthusiasm is contagious and everyone is on the same page, our performance gets a boost, and this is where one of Ceci's many virtues as an athlete came into play: with a wealth of wisdom, she was able to learn to live with my high levels of demand. She not only put up with me but also accepted me, even in situations where I might have upset her.

The initial energy of the newly formed team had its ups and downs during the training in Buzios. I had faith in the method and refused to budge, conceding nothing. Ceci had her doubts about the reaches of her athletic abilities, and wasn't sure whether the forearm problems were a sign from her body, which was demanding rest, or from her head, which was reaching its limits. Dani Espina was essential when it came to harmonizing our relationship. During our one-on-one sessions, he made us realize that the differences in our personalities could lead to a truly virtuous dynamic.

Finally, after spending many hours out on the water, we believed we'd reached the level we were looking for. Now we just had to confirm this belief in the European competitions we had coming up. We were chomping at the bit to test ourselves against our rivals. We wanted any success we achieved to be the result of dutiful, extended training and of a single inspired week. In the year leading up to the Rio Olympics, we were looking for victories that would add to our confidence as we continued along the path towards our ultimate goal.

All that preparation, however, collided with the health concerns I'd been dealing with during the first championship of the European season. The Princesa Sofía regatta, in Palma de Mallorca, inaugurates a string of important competitions, and I had wonderful memories from having competed in previous editions. Palma de Mallorca, after all, was the final destination of that long train ride I took with the Moth class mast back when I was studying in Southampton. It was also where Miguel Saubidet and I dominated the Snipe class, and where I sailed professionally in many large sailboat regattas. But none of that counted for anything now. This time I was feeling horrible. The cocktail of medications I'd prescribed myself wasn't enough to kick the almost chronic flu-like symptoms I'd been suffering.

I spent hours curled up next to the stove under several layers of blankets. Unable to sail, I distracted myself with the news. I remember following in great detail the terrible story of the pilot who, in a state of deep depression, crashed a commercial German plane into the French Alps. My sneezes echoed throughout the house. The tissues I left scattered about made the floor look like a cemetery. Considering the state I was in, we should have quit. I was in no condition to compete, but onward we pressed, and the experience was torturous. As was to be expected, the regatta didn't go well for us. Despite all the discomfort I'd been struggling against, I still flew to Jureré, in Brazil, to compete in the World Championships for the Soto 40 class: a boat in which I was competing as a professional. But I never recovered. I spent the entire time locked up in a hotel. They loaded me on board ten minutes before the race and got me off as soon as it ended. I could hardly stand anymore.

I realized that, if I wanted to continue as a competitive athlete, I would need to address my health. There was no denying the obvious: I'd been dealing with these symptoms since 2013. Lately, every time I got off a plane, I felt sick, as if I were incubating a nasty cold. I never paid much attention to these irritations until I finally realized that my body was trying to send me a message, and that it was foolish to continue ignoring it.

I spoke with the team and returned to Buenos Aires to get some tests done. While I didn't realize it at the time, I was about to embark on my long pilgrimage to doctors' offices.
First I went to see Bernardo de Diego, my general practitioner for the past twenty years, in whom I had enormous confidence. "Everything looks good here, I don't see any abnormalities," he said af-

ter viewing the results of the first tests he'd ordered. But my weakened state persisted. On a follow-up visit to his office, I could barely even walk. He checked me again and found nothing out of the ordinary, but he referred me to a doctor who specialized in sports medicine. Perhaps there was something about the demands of high-performance training that he was missing. At that appointment, a scan of my lungs was conducted. He was looking for signs of possible bronchitis or walking pneumonia. "There aren't any signs of that," he told me.

This was supposed to be good news, but I wasn't reassured. I could barely get up and down the stairs in my own house. Despite the fact that the doctors hadn't identified any problems, I knew something was wrong and the lack of certainty worried me. Checking my wallet, I found the receipt for my CT scan. Borja was living at home at the time and I asked him to get a copy of the results and take them to Dr. Bernardo. As soon as he read the report, he saw a strange growth in the upper lobe of my left lung. The "nodule"—that was the term the doctors used—had officially entered my life.

Armed with that information, I went to visit a specialist at the Austral University Hospital, a huge medical center surrounded by a park and located on the outskirts of Buenos Aires. Things were beginning to get serious. The doctor informed me that the nodule could be either benign or malignant. If the latter was the case, it would have to be removed immediately, the risk being that the disease could metastasize and spread to other parts of the body. In my particular case, we couldn't be sure as to what sort of nodule it was, although its size and contours pointed to a strong possibility that it was malignant. Carefully, using measured words in response to my questions, the doctor offered more details. But his cautious and selective use of terminology left me suspicious.

"When you say 'nodule,' are we talking about cancer?" I asked.

"Yes," he replied. "And we have to operate now in order to remove it."

The lung, he explained, is like a sponge, and due to the location of my nodule, it would not be possible to remove a small part and sew up the incision. The entire left upper lobe would have to be resected. The good news was that, over time, the remaining part of the lung would expand like a balloon and fill in the affected area. The loss of lung capacity was expected to be significant at first before the body would compensate for it. I was skeptical about that, however. After an operation of that sort, I knew it would be difficult to continue my normal lifestyle, much less return to high performance sailing. But first an endoscopy would have to be performed to better understand the nodule, confirm the diagnosis, and determine the proper course of action.

A tube with a camera mounted on it was inserted through my throat, but the nodule was in an unreachable area. The conclusion, though, remained the same: the doctors would have to operate as soon as possible. That was the message the doctor delivered to me during the phone call that Friday afternoon. The operation was set to take place in just forty-eight hours.

I spent an anxious weekend worrying about the imminent intervention. Although the possibility that it was cancerous was unsettling, I was actually more concerned about the prospect of having major surgery only to later discover that the nodule was benign.

"In that case," the doctor told me during a consultation, "it's better to just celebrate the fact that you don't have cancer."

Sure, but I'd still be missing part of my lung, I thought to myself.

I realize that, to the doctors, surgery was the option involving the least amount of risk. If they operated and there was no cancer, it would cost me my lung. But if they didn't operate, and the cancer metastasized, the consequences could be tragic. Using this logic, the lung capacity of an average fifty-three year old patient was expendable. But in my specific case, it was vital.

My lungs are my engine. From them springs the energy that gives me the strength to sail, go for a bike ride with friends, or play squash with my children. They are the organs through which air enters my body... the very same air that fills the sails of the ships on which I feel happy and free. I recoiled from the thought, after a lifetime of breathing sea air, the purest there is on earth, my lungs were now damaged.

Before my first Olympics, the 1988 Summer Games in Seoul, all the athletes representing the Argentine delegation were given a lung capacity test. I remember my surprise and joy when my results were fifth highest overall. Breath control is something I've always had naturally, and I always liked to develop it further in my training. On a good day, I could spend five minutes underwater without coming up for a breath. And now they were about to remove a part of my lung?

On Monday morning I dragged all these doubts, along with the lingering hope that the tumor would turn out to be benign, to the hospital. I went through the pre-surgical procedures before meeting the doctor in his office.

"All ready?" he asked.

"More or less," I replied.

"What are you thinking?"

I told him I wasn't convinced about the need for immediate surgery. That I would rather do another endoscopy to find out the true nature of the nodule.

"But the operating room is already prepped," he argued.

"Let's put it on hold for now. We can talk later about how to proceed," I insisted.

A number of my friends who were aware of the situation thought that I was crazy, that I was taking too much of a risk by postponing the operation. True, the most reasonable course of action would have been to operate immediately, but I wasn't denying the disease nor opposing the treatment. I just wanted to make the decision only when I was certain that there were no other alternatives.

During the following appointments, I learned that the size, shape, and behavior of the nodule could indicate whether it was benign or malignant. At twenty-three millimeters, the size was a concerning though not a definitive clue. The possibility still existed that it wasn't cancer. Either way, if it grew, we would have to operate. The plan I proposed, and which the doctors agreed to, was to schedule periodic check-ups to monitor its behavior. Meanwhile, I'd look for the best specialist to treat me.

I admit I wasn't an easy patient. I questioned everything. As a designer, I'm used to measuring volumes 3D, and one of the first things I asked was how could they determine the size of the nodule, which was an asymmetrical ball. I wanted to know how the measurements were taken so I could be sure that comparisons with the previous exam were correct. I went to every appointment with the expectations that it would show a contraction, a sign that that the growth was benign. When this turned out not to be the case, I began analyzing all the variables, secretly hoping to find some mistake.

In addition to medical science, I turned to some more unorthodox healing practices, from dietary game plans to visualizations with Dani Espina. I was open to trying even the most alternative of remedies, and one of them involved Gabi Mariani, my old friend and former business partner at the Optimist shipyard.

Gabi had been through a similar situation, and he was one of the first people I reached out to about what was happening to me. I was interested in both his experience and his advice. I truly enjoyed his company, and I called on him to join me on the most unusual of my forays into the world of non-traditional medicine: a trip to a town in the Buenos Aires province where I'd be scanned by a machine of Russian origin which apparently had the ability to analyze the state of the body's various organs. We got an early start one morning and, during the trip, we laughed at the madness to which we were about to subject ourselves. Still, though, there was a part of me that wanted to believe in it. We picked up Dani Espina along the way and, when we arrived, we introduced ourselves to the man offering the therapy. In the living room of his humble town home, he explained to us that organs have a particular vibration that gets thrown off when they're sick like my lung was. His machine would read those frequencies and correct the ones that were wrong.

The Russian machine was basically an old laptop connected to some sort of sardine can. First the man asked me a couple of questions. Then he stuck some electrodes to my chest and asked me to press my right thumb against the can. Then, some 1980's-style sounds blared out, not unlike the theme song from Knight Rider with David Hasselhoff, and on the screen appeared the images of two lungs peppered with small little dots. A serious look came over the man's face; he studied the images for a few minutes in silence, and then declared that I was healthy. I left the place with the same questions I had when I walked in.

After lunch at Dani's place, Gabi and I headed back to Buenos Aires. We had a nice talk in the car. We're both tech fanatics, and we're obsessed with efficiency when it comes to industrial processes. And yet we had just indulged in the improbable magic of a Russian machine. We chalked it up to the stress caused by this sort of disease. We talked about life and the possibility of death, which comes for us all, no matter how many treatments you undergo.

At first, the diagnosis left me shocked and feeling powerless, but over time I began to accept it. The same sort of thing that can happen during a race, I told Gabi during that trip. In our sport, you can do everything right, gain a comfortable lead, and yet you are still subject to sudden changes in nature that can alter the results. It might sound odd to say this, but it's the truth: I didn't suffer from cancer. On the contrary, I took it simply as one more learning opportunity offered by life. When surprised by an unexpected gale in the middle of the sea, where there's no place to seek refuge, all you can do is adjust the sails and prepare the boat to weather the storm until it passes. From a young age we learn to accept the winds that come our way. If they're in our favor, great. And when they aren't, you have to find a different way to take advantage of them.

In fact you never really know if it's for better or worse. When I got divorced from Silvina, I went to see a philosopher of sorts recommended to me by Spanish friends of mine. I left with a phrase, an expression, really, which I truly identified with: "Bad day, good day, who can say?" What could be interpreted as bad luck today might just end up taking you on a higher path than the one you've been traveling along. It is, ultimately, good luck.

Except for Gabi and a few close friends, at first I was quite discreet with the news about my illness. Doctors still weren't certain about the diagnosis, and I didn't want to stir up any unfounded fears. I was always open with my children about having a nodule in my lung. I used the same little strategy as the doctors did and avoided using the word "cancer" during our conversations. Yago, the oldest, and I did have a somewhat deeper conversation. He came to me one day and told me he needed space to grow, that it was hard on him to share the space and atmosphere of the Olympic circuit with me. I told him I understood, but I also mentioned the health concerns that were going to keep me away from competitive sailing for a while. Yago listened concernedly.

I had a similar meeting with Ceci, Mateo, and Dani. I explained that I was going to step back from the campaign to recuperate and that they'd have to continue on without me. The idea was for Mateo to take my place as helmsman on board the Nacra. That way, Ceci could continue her progress, and the team hierarchy would be a more horizontal one. Up to that point, I'd been responsible for making almost all of the major decisions, so this forced hiatus would present a good opportunity for them to gain confidence and grow.

They agreed and ran in some events together. But things didn't always go their way. At a regatta in Weymouth, in southern England, they were barred from competing. The problem had to do with an archaic rule requiring the helmsman be the one who accumulated the necessary points during the first stage qualifying events. Ceci rightly argued that, as a crew member, he had recorded the same score as I had, but it fell on deaf ears. Along with Mateo, they decided they'd use that time to train, but unfortunately Ceci suffered another injury to her arm.

In July of 2015, I managed to find a break in my busy schedule of medical appointments and went to the Nacra World Championships, which were being held in Aarhus, the same Danish city where I had competed in the Optimist some forty years ago. I hadn't sailed in months and it showed. It was a demanding experience, things didn't go well for us, and tensions and conflicts began to reemerge. We tried again in September, this time in Barcelona, where the European Championships were going to be held. We arrived ten days early to train in an attempt to make up for lost time, but once again, my lungs ended up changing the plan.

My uncle Wolfgang had always the person I consulted when it came to health issues. After he died, I turned to Manuel Galofré, Edu's father. The Galofrés are like my family in Spain, and every time I visited them in their home in Cabrera de Mar, I was surprised by the seriousness of Manuel's vocation. On the weekends he'd lock himself up either to study or to welcome prominent figures in his field of expertise. Gonzalo, one of his other sons, inherited these virtues. Both of them are renowned general surgeons affiliated with the Hospital Quirón in Barcelona. When I went to see them, they added Dr. Laureano Molins, a preeminent thoracic surgeon with an impeccable resume, to the consultation. He had operated on Juan Carlos, the King of Spain, when he was dealing with an issue similar to my own.

The first thing they did was confirm that my Argentine doctors had been up to the task and that I had been in good hands thus far. After running their own tests, they agreed with the original diagnosis and recommended that I undergo an operation without further delay. Once again I asked about the advisability of having follow-up tests run every three months and not rushing to any conclusions. They weren't very inclined to agree with me, but they respected my concerns. I decided to continue my treatment with them.

Edu was an active participant in the entire process and helped me sort things out during those appointments with his father and brother. He was very supportive even though he found himself in the difficult position of being caught between my reasoning and that of his own family. Neither of us had any medical training, but we applied the same scientific rigor that we'd acquired in design school: we asked, we analyzed, and we questioned.

While I was training for the European Championships, I went to one of my scheduled check-ups. I'd gone sailing in the morning and the idea was to be back out on the water again the next day, but that wasn't to be the case. The doctors explained that the tests were still inconclusive, that we still didn't know whether the nodule was benign or malignant. That being the case, I insisted on my plan of waiting and watching. They, however, stood their ground.

Dr. Molins spoke first. He made it clear that I was out of time. Dr. Gonzalo Galofré then stepped in and emphatically explained that all my reasoning was correct, but if I continued to put off treatment, and if the nodule was cancerous, as they suspected, it could metastasize at any moment. By that point, it would be too late, and I wouldn't be at risk of losing my lung but losing my life. If we didn't remove it now, they concluded, there was a danger that we'd never be able to stop the disease from spreading. Dr. Manuel, his father, was the last to speak. He took me into a corner of his office and explained the same concerns to me in calm, sensible language. I understood that I no longer had any real choice. His opinion was identical to that of the very first doctor I consulted. The only difference this time was that I was finally ready. I had walked the path I needed to walk in order to make the decision.

"Alright then," I said to the three of them. "Let's operate."

Molins then asked me when I'd be ready to proceed.

"If we're gonna do this, let's do it as soon as possible," I said.

The surgeon looked at his schedule and proposed a date.

"I've got an opening in five days, on September 22nd."

I grinned.

"That's my birthday. If you don't mind blowing out the candles in the operating room, let's do it."

Chapter Fifteen

Wounded Lion

The night before the operation we had a cookout at the Galofré's house in the hills of Cabrera de Mar. It was a way of celebrating my birthday, and—just as it was during the old days in Southampton—Edu took care of the cooking. The European summer was coming to an end and a cool breeze was sweeping up from the Mediterranean. We set up a big grill in the yard and my friend prepared fideuà, a typical Catalonian dish similar to a paella. His version included fish stock, chicken, short toasted pasta, mushrooms, along with his magical secret ingredient: vegetables from their garden, where they grew the richest tomatoes I've ever tasted.

It was a joyous night and we joked about the operation I was about to have in just a few short hours. The previous day we'd gone out for a celebratory bike ride. "Santi's last with two whole lungs" was the joke that circulated among the group. There were around twenty people at the dinner, including Edu's family, the Marianis, Ceci, and Mateo. Also part of the festivities were Theo and my brother Sebastián, who both share the virtue of generosity and dropped what they were doing in Buenos Aires to be with me. As soon as we said goodnight, after having blown out the candles, Ceci organized the drive to the clinic. As committed as she was to her managerial skills, I agreed to the schedule she had set.

The next day, at the hospital, many of those who had been celebrating the night before now gathered in the waiting room. Pololo poked fun at my gown. Lying there on the gurney as the nurses pushed me towards the operating room, Theo squeezed my hand. "You're a fighter, Dad. Don't worry. Everything will go just fine," he whispered in my ear. I don't remember anything after that moment.

They waited for a long time. We'd been told the operation should last around three hours, but it ended up being closer to seven. In addition to Dr. Laureano Molins, Gonzalo Galofré was also in the operating room, which gave me much peace of mind. Around eight in the evening, Dr. Molins summoned the group to let them know that everything had gone according to plan and that I was in recovery. The reason for such a long operation was that they had first tried to remove only a very limited piece of my lung. I'd been skeptical of the doctor's prognosis of fully recovering my lung capacity, and had insisted that the procedure be as minimally invasive as possible. But the nodule was in a difficult area to reach, and ultimately they were forced to remove the entire upper lobe of my left lung. Dr. Molins took out a sheet of paper, drew a set of two lungs, and pointed to the affected area.

"I hope you're a better surgeon than you are an artist," Pololo interjected in the middle of the explanation. "Otherwise, my brother's screwed."

Molins is a serious, highly formal doctor, and I doubt that he appreciated my brother's sense of humor. Ceci noticed that Theo was crying, the concern and fear welling up inside of him. She embraced him. The procession then moved to the intensive care wing where, little by little, I was waking up from the anesthesia and looking out at the world again. Gabi Mariani was the first to walk by.

"How much did they cut out? How much did they cut out?"

Apparently I repeated that over and over again from the threshold of my consciousness.

When Ceci came in I pulled the respirator away from my face and asked her the same question. She saw me tearing up and she broke down. "It was like watching your dad cry, and dads don't cry," she said recently, reflecting on the moment. Theo saw me lying there, my face pale, my body hooked up to machines and pierced by probes. But what struck him the most was my voice: it had been reduced to a thread, because during the operations, they had nicked the recurrent laryngeal nerve.

"We're here, Theito," I said with a sigh.

The next few days were tough. Pololo and Theo were staying at a nearby hotel and they visited me often. Ceci and Mateo, who had taken my place at the helm of the Nacra, would stop by after their training sessions. But at night I was left alone. In pain, I would press the call button to summon a nurse. But it was all in vain. Without a voice, I couldn't be heard. Nor did I have the strength to press the toilet button. When the hospital bed became unbearable, I'd spend long hours sitting in the armchair in my room.

The operation coincided with Yago and Klaus' training in Buenos Aires. After their fight in Santander, had relaunched their campaign for the 49er World Championships, which were to be held at the Náutico in November of that year and which represented their chance to qualify for the Rio Games. We'd talked on the phone and I told them not to come. I explained that I was being well taken care of, and that the most important thing was that they prepare to the fullest for the competition. And that's exactly what they did, although the going was tough. Yago was stressed and dislocated his neck during a bad yoga pose. It was stiff for a month. "Fortunately I don't have to tell the story of how my dad died while I was trying to qualify for the Olympics," he said in a post-Rio interview.

Theo was in charge of recording videos of my recovery process to share during the family chats. In one of them I'm dragging myself slowly through the hospital corridors with Theo by my side. "Okay guys, here we are with the old man, already walking like a champ," he says with an imposing Spanish accent. "We're here," I said again, smiling to mask the pain. "This is how I'll be jibing in in the Nacra," I joked when, still very weak, I made an awkward turn.

My friends followed all the ups and downs in the wake of the operation from Buenos Aires. They set up a WhatsApp group with my brother Sebastián, who was in Barcelona, keeping them up to date and answering all their questions. Pololo sent photos from the barbecue the night before, at the Galofré's house, and my arrival at the hospital. The chat group became something of a chronicle, and the name was changed to Reporte Lange. Everyone chimed in with encouraging messages when they received the news that the operation had gone well.

Still hospitalized, I was given a device to help restore lung capacity, and I began a few exercises. It contained three marbles that I had to suspend in the air using my breath, and I closely tracked my progress. My focus was already on the Olympics.

After I was discharged, I settled back into my house in Cabrera. Reinforcements had come to join the team in the form of Borja and my brother Martín. The doctors had suggested I start by walking, so we went down to the coast to take advantage of the only flat stretch in the area. Between Cabrera and Villasar, the next town over, there's a path nearly three miles long that we traversed dozens of times. The weather was mild. On one side we had the beach and the sea, while on the other we had the silent tracks of the commuter train to Barcelona and, beyond that, the foothills of the mountains. Along the way is a sailing school, a restaurant specializing in Mediterranean cuisine, and a couple of beach bars that only open during the summer months. The first walks I went on were with Carmen Galofré, Edu's sister, for whom I had a great deal of affection ever since my days as a student in England. Sensitive and serene, she was the perfect companion for the occasion. We maintained a slow yet steady pace, and when I started flagging, we would stop to rest and contemplate the sea. I was still barely able to talk, so Carmen and the twins, who often joined in, had to lean in close to hear me. Nine days after the operation, I offered a proposal.

"We're going to have lunch at Bárbara's. But we're going to bike there."

Natural, the restaurant owned by Bárbara, Edu's wife, is located in Villasar. It's downhill from Cabrera, so we wouldn't have to pedal much. We ate from the vegetarian menu, and afterwards I felt strong enough to face the return trip. The beginning of the journey is flat, but after that it's an uphill ride. I pedaled steadily, silently, maintaining my focus and flanked by Martín and my two sons.

"You got this, Dad. We're here. You can do it," Theo whispered to me, his voice trembling with emotion.

His hand on my back helped me to climb.

At my next appointment with Dr. Molins, I asked him how hard I could push myself. He told me not to be afraid. The incisions from the surgery were healed. Ever since the start of my recovery process, he'd encouraged me to keep moving. "How far did you walk today?" he asked me during every check-up. I like this philosophy: there's no better cure for the body than motion. I also asked him when I'd be regaining my voice. He told me he wasn't sure about that. In fact, there were some patients who never fully recovered.

My friends from Cabrera—Edu especially—joked about my aphonia, but I didn't like it in the least.

From what I gathered from Laureano's response, my voice was the least of our concerns. Lab results had confirmed that the nodule was malignant. Later, over dinner, he and Gonzalo confessed to me that I'd been a particularly difficult patient. At first, they thought my procrastination was due to some inherent mistrust in their recommendations, but later they came to understand my reasons. I wasn't about to just abjectly surrender myself without question; I preferred to be an active patient trying to understand the whole picture, up to and including the limits of what might be advisable. I needed to be certain that I was doing the right thing. One other thing they explained to me was that my recurring colds were not related to the lung cancer. In order to be rid of them I'd have to go see another specialist.

The best exercise they could prescribe to strengthen my lungs and aid my recovery was the bicycle. We would go for rides across the flatlands, on the path that runs along the coast, as well as through the mountains. Our house was a paradise for cyclists, surrounded as it was by rugged forest roads virtually devoid of cars. When I started feeling better, more people—Ceci, Mateo, the Galofrés—joined in. While later the climb up mount Òrrius would become a classic—a record of times and speed rankings was kept—during those first few weeks, the spirit between us wasn't a competitive one. Rather, they were curative rides in which I healed my body and grew closer to Theo and Borja. With my mind still firmly set on the Rio Games, I put everything into those exercises. The twins gave me the love and support I needed during that stage of the game. Their presence helped me manage my obsession with speeding up my recovery.

Theo was already a cycling enthusiast. For him it was more than a simple means of transportation. He took to bikes the same way I took to boats: when he is riding, he turns off this thought processes and connects with the experience in its moment. Borja, on the other hand, only discovered the benefits of cycling after coming to Cabrera. He'd been a diligent and careful student who won the "Best Citizenship" award, but when he arrived in Spain he was coming out of a difficult stage in his life. He'd been working as a server at a restaurant in San Isidro when my brother Martín insisted he come stay with me in Spain. He sensed that it would be good not only for me but also for him. And that's how it was. Our company, and our bikes, helped him out.

The twins shared a bedroom until they were eighteen years old. They've always been very close. Conversations about ships quickly bore them. Unlike athletes, who usually focus on performance, Borja and Theo know how to enjoy things without looking for signs of progress in everything they do. That attitude called me to question my own ideas, enriching me. They educated me through their freedom. "You have to execute," Borja sometimes jokes, parodying one of my catch phrases.

Thanks to them, and to the time we shared on our bikes, healing became something pleasant, a haven of peace in my busy life. In those days we'd have profound conversations and we came to know and understand one another on a deeper level. At twenty-four years of age, the twins had left the typical adolescent conflicts behind. We were now three adults, each with his own interests and perspectives, but always willing to support one another.

The house in Cabrera was the scene where that family reunion took place. It sits on the side of a mountain, and the window on the main floor offers a magnificent view. In the distance, above the treetops, stretches the sea. We'd spend entire afternoons in that spacious room with the kitchen to one side and the fireplace to the other. We listened to music, we sat by the fire, we cooked, we drank mate, and we slept a lot. There were only a few excursions to the movies or to a restaurant in town. Over the years, the house became our home. Sometimes, when Yago and Klaus are competing on the European circuit, the five of us will all gather there.

Theo and Borja both liked Cabrera and decided to stay. Theo was there for a few years before returning to Buenos Aires, but Borja made it his home. He's a musician who started out playing the violin before dedicating himself to guitar, bass, and trumpet. He studied at the Conservatori Superior de Música del Liceu, in Barcelona, and pursued a career as a music producer. He works part time as a server, and last summer he bartended at a surf camp in Cantabria, in northern Spain, where he also performed his own music.

I tell him to be methodical and dedicated, to practice at least six hours a day to become the best guitarist possible, but he simply replies that you don't have to be the best, that there are no medals in art. Every so often he presses me to retire, suggesting that I buy a boat in which we can sail around the world as a family, or that I set up a design studio in Cabrera. "Some day," I reply with a laugh.

I certainly wasn't thinking about retirement on that fall day in 2015 when Martín took me to the doctor in Barcelona and we took the opportunity to stop by the club where Ceci and Mateo were competing in the European Championships. My old rivals came over to greet me and wish me a speedy recovery. "Look at that smile on your face," my brother mentioned as we set out in the Zodiac to watch the races. It was true. I was starting to feel stronger, and my Olympic dreams for the coming year were reborn.

The doctors had told me to wait at least a month before getting on board a plane. As soon as those four weeks passed, I caught a flight to Buenos Aires to go sailing with Ceci. I was also excited to see my sister Inés. The only woman in a family filled with men, the two of us have shared a special connection ever since we were children when I was her protégé. In a strange coincidence that mortified our mother, she had suffered from cancer around the same time as me. A tumor was found in her breast, and went through sixteen rounds of chemotherapy between April and October of 2015. We spoke often on the phone and accompanied one another in our respective recoveries.

Inés' first grandson—soon to be born to Carolina, my goddaughter—was expected to arrive in mid-November, and she wanted to be there in Italy, where Carolina lived, to help with the new baby. While I was pedaling through Cabrera with the date of the Rio Games etched in my mind, she went for walks in Bariloche, the city in which she lived, with the goal of recovering in time to travel to Italy. She succeeded, and while she was on her way to Buenos Aires to catch her flight, we met up at a gas station. We were two cancer survivors recently freed from the hell of treatments and hospitals—she without hair and me without a voice—and we embraced one another in relief.

On November 16th, the first heat of the 49er World Championships was run in San Isidro, where Yago and Klaus were looking to qualify for the Rio Olympics. That was the goal they'd set for themselves when they first mentioned to me the prospect of teaming up together. At the beginning of the boys' campaign, I was part of the team as coach, but my role overlapped with that of being a father. I took it hard when the results didn't come, and I lacked the coolness necessary to address their mistakes. They continued working with Bambicha on the physical side of things, while I suggested they approach Miguel Saubidet, his uncle, about the possibility of taking over as coach.

Miguel hesitated at first after receiving Yago's proposal. He'd retired from professional sailing some twenty years ago, after his successful stint at the helm of the Argentine Optimist team, and was now dedicated to his work and family. He was well aware of how much travel would be involved in preparing for the Olympics. But ultimately this was outweighed by his desire to work with his nephews and develop them as athletes and as people. A man of few words, Miguel imposed his own reticent style. Rather than spinning their heads with directions and training plans, he prefers to be patient and wait for the opportunity to make just the right point. That tranquility was key to dealing with a complicated, unsettled duo like Yago and Klaus.

Yago is organized and has a great capacity to put in work. I think our personalities are quite similar in that regard. When he finished school, he moved in with me. We enjoyed some great times together and got along quite well.

Klaus is more of an intuitive athlete. And he has tremendous potential, as I was able to verify personally when we raced together in the 29er World Championships in Mar del Plata. When he embarked on his campaign with Yago, he was still relatively young—barely twenty years old at the time—and was learning to add professionalism and methodology to his talent.

The boys were progressing at a breakneck pace and soon became the rising stars on the circuit. They were more than capable, but as siblings they had two work hard on their relationship and on how they would deal with the pressure. Due to their relative lack of experience, it was a challenge to perform during the critical moments, and to roll with the punches when the results didn't go their way.

Miguel was the one who convinced them that, after their fight in Santander, they would fulfill their obligations and compete in the final event they had slated on their calendar. It was in Rio de Janeiro, and the two of them traveled alone, without much in the way of either equipment or hope. Nobody—not even they—expected much from that regatta, which was going to serve as a virtual farewell tour. However, once the pressure had been cleared, their natural abilities shone through and they finished third. It was the first time they'd reached a podium, and they liked the feeling. Emboldened, they decided to address their difficulties in communicating with one another and relaunch their campaign.

Now, with the renewed possibility of qualifying for the Olympics, they understood the key would be to sail relaxed and to isolate themselves from the excitement that was swirling around the club, which had then been invaded by teams from all around the world. They were quite fast: a talent which they put on full display during their training sessions. What they had to do was keep the tension of racing from getting in the way. They stayed at Miguel's house and we talked a lot... at least as much as my recovering vocal cords would allow me.

Yago went to the Náutico with his headphones on without making eye contact. They prepared the boat without wasting any time, and they left the club as soon as everything was finished. Thus, sequestered from the hustle and bustle of the competition, the boys had a magical week. Halfway through the competition they found themselves in first place and ahead of the two previous Olympic champions. They didn't get fazed, they kept their eyes on the prize, and in the penultimate race they crossed the finish line with their objective complete. The finals would determine the medal winners, but they had already punched their tickets to Rio.

I pulled up to their boat in the Zodiac. I hugged Klaus first before Yago joined in. Euphoria gave way to excitement and we embraced in silence. Klaus couldn't stop crying and Yago was struggling to hold back the tears himself. That coming together there in the middle of the river represented the relief of having qualified for the Games and the release of the stress of the operation. The years we shared together were present there as well. Many times, as children, they had wondered what their dad did and why he traveled so much, but at that moment everything made sense. The Olympics had become a family affair.

Ceci and I went sailing again one Wednesday morning. There was a strong southeasterly wind: the kind that the spring often brings to Buenos Aires. My voice hadn't fully returned yet—my weak, nasal whisper was lost in the noise of the sails—and it was impossible to communicate on board the boat. I was quickly getting worked up, and my shortness of breath was keeping me from making good decisions. To make matters worse, Ceci had a sprained ankle and wasn't at full strength either. We decided to avoid complicated maneuvers altogether. Instead, we'd sail in a straight line to one side, brake so I could catch my breath, and then we'd execute some slow and meticulous turns.

Getting back on the water was a great joy for me, but it was also a tremendous reality check. Once again, we were facing our limitations as a team, but on top of that we now had the added aggravation of being in a race against time. The 2016 Rio Games would begin on August 10th, 2016, and we were far from the level we wanted to be at. I was still extremely weak. Plus, we were lacking in hours spent on the water and the pace that comes from competition.

I was only too aware of this, and challenged the team accordingly, but the pressure created tensions. Yago called me for lunch one day and told me that my anxiety was making things unbearable.

"It's hard being around you, Dad. You've got to dial it down a notch," he suggested.

And he was right. We weren't enjoying it. Something had to be done... and and done quickly. Everyone was called to a meeting at my house. Mateo, Bambi, and Dani Espina were there, as well as Cole Parada, who had joined the team to lend his own experience.

The conversation didn't get off to a good start. I was tough and to the point: I said we weren't progressing fast enough and that we were making the same mistakes over and over again. Even high-performance athletes have the occasional miscalculation, but what was unacceptable was not learning from them. Ceci countered by saying she couldn't accept the tone I used while expressing myself on board the boat, the way I was communicating my frustrations. She pointed out the fact that, regardless of whether they were specifically directed at her or not, my harsh language and looks of disgust were undermining her performance.

"If I get angry, it's only because I'm convinced we can do better," I clarified.

"But all that anger just isn't helpful, Santi. Actually, it's starting to be detrimental," she countered.

To me, the conflict ran deeper than a simple problem with the way in which we communicated. We would have to redouble our efforts and create an environment that would allow us to actually enjoy the process through which we were putting ourselves.

My suggestion, then, was to dramatically increase our commitment to training. We'd gotten off to a late start compared to the other crews, and on top of that we'd lost a year to my illness. We were playing catchup and there was barely any time left. We had to arrive in Rio at a level that would at least give us reason to hope for a medal. As I put it, there's an abyss between third and fourth place. It's the difference between standing on the podium and being left out. If we weren't willing to make sacrifices in order to achieve that goal, I'd rather just give up the campaign, I said in conclusion. Ceci affirmed that she had no intentions of quitting, and that she was willing to put in whatever work was necessary to get us out of the doldrums we were stuck in.

The rest of the team was in agreement, so I presented my proposal: move to Rio as soon as possible so we could train there for the nine full months left before the opening ceremonies. I figured this was the best way to both save money on flights and gain extra hours on the course on which we'd be competing.

Ceci was listening carefully. She understood this was a risky gambit, and she wasn't entirely convinced. In fact, this was a virtually unprecedented move. No other team would even think of doing something like this, she said. Moving to Rio that far out from the Games would put a lot of pressure on the relationships among team members, to say nothing of the fact we'd be isolating ourselves from our friends and families.

But that was the whole point of it, I argued. We had to invest our time in becoming a true team—a level I didn't think we'd reached quite yet—and disengage ourselves from any and all activities that didn't directly involve sailing. There would be no time for family reunions or barbecues with friends. I'd rather lose out on a medal because of the internal conflicts arising from having everyone in camp together for an extended period of time than I would because we showed up unprepared, I said.

Everyone participated in this discussion. We were making one of the most momentous decisions of the campaign, a decision that would ultimately determine our failure or success. As the captain of the team, I could have tried imposing my will, but that would have been a mistake. Ceci was the key to all of this, and she would have to assume it as her own. She still had her doubts, but in the end she decided to put her faith in my experience.

"Okay," she said. "We're going to Rio."

Her vote of approval released some of the stress of the meeting, and we were then able to move on to other questions of methodology and planning. At the end, before adjourning, we drew up a list of the teams who would most likely be challenging for a spot on the podium: the French, the Austrians, the Spanish...

"There's one team missing," interrupted Cole. "Us. We're not there yet. We're cornered. We have no choice but to fight for our survival. We're like a wounded lion that can strike the winning blow at any moment."

The analogy got us so excited that we changed the name of our WhatsApp group. From that day forward, it was called Wounded Lion.

Chapter Sixteen

Recovered Lion

The Urca neighborhood is concentrated on the narrow spit of land left by the famous Sugarloaf Mountain before it sinks into the sea. This quiet peninsula, cut off from the chaos of the rest of Rio de Janeiro, was the place we chose to spend our long, intense months leading up to the Games. While the rest of the teams continued to compete around the world, racking up thousands of miles in air travel, we settled down into our training routine. We got to know our neighbors and discovered our favorite shops. But the most important thing was that it was just a five-minute walk down a tree-lined promenade to the Iate Clube do Rio de Janeiro: our home base.

Once we were set up there, in December of 2015, we ran in a couple of competitions. They didn't go well for us, and there was little more than six months left before the Games. We agreed that Ceci could take four weekends to fly back to Rosario to visit her family. As for myself, I scheduled three days for interviews with journalists in Buenos Aires. The rest of our time would be spent right there in Rio. The plan, an extreme version of the old KGB training camps, was the only way we could close the gap between us and our rivals while I finished recovering from my operation.

Our schedule was tight. A typical day began with some yoga and a visualization session. Then came the physical prep work. Since she needed to add to her strength, Ceci would hit the gym. Endurance was my weak point, so my training involved not only the gym but the bike. I especially liked the climb up Corcovado mountain to the statue of Christ the Redeemer. I'd start out at five in the morning to avoid traffic and would reach the top just in time to watch the sunrise. Everyone would meet back at the house around eleven for a light lunch, a meeting with Mateo, and in my case a short nap before leaving for the club. We put in anywhere from three to five hours on the water a day. Later, back at the house, we'd shower, have a bite to eat, take stock of the day, and prepare for the next. We'd have another yoga session, dinner at eight, and everyone had to be in his or her room by nine thirty. When wind conditions prevented us from sailing, we'd work on the boat and on logistics.

In order to increase the time we spent sailing, we'd occasionally do our physical training out on the water, exchanging the gym for a maneuvering course in and around the ships anchored in the port. It was a space marked by fluctuating winds and tight spaces. The tacking had to be perfect and we had to be extremely careful not to collide with the larger boats or get caught up in their anchor chains. We did this at eight in the morning so as to avoid prying eyes. These exercises helped us to not only quicken our movements but also to learn to sail while thinking outside the catamaran. We were looking to develop our sensitivity and automate our adjustments so we could focus on what was happening outside the Nacra, on the oscillations of the winds and the movements of our rivals. On other days we'd sail at night. Those workouts, in addition to being as innovative as they were effective, put an entertaining new spin on our daily routine and helped us stay fully motivated. Nearly fifty years later, they reminded me of my adventures with Martín Billoch at the Yacht Club Argentino.

Ceci, Mateo, and I were the permanent residents in the house, and we each had rooms of our own. Dani and Cole joined in for periods of time that gradually became longer as the Games drew near. We had a garage which we used to work on the boats, and we plastered the walls with charts and Excel spreadsheets. It was there that we recorded the different configurations for the sails, masts, and boats themselves as we tested them, the procedures for each specific maneuver, the terminology Ceci and I would use to communicate in specific situations, and the combinations of wind and tide in each of the seven courses on which we'd be competing. We referred to these records as the Bible, and they became our home décor. In the few square inches of free space left, Dani stuck cards with mindful quotes written in black and red marker. He'd change them according to our mood. "Make sure your worst enemy isn't living between your ears," one of them warned. "Fate shuffles the cards. We play with them," another read.

Both Ceci and I had to lose weight (she was at 139 pounds while I tipped the scales at 157). This proved easier for me because I had no problems throwing some noodles together with butter and cheese when necessary. Ceci, on the other hand, took great care in her cooking and felt it was impolite not to include others when she prepared something to eat. But when she got tired of always being in charge of the menu, she started preparing individual meals for herself.

That house was our refuge. We didn't invite very many people inside. We could have a long, intense day out on the water, but dinners were always a pleasant time of camaraderie. Sitting there at the table, we ceased to be a high-performance athletic machine and became more like a family.

There was one day, however, when the weather got rough. During a training run that didn't go well for us, I had pointed out to Ceci that she'd made a mistake during a particular maneuver, to which she responded by calling out a poor tactical decision on my part. And while being wrong about a technical issue and making a bad strategical choice of which side of the course to run on are two very different things, I didn't respond. The disagreement confirmed to me that we still had very different points of view when it came to certain critical issues. I knew the problem wouldn't be fixed by either a talk or an argument at the time, but neither did I want to simply sweep it under the rug. I chose silence. The next day was the same: we lived and sailed together but we didn't talk. The day after that was no different. With the help of Mateo, Cole, and Dani, the opportunity to speak up and resolve the conflict finally presented itself. It would be the last one we'd have during our preparations. There were only a few weeks left before the Games, and there was no time to waste on fighting amongst ourselves.

Our training partners were the Danes, the Swiss, and one of the Brazilian crews, João Bulhões and Gabriela Nicolino, who helped with local logistics. Many teams would finish their training and sail to shore feeling rested and relaxed. But we wanted to take advantage of every moment we had, and to better motivate ourselves, we set up a competitive little race around the club with João and Gabriela. The ships at anchor in the port, combined with the unsteady winds, added an extra layer of complexity. We kept a daily record of results and nobody was willing to ease up in the slightest. It was a game, but a challenging one that generated the pressure needed to perform well.

These sessions helped us measure ourselves against our rivals, but when they left Rio, we were left alone with the Brazilians in our

Rio retreat. Far from slowing down, we instead spent those days making detailed adjustments to the maneuvers in which we'd been bested. If we were having trouble calculating our approach to the various buoys, we'd practice for days until we began to notice significant improvements.

In our first series of training races we were awkward and slow. We couldn't beat anyone. Two months later, when the Olympic qualifiers returned to Brazil, we were already in the middle of the pack and, on some occasions, nipping at the heels of the leaders. By the third practice session, in April, we were winning races, having established ourselves as one of the fastest teams in the fleet.

There was one maneuver in particular, however, that continued to cost us. Speed jibing—quick changes in direction with the wind coming from stern—is critical in a catamaran. The boat is sailing at flank speed, leaping over the waves, and if the maneuver fails, all the momentum is lost and it's very hard to get back up to speed. Errors in execution caused us to lose our position in many of our races. Jibing requires coordination and athleticism. Since I was having trouble bending down, I was lacking in my agility. Ceci was having trouble finding her balance at the end of the move, when she swings from the lower side to the higher side of the boat hooked in her harness. Our execution was uneven at best. We worked hard, both on the water and in visualization exercises with Dani, but still we didn't feel like we were progressing fast enough.

One morning in May we'd agreed to a training session at noon, so we left at ten to get in some early practice. The conditions were ideal: the wind was coming out of the south at around fifteen miles per hour and the surface of the sea was calm. We started out with a tailwind from Ilha da Laje, a small rock formation in the middle of the bay, to the Niteroi bridge. Cole was operating the Zodiac and

Mateo would signal it was time for some speed jibing with a whistle. We got through the first few without any problems and were gaining confidence. The whistles increased in frequency, but we stayed coordinated and got into a rhythm. Ceci, the boat, the sails, the sea, the wind, and myself all became a sequence of movements in harmony with one another. Over the span of about half an hour, we completed roughly forty speed jibes, all of which were tightly executed and free of errors.

After the last maneuver, underneath the bridge, we turned the Nacra into the wind and embraced in the certainty that our efforts had not been in vain. The move to Rio had given us the chance to win our race against time, and now we were a fully-fledged team, confident and ready to compete. The energy from that hug would stay with us through to the end of the final race of the Games. Mateo looked on with pride from the Zodiac. Cole says it was one of his happiest moments as a coach, and that the hug meant as much to him as any Olympic medal.

That night I invited the entire team out to dinner to celebrate. We renamed our group chat as Recovered Lion, cracked open an ice-cold beer, and I proposed a toast.

"At the Games, there will be around eight teams competing for a medal," I said. "And we are now one of them. We've punched our ticket!"

My conviction was due to our near perfect speed jibing workout, to the confidence we'd gained from our training races, but above all to the progress I saw on the charts and tables that adorned our house. A special section of wall was dedicated to tracking our mistakes, and the objective was to eventually find it empty. This isn't to say that we'd never do anything wrong again, but what it did mean was that we were able to complete a full race from start to finish without any miscues.

A month before the Games began, we moved into an apartment closer to the Olympic marina, the venue for the sailing competitions. It was our way of marking a clean break from the long and arduous preparatory course that we'd been on up to that point. We had to shift from training mode into competition mode. The change of environment marked the end of a stage, and would provide a bit of a refreshment to the team. The apartment was smaller than Urca's house, and all five of us—Ceci, Dani, Mateo, Cole, and I—settled into what would be our quarters until the end of the competition. Our new home was the sacred place in which we would prepare for battle.

That was the time when Galarza came, along with his wife, María Inés. We'd discussed the possibility of moving him in with us for the last phase of the game, but his mother had been ill and we were forced to make do with a weekend visit. Despite the fact that we hadn't lived together since the 2008 Beijing Games, we immediately picked back up with daily life. Galarza brought a touch of warmth to our state of coexistence. While we could have functioned without him, he was the last piece of the puzzle that was our winning formula, and we missed him dearly when he left. Two weeks after Galarza left, I was walking around the club with him on my mind when my phone rang.

"Good morning, Comrade Lange. Comrade Galarza here, reporting for duty!"

"Mariano, what a surprise! Where are you?"

"I just landed in Rio. I couldn't help but notice the guys were looking a little hungry and I thought I might be able to help. I'll grab a taxi and be right over."

The final decision we had to make was selecting the materials with which to compete. Unlike the Tornado, there's no room for tweaking the design on a Nacra. We all use the sails, masts, and boats that the supplier sells us. But there are always certain differences, and the key to success is figuring out the fastest combination based on the expected wind and wave conditions. For Rio we had three boats, eight masts, and around fifteen mainsails—the biggest one—but we could present only one single outfit for the official measurements. We had no problems with the boat and the mast. But when it came to choosing a mainsail, on the other hand, there was a lot of doubt in our minds.

We identified each with a number on an ascending scale according to their date of manufacture, and the one we liked the most was the M1. It was the first sail we bought, the one we trained with, and the one with which we finished second at the World Cup in Santander. But it was old, and due to the effects of wear and tear, there was a distinct possibility that it might break. This concern forced us to use it sparingly in the days leading up to the start of the Games, a fact which complicated the set-up and tuning of the boat. A third drawback was the fact that this particular sail was very fast in light to medium wind conditions, but in strong winds it was significantly less efficient.

Although the choice of materials with which to compete had to be made by the team as a whole, I was the one it ultimately came down to. Towards the end of our selection process, we went out for a test run with Mati Bühler, bringing with us both the M1 and the M15, our other top candidate. We tried the M15 first, and found that Mati and Nathalie had a bit of an advantage over us. When we tried the M1, we began to impose our will on them instead. That was all the confirmation we needed. I marked the weak areas of the sail with sky blue tape and we sent it to a sail shop in Buenos Aires to be reinforced.

We had already decided to compete with the M1 when Elena's forecast for the games came in. It was bad news: they were predicting two very windy days. If the forecast turned out to be correct, racing with the M1 was saying goodbye to the medal podium. But there was still just over a week before the start of our competition, and forecasts are always subject to change.

I spent the next three nights unable to sleep. I was well aware of the fact that, after months of preparation, winning a medal depended heavily on choosing the right mainsail. If you're fast, you might win and you might not, but at least you're in the race. If you're slow, victory is out of the question. A later, updated forecast dampened the expectations of wind and encouraged us to stick with our decision. We'd be going for gold with our dear old M1.

During those months in Rio, in addition to getting the boat ready to be as fast as possible, we also got ourselves physically ready to compete. Both our technique and our equipment were prepped to the fullest. Confident in the work we'd put in, all that was left for us to do was sail calmly and execute. We decided to take a couple of days off. Cole flew to Europe for a big vessel championship. Mateo took his girlfriend for a walk around Rio. Ceci was so motivated that she cancelled a scheduled trip to Rosario so she could stay and work with Dani.

I returned to Pedro Bulhões' Casa dos Ventos in Buzios. It was three days of solitude and introspection during which I barely spoke to anyone and didn't use the phone at all. Instead I'd visualize segments of the race, writing down strategies on napkins as a way of mentally preparing myself for the competition. I tried to keep my mind clear and focus only on the essentials, the most basic concepts that would have me performing at my best. There was also some yoga, I went for a run, and did a bit of walking. One night I had fish for dinner at one of the bars on Manguinhos Beach. The season was over and the place was almost empty. As a lone musician played bossa nova classics on his guitar, I realized that I was ready. I was ready for what was to come.

When I returned to Rio, the rest of the delegations were starting to settle in and make their own final adjustments. There was an Olympic feeling in the air. Yago, Klaus, and Miguel rented a house five blocks from ours and we organized a barbecue to welcome them, but everyone was focused on their own tasks to be done. I asked them if we could march together in the Opening Ceremonies. It's one of the things I had enjoyed most in my previous Games, and I was excited to share that experience with the boys. I'd been thinking about the moment for over a year, ever since an English journalist interviewed me at the Maracana stadium, where the Opening Ceremonies would be taking place. When I was a young boy, all the dreams I had of sailing were of world championships and ocean crossings. Never did I imagine the possibility of entering the Olympic stadium as part of the Argentine delegation alongside two of my children. We were a family, and we were also three athletes ready to represent our country.

That day found me in equally captivated and aggravated. I wanted the three of us, plus Ceci, to march together during the Parade of Nations. The boys' eyes were popping out of their heads in awe of all the elite athletes around them. Klaus was commenting on the outfits worn by the various delegations, and Yago was trying his best to keep all his emotions in check. During the bus ride and while congregating with the rest of the Argentine athletes, the rousing soccer chant of "Vamos vamos Argentina" broke out, but Yago was deeply immersed in a long conversation with Sergio Hernández, coach of the basketball team.

August 10th, 2016, was the first day of sailing of the Games. It was a set of twelve contests over the course of four days involving the entire fleet. The fifth and final day was designated as the medal race which would be contested among the top ten teams. Two days of rest were also factored into the schedule. With so many races on seven different courses, one bad result was bound to happen. The key to success lies in the ability to recover. This long style competition rewards perseverance.

We started on the course laid out at the foot of Sugarloaf Mountain in a part of the bay we knew by heart. It was here that we had raced against our Brazilian friends back to the club after training sessions. It was a day of low but shifting winds, which would force us to be ever vigilant. We flew off the line and took an early lead. This was a regatta involving plenty of maneuvering, which gave my younger and more agile competitors an advantage, but still we were able to hold onto the lead for most of the race until we found ourselves in a windless patch of water. We watched, powerless, as other crews with better wind passed us by while we hobbled home in eleventh place. With no time for critiques or criticisms, we approached the second race of the day with the weight of that first bad result on our shoulders. And we responded well. We got off to a difficult start, but we hit the right marks and nailed all our maneuvers. We passed the Greek crew right before the finish line for second place. Right from the very first day of the competition, we proved we had the mettle to recover and respond.

The next day we faced the dreaded high wind conditions. On top of that, during the first race of the day, we made a mistake very uncharacteristic of us in a major competition: we aimed for the wrong buoy and had to retrace part of the course, the result being we finished thirteenth. But we responded well yet again and followed it up with another second-place finish. The third and fourth races of the day, which would be our weakest, resulted with us finishing twelfth and a sixth.

Friday, August 12th, was a day of rest. Cole and Mateo looked after the ship while at night Galarza worked his magic and relaxed us with a memorable meal and several of his famous stories. We were smack in the middle of the competition, and while we'd shown our speed and ability to overcome bad situations, we were still lacking a victory. Ceci worked with Dani and envisioned us winning a race.

On the third day, the competition moved outside the bay. There were moderate winds and big waves: my favorite conditions. It was exactly what we'd planned for when we chose the older mainsail. This was our chance to make an impact, and we did. We finished the three races first, sixth, and ninth. We went to sleep that night in second place in the overall standings.

And then there was the fourth and final day of competition before the medal round. With three races scheduled, we were entering the defining stage of our event, and pressure was beginning to become a factor. And we couldn't have gotten off to a worse start: we were disqualified from the first race for starting early. Each crew is allowed to discard their worst result, so we wouldn't have to add those points to our scorecard, but that left us with two remaining tests and no room for error. If we wanted a medal, we'd have to do everything right. Because of the wind conditions, these races would come down to the tiniest details. The Australian crew of Jason Waterhouse and Lisa Darmanin had just secured their third outright victory and were locked in to first place.

Before the second race of the day, we spoke with Cole and Mateo to determine our starting strategy. Our options were limited. If we were overly aggressive, we'd run the risk of another early start, but if we took a more conservative approach, it would be harder for us to be among the first off the line, which is what we needed if we were to get back in contention. Mateo proposed starting near the Olympic officials' motorboat and angled towards the right side of the course, which is one of the alternatives we had trained for. That would force us to let all boats heading in the other direction pass, but it also ensured that we wouldn't be passed ourselves. It also took us to the side of the course on which we wanted to sail. It turned out to be a great decision. We crossed the finish line in second place, just behind Mati Bühler.

Still, though, we faced the same pressure for the final race of the day. We couldn't afford any mistakes, and decided to adopt a similar strategy. Most of the top teams had decided to veer to the left, making the first leg a test of pure speed, an aquatic horse race to see who could break out and cross the line ahead of the rest of the fleet. We started well and fought for every inch of the way with Mati and Nathalie. Suddenly we found ourselves with a bit of an advantage: we saw a gap and we went for it. The move worked. We got to the buoy first, maintained our lead throughout the race, and won. Mati and Nathalie were never able to catch us, and in fact collided with the Brazilian crew, resulting in a penalty and a tenth-place finish.

The fallout from all of that was this: at the end of the day, we were alone atop the standings—the first time we'd occupied first place—with a five-point margin over second place.

There was a strong storm on the day off before the championship final. I was worried about Yago and Klaus, who were competing on one of the open ocean courses. I went to see them at the marina, and was relieved and happy to hear they'd had a great day and were in fifth place in the standings. I washed their boat so they could go and meet with the press. Upon their return, we learned that the Irish team had filed an appeal against them. The appeal was granted, meaning Yago and Klaus were officially disqualified from that race, their seventh of the competition. I returned to the apartment with a heavy heart. Competitive sports is a ruthless business in which a single number determines the merits of your effort. I had dinner and went to bed early. I was expecting a long day ahead of me.

Chapter Seventeen

Work Your Magic, Old Man

Last. That's the position we find ourselves in minutes after the start of the medal race, the defining test of the Rio de Janeiro Olympic Games in which only the top ten remaining teams compete. Yesterday, as we were preparing for this championship final, where scores are doubled, we had analyzed possible combinations of results. We were atop the leaderboard, and our five-point lead over the second-place team had left us in a very good position for winning the gold. In fact, if we finished in the top three, the gold was ours. After that, everything depended on the results of our rivals. We agreed that I could concentrate on tactics while Ceci would assume the task of monitoring the positions of the ships during the race.

Still, there was no mathematical equation for solving the disastrous position in which we found ourselves. Seconds before the start of the race, a poor maneuver by the English team triggered a cascading series of events that ended with a penalty being handed down from the judges against us. We hadn't committed any infraction—the ruling was entirely unfair—but there's no arguing in sailing. We do the penalty turnaround, after which I confirm the magnitude of our disadvantage: the rest of the fleet is far, far ahead of us. The race is a relatively short one—no more than twenty minutes—and there's no time for regrets. All we can do is sail well, better than we ever have, and put everything into our recovery. The unsteady, shifting winds will provide us with opportunities to attack.

I check to see if my coordination with Ceci is still intact, and indeed she is tending to the sails and attentive to the speed of the boat. I look up and analyze the course, looking for signs that might allow us to reach a patch of better wind before the rest of the fleet. When you're last, desperation can cause you to take extreme measures and tempt you into taking the opposite side of the course as your rivals. More often than not, this is a bad decision. The time for risks must only coincide with the appearance of an opportunity. We trained with Dani for years to get through situations like this without letting our minds fool us with false hopes.

Steadfast, we hold out for quite some time, only making up ground on the fleet when we spot a gust of wind. The tactic works. We're still in last place when we reach the first buoy, but we've caught up with the pack. Now we can look to attack.

"Both options are open," I announce to Ceci as we approach the mark. This means I still haven't decided on which side of the course we'll be running the second leg of the race, when the wind will be at our backs. We can either stick to the path we're on, or we can jibe and go left.

Ahead of us, most of our rivals are breaking to the left, and I see an opportunity. We're near Sugarloaf, our regular training grounds. The long months we spent sailing in these waters help me to see, off to the right, a gust of wind that can save us.

"Let's go, Ceci!" I yell.

"Work your magic, old man," she calls back, well aware of the fact that, by separating ourselves from the rest of the fleet, we're taking a huge gamble.

"It's okay, we're doing great."

With good wind and a good angle, jibing is the key now. We need to hit it at just the right point that allows us to reach the next buoy at full speed without having to make any new maneuvers. At first, this is a challenge for us, but our practice pays off and the results are perfect. We converge on the marker with the rest of the fleet: our gains are enormous.

At that moment, a new danger presents itself. Mati and Nathalie are approaching with the right of way, and the crossing is going to be a matter of inches. I grit my teeth and we pass with barely any room to spare. Mati could have raised a flag in protest, but it could have gone either way, and he chooses not to.

We finish the turn in fifth place. My goal is to keep passing boats until we're in the top three, guaranteeing us the gold. And in fact, we were already in a winning position. But due to the intensity of the situation, Ceci doesn't realize it. Based on a lack of information, we continue to attack when we should be concentrating on defense.

At one point, Ceci sticks her head out of the boat to locate our rivals and figure out our position.

"Just worry about speed," I tell her.

We continue gaining ground, passing the French who were in fourth. We reach the next buoy in a very close contest with the Austrians for third place. They have the right of way.

"Don't push it," Ceci says.

"We're passing them," I insist.

Ceci doesn't argue. There's no time for debate, and it's always the helmsman who makes the final call in these tight situations. My obsession with taking over third place is causing me to make a serious mistake. If we let the Austrians pass and remain in fourth place overall, we would still take home the gold. But Ceci doesn't tell me this, and I don't know.

We cross in front of the Austrians, and during the turn we force them to change their course: a foul on our part.

"Don't protest, Tom! Please don't protest!" I plead with Thomas Zajac, the Austrian helmsman.

I've known him for years. He was part of his country's junior Tornado team when we were training with Hagara and Steinacher, but my pleas fall on deaf ears. He pulls the red flag out of his life jacket, and I prepare myself to hear the judge's damn whistle announcing that we'll have to do a second penalty turnaround before continuing on to the finish line.

We're still very close to the Austrians, and maneuvering gets messy. Both crews are jibing almost simultaneously, and this time they're the ones who put themselves in a risky situation. I take the opportunity to raise my own red flag in protest. The judges are still focused on our penalty and don't see the one committed by Tom and his crewmember Tanja Frank, but the confusion helps us save a few seconds of precious time. A whistle blows yet we continue racing. The rule states that the penalty turn must be completed as soon as the judges call the foul, but since there were two protests, it isn't clear whether the call is against the Austrians or against us.

"Santi, it's us. We have to come clean," Ceci tells me when she sees the race official pointing the flag at us. Timing is critical. The judges could disqualify us if they think we're delaying the execution of the penalty turnaround.

A sudden noise grabs my attention. I look back and confirm that one of our rudders is up. I'm losing control of the catamaran. We've hit some of the plastic that floats throughout Guanabara Bay. It has happened to us dozens of times in training and we know how to respond, but it's not easy. I hunker down and look back, steadying the boat while trying to jam the rudder back into position. Only on my second attempt do I manage to get it hooked back into place.

Now we do lower the spinnaker and begin the penalty turn. Ceci arranges the sails to speed up the process. We execute the maneuver to perfection, much better than the first one.

From the Zodiac, Cole looks at the list of results and crunches some numbers. Through his binoculars, Mateo tries to figure out who's in the lead. Our chance at victory—and everything else—depends on that.

"So? Is it Australia or New Zealand?" Cole asks.

"I don't know, I can't tell. The flags are almost identical," Mateo responds nervously.

Cole looks up and sees Dani sitting in the other end of the boat with his eyes closed. He smiles as he murmurs what sounds like a prayer.

"What is he, some sort of alien?" he askes Mateo.

We pass the final buoy in the middle of a tight grouping. All that remains is the final attack on the finish line. We cross the line in sixth place with no idea whether we've won gold, silver, bronze, or nothing at all. We look for any indications around us, but the confusion is widespread across all the teams. Cole, Mateo, and Dani are in the Zodiac, confined to a remote section which they cannot leave until the final competitor crosses the line.

"I think we're silver," Ceci says with a heavy heart.

She's convinced that Australia has won the medal race and snatched victory from us. She understands that our second penalty cost us a certain victory, and she regrets not having been able to gauge the positions of our rivals and see where we were sitting. That would have allowed her to indicate to me that we didn't need to pass the Austrians after all, that we could let them pass before us and sail calmly towards our triumph.

The Australian team embraces, celebrating what should be their Olympic victory. The sight of them celebrating confirms to me that we've lost. I went for all the glory and came away empty-handed, with nothing to show for it. Surely we have also missed out on silver and bronze, I think to myself. We've fallen into that terrible abyss of fourth place: the first of those for which there is no trip to the podium. With the adrenaline from the race still coursing through my veins, I process the information without any emotions. I am neither sad nor angry.

The roar of an outboard motor yanks me out of my thoughts. The coaches have finally been released from their holding pen, and Cole, Mateo, and Dani pull up, euphoric.

"Gold! It's gold!" Cole shouts.

"You won the gold!" cries an Argentine journalist who's approaching in a second boat.

"Gold? Are you sure?" I ask Cole.

Ceci grabs me in celebration without fully understanding the situation.

"What about Australia?"

"They finished second. It was the New Zealanders who won," Mateo replies, extending his hand to pull the boat closer.

Ceci puts her hands to her head and collapses into a hug with Mateo, which is quickly joined by Cole and Dani. The four of them celebrate as I stretch out my body and reach for the sky. I feel like I could levitate. I am completely at peace. Twenty-eight years after my Olympic debut, I've finally made it. After just a few seconds of solitary celebration, Dani snatches me out of my reverie with an embrace.

"I love you," he tells me.

On our way back to the marina, we sail past the grandstands filled with spectators that had been set up on the beach. We weave our way through a maze of boats and launches. As we wave to the crowd, Ceci points out a couple of figures swimming towards us. It's Yago and Klaus. They're still in their racing uniforms and struggling to make it across the wide strip of water separating the coast from our catamaran. It seems to me that they must be violating some sort of rule, but everyone is overflowing with too much joy to care. We haul them on board and I hug them both. Two of Ceci's friends, Juan Pablo Bisio and Nicolás Schwindt, are also swimming towards us. After celebrating with them, Ceci wraps us tightly in her arms as we stammer out a few words of excitement and gratitude. When we calm down again, I ask the boys how it went with them. They had just finished their last day of general racing and had been on the verge of qualifying for the medal race.

"We made it!" Yago exclaims.

"Hell yeah!" I shout.

Once we hit land, a full on festival of hugs and congratulations breaks out. Theo is there and shares in the euphoria. Borja will be arriving tomorrow. Galarza greets me with a sapucai: the joyful cry of the gauchos from Corrientes, a tradition he inaugurated at the Athens Games when we won our very first Olympic medal. My brother Sebastián reminds me that he's still undefeated: he's come to three of my Olympic competitions, all of which resulted in medals. My mother is making her debut as a triumphant Olympic spectator, as was my brother Martín. Ceci's family and many friends are also part of the festivities. The WhatsApp group that Sebastián had set up with my schoolmates during my operation in Cabrera is blowing up again amidst the celebrations.

Ceci pressures one of the volunteers for the chance to take a shower before the medal ceremony. I have to go through the anti-doping control process, and everyone's heads are spinning, but during the few minutes of down time we have, I talk to her.

"I'm going to give you the same advice that Camau gave me when I won my first medal," I tell her. "Pay close attention and remember to enjoy this moment, because it's all going to happen so quickly."

The ceremony is set for sunset on a stage on the beach surrounded by hills and palm trees. Ceci rests her hand on my shoulder as the Australians and Austrians are awarded the silver and bronze medals, respectively. Then she whispers something in my ear just before it's our turn. I don't recall the exact words, but what I do remember is that it made me turn to look at her and smile. Arm in arm, we step up on the podium. Ceci is beaming. As the Argentine national anthem is being played, I place my hand over my heart and close my eyes. After two bronze medal finishes, I finally have the enormous pleasure of seeing our flag flying above all others. A tear trickles down a wrinkle that years of surf and sun have etched on my face.

We celebrate long into the night with a group of Brazilians and Argentines at the Iate Clube, which has been our headquarters for the last few months. I'm exhausted. When I finally get home, my head continues to spin with the emotions of the day.

I set the gold medal on my nightstand, lie down, and try to sleep. But all I do is toss and turn. The feeling of culmination that has been with me since our triumph has yet to leave. My body needs rest and sleep, but another part of me wants to prolong the feeling as much as possible. I relive the moment when we took risks and passed five boats on the downwind stretch of the race, the vertiginous near collision with Mati Bühler, the infinite waves of joy that washed over me when it was confirmed that the gold medal was ours. I'm looking to record each and every image from this day in my mind, and to feel this way for the rest of my life.

The next morning, I wake up early and turn on my phone to call some friends, but it keeps buzzing and buzzing with requests for interviews. I decide to turn it off for the time being and have some breakfast. Ceci is the first to appear in the kitchen.

"Ready for the 2020 Tokyo Games?" I ask, offering her the day's first cup of mate.

Epilogue

The gold medal from Rio represents the realization of a dream I'd pursued for quite some time. That spot on the Olympic podium not only marks the peak of my career but it's also tied to the most important decisions I made in my life. Without my realizing it, the line dividing my days on the water and my days on the land was beginning to blur. For that reason, when the medal was draped around my neck, I felt that my entire life's story was coming together at that very moment.

For many, the crowning achievement of my career was a happy ending. It's a completely reasonable thought. However, I have always known that the show must go on, even if everyone told me I was crazy. I'd heard the same thing years ago when, having already retired once from my Olympic career, a young athlete came knocking at my door in search of advice, and instead I suggested we sail together. Without that sudden, crazy impulse, Rio never would have happened. And Rio, in turn, confirmed my commitment to keep on doing what I love to do. It's not about the medal. I've already got it. But when I'm on the water, my mind is empty and free and time comes to a stop. I feel a wave rising under the hull, a slight variation in the wind, the tightening of the rudder indicating a need to change course or trim the sails, and everything else just melts away.

I've been competing for fifty years. Early on, after a victory, the joy would stick with me for a month or so. If I lost, I'd spend that same period of time turning my frustration over and over in my mind. A long athletic career has allowed me to understand that the true value of sports lies not in winning. What's driving us toward the Tokyo Games, my next goal with Ceci, is the same thing that drove us to Rio: improving ourselves. Stone and Road, as Yupanqui says in his folk song. Keep moving forward and learn from the obstacles that appear along the way.

Would we have won gold in Rio without the stone of disease? It's impossible to say. My health problems were an Everest that we had to climb. There was no choice but to go out and conquer it. Our success gave us a wealth of confidence. And at the same time, a life of athletics had prepared me to face the disease. Especially when it comes to the sport in which I compete. With sailing, you're in nature's hands. You're in the hands of the wind, the waves, the tides: superior forces that are far beyond our control and which must be accepted. There is no other alternative than to recognize yourself as vulnerable.

I remember a thought I had during the days I spent recovering from the surgery in Cabrera de Mar. It was in the middle of one of those first bike rides I did with my children through the narrow streets climbing up the mountain. I was still very weak. I felt what seemed like centuries of fatigue bearing down on me, and I had the sensation that the machine—my body—could explode at any given moment. Was it unwise of me to demand so much from myself? Was I putting my life at risk? Regardless, we had to press onward. Because there was also a strength, a passion, that was washing over me.

For me, there was no beginning to my love of boats. It was simply always there. I first experienced it as a game. Then came the competitions in which I learned to seek excellence more than mere results. It's all there: determination, demand, perseverance. All the values I'd taken on naturally turned out to be those of the Olympic spirit itself. It's no coincidence that the Games have taken on such a significance for me.

There are two other Olympic values with which I closely identify. One of them is respect. First comes self-respect, which I believe I showed when I followed the path of my ideals and my freedom. Then there's the respect you show to your rivals, who drive us to always give just a little bit more in the spirit of competition. And, finally, there's the pride I feel when representing Argentina, and the love that a job well done arouses in me. Those are forms of respect as well.

Friendship, the third Olympic value, has defined me ever since I was a child. At the Games, it signifies the fellowship of athletes over their differences, whether political, economic, racial, or religious. But, for me, friendship also has a more intimate meaning. My friends represent the foundations of me as a person. Since the days of elementary school, they've been with me for every step along the journey of my life. Or, rather, we've accompanied each other through thick and thin, through the joys and sorrows, recognizing each other in the changes time has brought. Some time ago, we also learned to love one another in our differences. I'm proud of the friends I have who have forgiven me for the absences which my life as a sailor has imposed upon me (and them), and who welcome me, every time I return home, as if I never left in the first place. I learned, from that first friendship, how to make new ones in every port.

The most solid of all things, the rock I cling to for balance, are my children, all of whom taught me how to experience true love. Many times, when I felt lost in the middle of rough seas, they were the beacon that charted my course.

I thought of them when the idea of writing this book first came up. It was an opportunity for me to talk about many things they never knew about their father. I was excited about the project, but quickly realized I'd gotten myself into a bit of a jam. The first attempts at having a German journalist write it were unsuccessful. How to explain the color of the Río de la Plata or the hardness of the cobblestone streets of my suburban neighborhood.

We needed an Argentine writer. After a brief search, we were lucky to find Nicolás Cassese, who immediately got to work. We had long conversations, both in Buenos Aires and at a distance, and he started putting in the legwork, interviewing dozens of people in order to reconstruct the events of my life. In time, he sent me the first two chapters. As I read them a sense of strangeness came over me. It was hard to recognize myself in the person narrating a series of events that didn't happen in quite the same way in my memory.

I called Héctor Guyot, a childhood friend of mine and, like Nico, a journalist for the newspaper La Nación. I emailed him the chapters and the next day he came over to my house. "You're in very good hands," was the first thing he told me. We spent the morning talking about the book and those first two chapters. Héctor told me I could count on him as a consultant and as a reader as the book progressed. We were already in the process of hiring an editor, but right then and there I brought him on board to add one more perspective.

A few days later, Nico, Héctor and I traveled to Corrientes where the members of the KGB had gathered again. Beyond just the information to gather, I wanted both of them to get to know the team spirit that has been so fundamental in my career. We spent three incredible days together and, by the end of that trip, we had started to form a new team—a team of writers—that would hone its own method of advancing, chapter by chapter, through the adventure of narrating this story.

With the project well underway, I went from the stress of those early readings to learning and enjoyment. Nico wrote. Héctor edited the chapters before passing them along to me. I responded with observations and comments in the margins that would later be incorporated into the text. We had regular three-way conversations on WhatsApp. We tweaked the first half of the book during a week of marathon days at my house in Cabrera. Later, during a retreat in Buenos Aires, we reviewed the second half. There we were joined by Olivia Pollitzer, who had helped Nico transcribe the interviews and now contributed her acute eye for detail to the final edits.

It was a demanding yet passionate job. We talked a lot and even argued at times over the importance of a particular scene or the use of a specific word, though always in a climate of great generosity and mutual trust. The process brought me a number of discoveries and even revelations. By entering into a dialogue with my past, I returned in some way to the people who populate it. I was able to deepen my relationship with my father and resume conversations with friends who, unbeknownst to me at the time, were still waiting. It was a journey rife with emotions, and yet throughout all of it, there was a question that was nagging me: who is going to be interested in this story? This book, which will take on a life of its own once published, will have to answer that question.

The story I will tell is the story as I remember it. In order to fill in certain gaps, my mind sought out many of those people who have accompanied me through the various stages of my life.

Acknowledgements

This book, representing my entire athletic career, would not have been possible without the help of countless people and institutions. To my siblings—Máximo, Martín, Inés, and Sebastián—and my mother, Ana María Robertie de Lange, I thank you for your patience in the face of my lengthy absences. With this book as an excuse, we gathered for a cookout filled with the stories and anecdotes that enrich these pages. My children, Yago, Theo, Borja, and Klaus, shared their memories and showed me, yet again, their love. At Red Bull I found another family whose unconditional support spanning over twenty years continues to play a fundamental role in my development as an athlete. It was they who came up with the idea and initial push for this project. I joined the team thanks to Roman Hagara and Hans-Peter Steinacher, who started out as my rivals before becoming training partners at a pivotal stage of my Olympic career, and who eventually became my friends.

Carlos Bayala used his enormous talent to sketch out the early cover designs. It was also his idea that the book be called Breathe. Martín Ainstein and Pep Blay shared the interviews they'd conducted for documentaries about my career. With great care and sensitivity, Gustavo Cherro selected the photos for the book.

Nicolás Cassese, Héctor Guyot, and Olivia Pollitzer spent long hours writing with me. I already miss them. The Club Náutico San Isidro and the Yacht Club Argentino, along with many others, have always supported me, as did Argentina's Ministry of Tourism and Sports and the National High Performance Sports Agency.

The story I will tell is the story as I remember it. In order to fill in certain gaps, my mind sought out many of those people who have accompanied me through the various stages of my life. Special recognition is due to Ceci Carranza, Camau Espínola, and Cole Parada, my fellow Olympic adventurers. I would also like to thank Ferdi García Guevara, Mateo Majdalani, Martín Billoch, Mariano Galarza, Edu Galofré, Gabi Mariani, Miguel Saubidet, Dani Espina, Thomas Zajac, Angelo Glisoni, Matías Bühler, Ramón Oliden, Fernando Echávarri, Mikel Pasabant, David Vera, Tati Lena, and Tobal Saubidet for their incredible willingness to join us on this project.

There are also those fellow travelers who, despite my deep affection for them, and for different reasons, do not appear in this book. Both those who I mentioned and those who I didn't are equally very important to me. I feel immense gratitude to you all.